RECLAIMING JIHAD

Dedication

To Magdah, Ziyad and the twins

RECLAIMING JIHAD

A Qur'anic Critique of Terrorism

ElSayed M.A. Amin

THE ISLAMIC FOUNDATION

Reclaiming Jihad: A Qur'anic Critique of Terrorism

Published by
THE ISLAMIC FOUNDATION
Markfield Conference Centre,
Ratby Lane, Markfield, Leicestershire
LE67 9SY, United Kingdom

Qur'an House, PO Box 30611, Nairobi, Kenya

PMB 3193, Kano, Nigeria

Distributed by
KUBE PUBLISHING LTD.
Tel: +44(0)1530 249230, Fax: +44(0)1530 249656
E-mail: info@kubepublishing.com

Cataloguing-in-Publication Data
is available from the British Library

ISBN 978-0-86037-593-7 *paperback*
ISBN 978-0-86037-588-3 *casebound*
ISBN 978-0-86037-598-2 *ebook*

10 9 8 7 6 5 4 3 2 1

Cover design and typesetting Nasir Cadir

Printed by IMAK Ofset, Turkey

CONTENTS

TRANSLITERATION TABLE

Arabic Consonants

Initial, unexpressed medial and final: ء ’

ا	a	د	d	ض	ḍ	ك	k
ب	b	ذ	dh	ط	ṭ	ل	l
ت	t	ر	r	ظ	ẓ	م	m
ث	th	ز	z	ع	‘	ن	n
ج	j	س	s	غ	gh	هـ	h
ح	ḥ	ش	sh	ف	f	و	w
خ	kh	ص	ṣ	ق	q	ي	y

With a *shaddah*, both medial and final consonants are doubled.

Vowels, diphthongs, etc.

Short:	ـَ	a	ـِ	i	ـُ	u
Long:	ـَا	ā	ـِي	ī	ـُو	ū
Diphthongs:			ـَوْ	aw		
			ـَيْ	ay		

FOREWORD

THERE CAN BE little doubt that terrorism is one of the major problems that confront humanity today. Since the bombings at the World Trade Center, New York, on 11 September 2001, and the declaration a few days later of a "war on terror" by US President George W. Bush, the problem of terrorism has been seen as a critical factor in relations between Muslims and non-Muslims, and also (although this is often overlooked by non-Muslims) between different Muslim groups as well as between different non-Muslim groups. The notion of a "war" carries the implication that there are just two sides to the conflict, perhaps together with neutral parties who really ought to declare themselves for one side or the other. In reality the problem of how we should understand and react to terrorism is far more complex.

As Dr ElSayed Amin points out, the meaning of terrorism has changed much in recent times. Today it is a strongly pejorative term, although this was not always the case. Still, in its current usage there is considerable doubt as to its precise meaning, and various problems in determining its applicability to specific acts. It seems certainly to include acts of violence which are perpetrated against victims who are, or who include, innocent persons, in the sense of persons other than enemy combatants. The major systems of moral belief have often condemned such acts. Nevertheless, popular acceptance even of that condemnatory principle has been selectively abandoned, or has been heavily qualified, through the wars of the twentieth century, in which civilian populations have been repeatedly targeted by military action, notwithstanding some progress in the development of the international laws of war.

Since the notion of terrorism is today often referred to in debates concerning the practice of Islam, it is vital for anyone who wishes to act morally to know and understand the Islamic position on terrorism. The many millions of Muslim believers obviously need to know this so as to be sure how their religion requires them to act. But everyone else needs to know that as well, so as to understand the Muslim position and to know how they should act towards Muslims. This is especially important in view of the widely-publicized implied or expressed allegations outside the Islamic world that Islam is inherently supportive of terrorism. The issue is vitally important with regard to international relations between those states which are predominantly Islamic and those which are not. But in today's globalized world, in which the population of virtually every state contains both Islamic and non-Islamic communities, and in which different socially-accepted religious beliefs and systems of morality and law co-exist, mutual understanding and respect are also essential in intra-state arenas.

It is extremely difficult to decide what is the correct definition of terrorism in Islam, or what exactly are the Islamic injunctions in respect of terrorism. There are variations of opinion on these matters within the Islamic world. There is a huge amount of literature in Arabic, English and other languages, written by both Muslims and non-Muslims. Dr ElSayed Amin's work seizes on the crucial, central part of the debates. It studies exegeses by leading scholars of the Qur'anic provisions which refer – or have been taken to refer – to terrorism. While it rightly aims for general validity within Islamic thought, it focuses particularly on the views attributable to Sunni teaching, and especially (although by no means exclusively) on pronouncements made from, or with reference to Egypt. Even with these foci, which are entirely justifiable, the bibliography of literature cited is remarkably large.

The questions on which this work concentrates are the most

difficult questions arising from the problem of terrorism. The work asks both how terrorism should be defined for general purposes, and how it should be understood to be defined in the Qur'an. The concept bears a certain relationship to the Qur'anic notion of *fasād* (corruption, or a negative use of force), although that relationship seems to be initially unclear and contested. This needs to be investigated, and the uses of *fasād* elucidated, with a full study of the views of classical and modern exegetes. Since Islam is not a totally pacifist faith, there needs next to be a consideration of the circumstances in which the Qur'an enjoins arming as a deterrent to wrongful attack, an injunction sometimes represented as a call to engage in terrorism. There are strong arguments for holding that this is a serious misinterpretation. The relationship between (prohibited) terrorism and (authorized) jihad, again frequently confused by critics and some believers, is meticulously investigated, with a full study of relevant exegeses and academic debates. Finally the work considers whether terrorism is punishable according to the Qur'an as the crime of *ḥirābah*, and, if it is, how it is to be punished.

I first met Dr ElSayed Amin, and had the privilege of discussing his work with him, when he was working at the University of Birmingham on the PhD thesis on which this book is based. He brings to the work some years of experience at the Azhar University, the leading university in this field in Egypt, and as a Member of the Egyptian Supreme Council on Islamic Affairs, as well as in other expert advisory capacities. He is an expert on Islam in English, and has significant international experience. I would commend to readers, both believers and non-believers, the importance of this work as a scholarly contribution to understanding, harmony and peace in the modern world.

Gordon R. Woodman
University of Birmingham
January 2014

INTRODUCTION: WHY DOES THE QUR'AN MATTER IN CONFRONTING TERRORISM?

THE QUR'AN TODAY is widely misused and misunderstood in respect of terrorism. For some extremist Muslims, it is misused to justify terrorism; its verses are quoted out of context to justify conflict as the permanent norm between Muslim and non-Muslims. And for some non-Muslims it is misunderstood as a book that preaches hate and calls for the killing of innocents. Given that today's terrorist groups such as al-Qaeda rely on the Sunni Qur'an exegetical genre (*tafsīr*) for justification, it is necessary to go back to this commentary tradition, and take into proper consideration the historical and circumstantial contexts in which these commentaries were written. This can hardly be misconstrued as an idle academic exercise. as the misappropriation of Sunni exegesis has not only brought this venerable and subtle genre of Islamic scholarship into question but has marginalized it in the discussion of Islam and terrorism. Indeed, it can be seriously considered whether this misappropriation has tarnished the image of the Qur'an and indeed Islam itself. In order to offset this, the classical and contemporary *tafsīr* tradition needs to be put into its proper contexts to show how terrorists fail to do this when they misappropriate it.

Since the 11 September attacks of 2001, some in the West consider Islam and the Muslim world "as sources of threat to the international order and as the main source of terrorism and violence in the name of religion".[1] The Qur'an, seen as a Divine book by a fifth of the world's population, has been the subject of extreme interpretations by some Muslims and non-Muslims whose research is based on ill-informed sources and, therefore, lacks due rigour and objectivity. Many Qur'anic verses are intentionally quoted out of their original contexts to suit the political and ideological agendas of individuals or groups whose objective is to disseminate fear and terror in our already troubled world.[2] The Qur'an has come to be misperceived as a book from which so-called "Islamic terrorism" is originally derived, as a result of extreme interpretations by some Muslims.[3] As a result, "Qur'anic exegesis has become an ideological weapon employed by various socio-political powers to maintain or to change the *status quo*, a conservative weapon to maintain and a revolutionary weapon to change."[4]

This book therefore sets out to examine terrorism from a Qur'anic perspective. It attempts to elucidate how terrorism is defined, whether or not it is related to other concepts that are Qur'anic, such as jihad and deterrence, and whether or not the Qur'an offers punitive measures to combat it. The starting point of my research is the Qur'an itself,[5] as interpreted by a careful selection of classical and modern exegetes. As a committed Muslim, my working premise in this book is to take as read the fundamental Muslim conviction that the Qur'an is the Word of God revealed through the Angel Gabriel to Muḥammad (d. 11/632).[6] As the Qur'an is the central book in the lives of Muslims, it is (ab)used by some extremist Muslims to justify their acts by cloaking them in religion. Both Muslim and non-Muslim readers therefore need to know how this appropriation of the Qur'an by extremists and terrorists lacks objectivity. It is therefore essential to take a journey through a representative selection of the Qur'anic interpretive corpus to critique these biased explanations by extremists by setting them against the mainstream interpretative understanding.

For reasons I shall elaborate below, of the various Qur'an exegetical genres, this study restricts itself to the thematic exegesis of terrorism. Eight select classical and modern exegeses constitute the main sources for this research. The period of the study, as far as these are concerned, is from the first quarter of the second/eighth century up to the end of the twentieth century. On the basis that the starting point of all exegetical genres is the text of the Qur'an itself, this study attempts to analyse the interpretations of the selected exegeses of words thought to be related to terrorism, taking into account whether or not they occur in the Qur'an, what relation, if any, they have to jihad and to deterrence, and how the Qur'an deals with the punishment for such actions. Importantly, the structure of this study focuses in detail on some highly relevant verses, and sometimes verses are divided into various sub-themes, as in Chapters 2, 3 and 5. The fact that this study depends mainly on the Qur'an does not belittle the significant contribution of the Prophetic hadiths in not only combating terrorism but also explaining many of the important issues left unresolved by the Qur'an in this regard, although it is beyond the scope of this study to consider the importance of the hadith literature here.[7]

Since the first century of the Islamic calendar, it has been widely acknowledged that the Qur'an needed exegesis (*tafsīr*) even in the time of Muḥammad.[8] The Qur'an was revealed piecemeal over a period of twenty-three years, and its exegesis "started from the very first day of its revelation" and "will continue to the very last day of its existence as a Scripture".[9] During Muḥammad's lifetime, his Companions used to ask him about the meanings of certain verses or words that they found difficult to understand.[10] While we may accept that Muḥammad was the first exegete of the Qur'an, he did not, however, explain the whole text to his Companions.[11] After his death, some of them became famous for interpreting the Qur'an, prominent among them being ʿAbdullāh ibn ʿAbbās (d. 68/687), Ubayy ibn Kaʿb (d. 20/640), and ʿAbdullāh ibn Masʿūd (d. 32/653).[12]

Some of the Successors (Tābiʿūn) who followed their teachers among the Companions are al-Ḥasan al-Baṣrī (d. 110/728), Muqātil ibn Sulaymān (d. 150/767) and Sufyān al-Thawrī (d. 161/778).[13] It was only during the post-Successor period, in the first quarter of the second/eighth century, that Qur'anic exegesis started to become an independent genre, especially when it was crowned by the exegesis of al-Ṭabarī (d. 311/923).[14] Subsequently, a great number of exegetical works were written during the classical period, enriching the discipline of Qur'an exegesis, which started to grow steadily thanks to notable exegetes such as al-Zamakhsharī (d. 538/1144), al-Rāzī (d. 606/1209), al-Nasafī (d. 710/1310), Ibn Kathīr (d. 774/1373), al-Bayḍāwī (d. 791/1389), and al-Suyūṭī (d. 911/1505), among many others.

The modern phase of exegesis started after World War Two and the independence of Muslim countries from the colonial powers, resulting in the evolution of "literary exegesis with political leanings, as well as the emergence of scientific tafsīr which has emerged as a result of the scientific and medical developments during the twentieth century".[15] The efforts of Muslims in interpreting the Qur'an continue until today with the aim of making it "more accessible to an increasingly literate but not necessarily formally religiously-trained population".[16] This brief sketch of the development of Qur'an exegesis divides the history of *tafsīr* into roughly three stages: (1) the formative, from the lifetime of Muḥammad until the second/eighth century; (2) the classical, from the first quarter of the second/eighth century to the pre-modern period; and (3) the modern, from the late nineteenth century up to the present.[17]

In the development of Qur'an exegesis, the following five genres can be identified on the basis of the methodology applied by exegetes:[18] (1) Analytical exegesis (*al-tafsīr al-taḥlīlī*), in which all the verses are interpreted according to their arrangement in a given chapter (surah); this is also called verse-by-verse/serial/sequential exegesis (*al-tafsīr al-musalsal*). (2) Synoptic exegesis (*al-tafsīr al-ijmālī*), in which an exegetical outline of the verses is given according to their arrangement in a certain surah. (3) Comparative exegesis (*al-tafsīr al-muqāran*), in which the exegete analytically compares the different views of exegetes on an exegetical problem in a given verse. (4) Literary exegesis (*al-tafsīr al-adabī*), which interprets the Qur'an using a simple language and style in order to make it more accessible to the ordinary reader. (5) Thematic exegesis (*al-tafsīr al-mawḍū'ī*), in which the verses in one or more surah thought to share the same theme are collected together for purposes of exegetical analysis.[19] Out of these five types, thematic exegesis is the most strongly relevant and applicable to terrorism, as the main focus of this study.

Thematic exegesis is a relatively new term in Qur'an scholarship; even today, its existence as an independent category of exegesis is hardly discernible in modern Islamic libraries, even though it is of vital importance to Qur'an scholarship in general and exegesis in particular.[20] Two explanations are given about the origins of thematic exegesis in the modern period.[21] The first is that the term became known in the 1960s as a result of widespread controversy related to the submission of a doctoral thesis at the Azhar University by Muḥammad Maḥmūd Hijāzī (1914–1972), "Al-Wiḥdah al-Mawḍū'iyyah fī al-Qur'ān al-Karīm" ("Thematic Unity in the Ever-Glorious Qur'an"). It is claimed that as this topic at the time was unfamiliar to the examination committee, the degree was not awarded to the student. The second explanation traces the modern origin of the term to the 1980s, when a course on the thematic exegesis of the Qur'an was introduced into the curriculum of the Department of Exegesis at the Faculty of Uṣūl al-Dīn at the Azhar University in Cairo. Whichever of the two explanations is most authentic, both point to the scholarly precedence of Azhar scholars in this field. It is also clear that thematic exegesis as an independent genre is relatively new, a fact widely acknowledged in more than fifty research papers submitted to an important two-day conference on the "Thematic Exegesis of the Qur'an: Reality and Prospects", held in 2010 at the University of Sharjah in the United Arab Emirates (UAE).[22]

Thematic exegesis is of two types. The first, is the thematic genre of surahs, in which the exegete reflects on the surah as an independent unit, explaining how its verses are linked together.[23] The most famous of the many modern scholars who took great interest in this genre of exegesis are Muḥammad 'Abdullāh Dirāz (1312/1894–1377/1958) in his *al-Nabā' al-'Aẓīm*, and Muḥammad al-Ghazālī (1335/1917–1417/1996) in his *Naḥwā Tafsīr Mawḍū'ī li Suwar al-Qur'ān al-Karīm*.[24] The second is the thematic genre of verses, in which the exegete is concerned with collecting verses that deal with the same topic in an attempt to clarify the Qur'anic view regarding a specific issue.[25] According to the modern Egyptian philosopher, Hassan Hanafi, "All of the verses sharing one thematic interest are gathered, read in conjunction and understood together, if necessary several times over until the major orientation of the texts as a whole becomes apparent."[26] An example of a modern academic study that deals with this latter type of thematic genre is Kāmil Salāmah al-Daqs's *Āyāt al-Jihād fī al-Qur'ān al-Karīm: Dirāsah Mawḍū'iyyah wa Tārīkhiyyah wa Bayāniyyah* (*Jihad Verses in the Ever-Glorious Qur'an: Thematic, Historical and Rhetorical Study*).[27]

It is this second type of thematic genre that I shall adopt in this book because through it all verses widely considered to deal with terrorism from a Qur'anic perspective, as well as other allied themes such as jihad and deterrence, can be easily identified. The selected exegeses employed this study will also use, even if indirectly, this type of thematic genre, as will be shown in the biographical sketches of the exegetes given below.

In this study, eight selected works of classical and modern exegesis from the first quarter of the second/eighth century up to the end of the twentieth century constitute the main sources for the examination of terrorism from a Qur'anic perspective. The main sources from the classical period are the exegeses of al-Ṭabarī (d. 310/922), al-Rāzī (d. 606/1209), al-Qurṭubī (d. 617/1272), and al-Alūsī (d. 1270/1854). The main references from the modern period are 'Abduh (d. 1323/1905), Riḍā (d. 1353/1935), Darwazah (d. 1404/1985), Quṭb (d. 1385/1966), and al-Sha'rāwī (d. 1419/1998). Four other classical exegeses, namely those of al-Jaṣṣāṣ (d. 370/981), Ibn al-'Arabī (d. 543/1148), Ibn Kathīr (d. 774/1373), al-Suyūṭī (d. 911/1505) and one from the modern period, namely Mawdūdī (d. 1399/1979), are also referred to, especially when they offer original ideas or when the verses under discussion are not interpreted by some of the main selected exegetes.[28]

The rationale for my selection of the above exegetes from the vast *tafsīr* literature is because of the following reasons. Firstly, unlike others, all of these exegetes have paid close attention to the context of verses talking about jihad and other issues related to the topic of this study. Secondly, most of them wrote in historical periods in which the relations between Muslims and non-Muslims were hostile. This may explain why the interpretations of some of them were a reflection of their lived realities. Thirdly, some Muslims who unjustifiably adopt violence and call for killing others quite often refer to the above exegeses to establish authority for their baseless claims. Fourthly, some of the above exegetes, especially the modern ones such as al-Shaʿrāwī, were personally involved in combating terrorism. Therefore, it is necessary to highlight this vital role and to see how terrorism is discussed in their exegeses. Fifthly, the interpretations of some of them were revolutionary such as that of Quṭb's, and, therefore, they had a real impact on those Muslims who adopted violence and attempted to provide a Qur'anic pretext to justify their illegal actions. Finally, some of them, such as Darwazah, have referred to the punishment for terrorism from a Qur'anic perspective in clear unequivocal terms. As a way of providing further backing for my selection, I provide a brief, chronological sketch of the main selected exegetes, with some notes on their biographies as well as on some aspects of their interpretative approaches.

Al-Ṭabarī was born in Tabaristān in northern Iran in 224/839, which he left at the age of twelve to seek Islamic knowledge, touring countries such as Egypt, the Levant and Iraq. After many years of study, he settled in Baghdad and spent most of his life there until he died in 310/922. Al-Ṭabarī is widely associated with having had a real impact on three Islamic sciences, namely Qur'an exegesis, history and Islamic jurisprudence (*fiqh*), although he is best known as a historian and exegete.[29] In Islamic jurisprudence, he was the founder of a successful school of law (*madhhab*) known as al-Jarīriyyah, which continued for some years after his death but eventually died out. In history, his *Tārīkh al-Rusūl wa al-Mulūk wa al-Khulafā'* is an extensive world chronicle. In *tafsīr*, his magnum opus, *Jāmiʿ al-Bayān ʿan Ta'wīl Āy al-Qur'ān*, is the "summative repository of the first two-and-a-half centuries of Muslim exegetical endeavour".[30]

One of al-Ṭabarī's main exegetical methods is to rely on citations from earlier generations of exegetes. Another is to present different interpretations regarding a particular point and then to follow this with his own view. One of the distinctive features of his exegesis relevant to this book is that he pays special attention to the context of verses and how they relate to each other in different surahs of the Qur'an. While he did not call this "thematic exegesis", his approach definitely carries one of the latter's main features. Al-Ṭabarī's exegesis has been widely critiqued by many Western scholars, especially with regard to his view about Muslim–non-Muslim relations and suicide in Islam, as will be explained in Chapter 3 of this book.[31]

Al-Rāzī was born in Rayy, east of Tehran in 544/1150. After receiving basic religious instruction from his father, Ḍiyā' al-Dīn, himself an erudite scholar, al-Rāzī travelled to various cities in Transoxiana (Mā warā'a al-Nahr), such as Bukhara, Samarqand and Khaznah as well as other cities such as Khawārazm until he settled in Herat, devoting the rest of his life to teaching and writing until his death in 606/1209. His religious upbringing and his father's interest in jurisprudence and theology seems to have encouraged al-Rāzī to master these two sciences by getting involved in theological debate. On the basis of this debating, he was considered by some to be an erudite scholar and philosopher who influenced later thinkers, especially in theology and exegesis, while others considered him to be a heretic. However, it is not my purpose in this study "to fall into such value judgments".[32]

In his famous exegesis, *Al-Tafsīr al-Kabīr aw Mafātīḥ al-Ghayb*, al-Rāzī relied on revealed sources such as the Qur'an and the Sunnah. However, his reliance on rational considerations, which developed as a result of his exposure to a wide range of sciences such as theology, mathematics, jurisprudence, history and biography, logic and philosophy, is a major distinctive feature of his exegesis. In his exegesis, he usually begins by stating the main theme of his discussion, blending, whenever necessary, *al-tafsīr al-taḥlīlī* and *al-tafsīr al-mawḍū'ī*.[33] He then divides each theme into subdivisions and sub-subdivisions. Al-Rāzī's character, which had an impact on his exegesis, has led some modern scholars, such as 'Abd al-Mun'im al-Nimr, to state that his exegesis can be described as a mixture of "thematic, linguistic, juristic and creedal exegesis".[34] The encyclopaedic nature of al-Rāzī's approach has also led some modern researchers to attack him as an ideologue of the philosophy of terrorism, an accusation that Chapter 1 of this study refutes. In addition, in Chapter 2, I will attempt to mount a critique of al-Rāzī's discussion of the objectives of the Qur'anic phrase "to frighten off" (*turhibūna*), in his interpretation of 8: 60, a key verse cited by terrorists of a Muslim background today.[35]

Al-Qurṭubī, whose date of birth is uncertain, was born in Cordova in Spain, where he received his early religious education. He then travelled widely until he settled in Minyat ibn Khaṣīb, a small town close to the city of Asyut in Upper Egypt, where he died in 617/1272. Al-Qurṭubī's most famous work is *Al-Jāmiʿ li Aḥkām al-Qur'ān*, one of the best-known books of traditional exegesis in which the interpretation of juristic issues is one of its distinctive features. His study provides an early example of a tacit approach to *al-tafsīr al-mawḍūʿī* from a juristic perspective. In his exegesis, al-Qurṭubī was influenced by his Andalusian predecessors, especially the Mālikī exegete Ibn al-ʿArabī, but in such a way that he also accommodates the views of the opponents of the Mālikī school. While also being influenced by al-Ṭabarī and al-Rāzī, al-Qurṭubī left his impact on later exegetes such as Ibn Kathīr and al-Alūsī.

The historical period in which al-Qurṭubī lived in Andalusia was marked by tension in Muslim–non-Muslim relations.[36] This may explain why he attempted to provide a detailed explanation of the Qur'anic *casus belli*, projecting a hostile attitude towards non-Muslims as the underlying basis of relations between Muslims and non-Muslims. His view is discussed in Chapter 3 of this study. I want to argue that al-Qurṭubī's views should be read and quoted giving due regard to their historical and circumstantial contexts, but, as I will show in Chapter 3, they are unfortunately misquoted, (ab)used and misinterpreted by Bin Laden and other terrorists.[37]

Al-Alūsī was born in Baghdad in 1217/1802 to a family of scholars in various Islamic sciences. In this distinguished scholarly environment, al-Alūsī received his early religious education from his father as well as from other notable scholars based in Baghdad.

He also travelled to Beirut, Damascus and Turkey to seek more Islamic knowledge, before returning to Baghdad, where he died in 1270/1854. During his lifetime, many parts of the Muslim world were under military occupation and he tried his best to encourage Muslims to revive the spirit of jihad by authoring *Safrat al-Zād li Safrat al-Jihād*.

Al-Alūsī's *Rūḥ al-Ma'ānī fī Tafsīr al-Qur'ān al-'Aẓīm wa al-Sab' al-Mathānī* is well known as one of the comprehensive exegeses of the classical period. Al-Alūsī read many of the classical exegeses who preceded him before writing his own exegesis. In *Rūḥ al-Ma'ānī*, he uses reason to interpret the meanings of the Qur'an, and takes much interest in explaining various religious terms, especially juristic ones, which indicates that his exegesis also contributes tacitly to thematic exegesis.[38]

Muḥammad 'Abduh was born into an educated family in 1226/1849 in the village of Maḥallat Naṣr, in the Buḥayrah Governorate of Lower Egypt. By the age of twelve, he had memorized the Qur'an and joined the Aḥmadī al-Azhar Institute, in the Ṭanṭā Governorate of Lower Egypt, second only to al-Azhar as a centre of religious learning at that time. After a while, he stopped studying there because of his dislike of the less than innovative teaching methods that were common at that time. Thereafter, he resumed his religious study at the Azhar in Cairo, where in 1872 he met the well-known social reformer Jamāl al-Dīn al-Afghānī (1254/1838–1314/1897), which was a turning point in his life, as 'Abduh was introduced to both classical learning and European works available in translation.

In 1294/1877, 'Abduh graduated from the Azhar and was appointed as a lecturer in history at Dār al-'Ulūm al-'Ulyā.[39] He started to write in local newspapers and became a political activist in the liberal national party along with al-Afghānī, who was banished from Egypt in 1296/1879. 'Abduh was also barred from teaching until he was pardoned and appointed as the chief editor of *Al-Waqā'i' al-Miṣriyyah* gazette. He joined the 'Urābī Revolution, which was defeated by the British in 1882, and was then banished from Egypt. Outside Egypt, he went to Beirut and then, in 1884, to Paris, where he met al-Afghānī and they established the periodical *Al-'Urwah al-Wuthqā* together. When 'Abduh was permitted to return to Egypt in 1889, he assumed many positions, including notably as Mufti of Egypt. In Egypt, 'Abduh committed himself to reform (*al-iṣlāḥ*) in three main domains: the Azhar educational system, the presentation of Islam in mosques, and the Egyptian legal system of Shariah-based courts. 'Abduh authored many important works, among the most popular of which are *Risālat al-Tawḥīd* (1315/1897), *Al-Islām wa al-Naṣrāniyyah ma'ā al-'Ilm wa al-Madaniyyah*, and a sizeable part of *Tafsīr al-Manār*. 'Abduh died in 1323/1905.[40]

Riḍā was born in al-Qalamūn, a village near Tripoli in northern Lebanon, in 1282/1865. After a year of study at a local Turkish school in Tripoli, which he did not enjoy, he joined the National Islamic School founded by an enlightened Tripoli Sheikh, Ḥusayn al-Jisr (1845–1909), and then the religious school. In both schools, he had a religious education and studied French, Arabic, Turkish, mathematics and the natural sciences. By the end of 1897, and after finishing his undergraduate degree in Tripoli, Riḍā left his birthplace for Egypt. Riḍā furthered his studies by attending the Azhar, then under 'Abduh's supervision, and he soon published the first issue of his journal *Al-Manār*. He remained attached to 'Abduh as a student and later as a colleague until the latter's death, when "Riḍā established himself more as a leading heir" of 'Abduh's reformist ideas "by taking over the commentary of the Qur'an known as *Tafsīr al-Manār*, which Abduh had begun."[41] He also continued his efforts at political and social reform until he died in 1353/1935.[42]

Three main influential figures inspired Riḍā's thought. The first is Sheikh Ḥusayn al-Jisr, who instilled in Riḍā the idea that "the progress of the Muslim nation was through a synthesis of religious education and modern sciences".[43] The second is al-Afghānī, whom Riḍā came to know about accidentally when he happened to rummage through his late father's papers and discovered some issues of *Al-'Urwah al-Wuthqā*. The third is 'Abduh, with whom Riḍā associated after al-Afghānī's death.

Tafsīr al-Manār, which is incomplete, consists of twelve volumes. Four of them were a transcription of 'Abduh's lectures by Riḍā from *Sūrah al-Fātiḥah* up to *Sūrah al-Nisā'* 4: 125.[44] Riḍā continued this exegesis up to *Sūrah Yūsuf* 12: 52. According to al-Dhahabī (1915–1977), Bahjat al-Bayṭār (d. 1976) completed the exegesis of *Sūrah Yūsuf* and published it separately under Riḍā's name.[45] In this study, Riḍā is considered the main author of *Tafsīr al-Manār*, but, whenever an opinion of ʿAbduh's is referred to, it is either attributed to him directly or I have noted where Riḍā has quoted ʿAbduh or attributed an opinion to him.

As far as thematic exegesis is concerned, it is clear throughout *Tafsīr al-Manār* that Riḍā does employ it, especially when he criticizes the classical exegetes for not exerting as much effort in presenting the Qur'an as a source of guidance, as they did, for example, with theology and jurisprudence.[46] Given that ʿAbduh and Riḍā lived in an era when many parts of the Muslim world were under foreign occupation, it is necessary to investigate their understanding of jihad in the Qur'an, and how they attempted to identify and assess perverted and extremist acts in their times, which are thought to be similar to acts of terrorism in ours.

Darwazah was born in Nābulus in Palestine in 1305/1887, and there he received his early education until he graduated from high school in 1905. After graduation he joined the Ottoman civil service and was promoted to deputy of the Nābulus post office. At that time, his cultural background started to take shape, especially through his regular reading of the many periodicals and magazines in circulation in the Arab world. He moved to Beirut to work for the postal service and then returned to Nābulus in 1918 to briefly work as the manager of the Palestinian endowments (*awqāf*) before administering the Najāḥ National School in Nābulus from its inception in 1922. During the period of unrest in Palestine in 1936, while on a visit to Damascus, he was barred from returning home and was imprisoned for some time. On release, he left for Turkey, where he remained until 1945. He then returned to Damascus, where he stayed until his death in 1404/1985.

Darwazah was a prolific author who wrote more than thirty books in various disciplines. However, his *Al-Tafsīr al-Ḥadīth: Tartīb al-Suwar Ḥasab al-Nuzūl* is one of his remarkable achievements.

In this exegesis, Darwazah interprets the Qur'an according to the chronological arrangement of the surahs, allowing "the Qur'an to speak for itself and be understood in the way it was understood by the Meccans of the Prophet's time."[47] He is also concerned with how verses of the Qur'an are contextually and thematically interrelated because, in his view, this leads to a better understanding of the Qur'an.

Darwazah is the only exegete of the classical and modern period dealt with in this study to have clearly tackled the problem of punishment for terrorism with clear reference to the Qur'an. In his exegesis, he maintains that peace is the underlying principle governing relations between Muslims and non-Muslims, a point clearly opposed by Quṭb, who considered both Riḍā and Darwazah to be "defeatists" and "apologetics", as discussed in Chapter 3 of this study.[48]

Sayyid Quṭb was born in 1323/1906 in the village of Mūshā in the Asyūṭ Governorate of Upper Egypt. He memorized the Qur'an at the age of ten before joining the government school, from which he graduated in 1918. He moved to Cairo to pursue his secondary education, joining the Faculty of Dār al-ʿUlūm in 1930 and graduating in 1933. Between 1933 and 1951, he worked as an employee in the Egyptian Ministry of Education, where he served as an inspector for some years. During this period, he was sent on an education mission to the United States for two years. On his return journey to Egypt in 1950, he visited England, Switzerland and Italy. After his return, he joined the Muslim Brotherhood (*al-Ikhwān al-Muslimūn*) and worked as the editor of the group's magazine *Al-Risālah*. During the 1950s and 60s, he was the Brotherhood's chief ideologue. During his lifetime, Quṭb was arrested and imprisoned three times. His first imprisonment, in early 1954 together with prominent leaders of the Muslim Brotherhood, lasted for three months. His second took place in October 1954, when shots were fired at the late Egyptian President Gamal Abdel Nasser (1918–1970). The intervention and mediation of the Iraqi President ʿAbd al-Salām ʿĀrif (1921–1966) led to Quṭb's release, after he began to suffer from poor health as a result of brutal torture. He was rearrested for the third time in August 1965 and charged with attempting to assassinate Abdel Nasser; he was sentenced to death on 21 August 1966 and executed a week later. Since his death he has been regarded as a martyr by his supporters.

During his period of imprisonment, Quṭb is widely believed to have "developed a radical approach, rejecting the then state system as illegitimate and 'un-Islamic'."[49] As a result, some see him as the ideologue of most modern terrorist groups, going as far as to include the perpetrators of the 11 September 2001 attacks as well as al-Qaeda and its erstwhile leader Osama bin Laden (1957–2011). Others see him "as a victim of state persecution who developed a theology of liberation in reaction to his maltreatment".[50] Importantly, these opinions are presented in detail, along with other controversial views of Quṭb in Chapter 3 of this study. No less important is the ongoing controversy surrounding Quṭb as a personality who, perhaps unlike many others, became more famous after his execution than he was during his lifetime by living longer than his executioners did in the memories of succeeding generations.

While Quṭb was a prolific author, his *Fī Ẓilāl al-Qur'ān* remains, without doubt, his most important work. It first appeared during the 1950s, serialized in *Al-Risalah* magazine until it was banned. Quṭb continued to publish the *Ẓilāl* over a period of two years afterwards and managed, despite harsh conditions in detention, to continue writing it. A closer look at the *Ẓilāl* reveals that it is not a traditional commentary on the Qur'an, but rather "a free expression of the author's feelings while reading the Qur'anic verses".[51] While giving attention to the occasions of revelation of specific verses, Quṭb did not take much interest in interpreting the juristic aspects of verses. He is more concerned to relate the verses to contemporary social and religious contexts, which is an aspect of thematic exegesis. Of all the exegeses selected for this study, the *Ẓilāl* is perhaps the only work that has been translated into English – evidence that the *Ẓilāl* is one of the most widely-read exegeses of the Qur'an today.[52]

Al-Shaʿrāwī was born in early April 1329/1911 in the village of Daqādūs of the Daqahliyyah Governorate in Lower Egypt. He received his primary education at the Azhar institutes in al-Zaqāzīq and Ṭanṭā in Egypt. He then travelled to Cairo to pursue his studies at the Azhar University and was granted a licence to teach (*ijāzah*) Arabic and Islamic studies in 1943. He then taught at the Azhar institutes of al-Zaqāzīq, Ṭanṭā and Alexandria. In 1950, al-Shaʿrāwī taught at King ʿAbd al-ʿAzīz University in Saudi Arabia, after which he returned to Egypt and assumed many leading positions within Egypt's religious institutions, such as director of Islamic preaching (*daʿwah*) in the Egyptian Ministry of Endowments in 1961, chairman of the Azhar mission in Algeria in 1966, and Minister of Endowments in 1980.

In Egypt, al-Shaʿrāwī was a public figure who "was seen more often on the Egyptian television screen than [the late Egyptian president] Anwar al-Sadat himself [(1918–1981)]."[53] He was engaged in brokering peace between the Egyptian government and extremist groups of the time, as clarified in Chapter 4 of this study. Although dozens of authored works, including his exegesis, bear his name, some of them were actually edited transcripts of his recorded interviews on television and elsewhere. His charismatic appeal was more apparent in his television appearances than in his writing.

Of all his works, *Tafsīr al-Shaʿrāwī* remains the main source through which his thought has been disseminated. His exegesis came as a result of his regular weekly television programme, aired in Egypt every Friday. In a show of humility, he named his exegesis *Khawāṭirī Ḥawla al-Qur'ān* (*My Reflections around the Qur'an*), arguing that were the Qur'an intended to be interpreted as Allah wants it to be, the Prophet would have assumed this task par excellence, but he only explained to his Companions what they asked him about. Nevertheless, his reflections (*khawāṭir*) remain one of the recent contributions to Qur'anic exegesis. It is incomplete and the printed text goes as far as 37: 138. His commentary on other surahs is only available in audio format on his personal internet website, which was probably developed after his death in 1419/1998.[54]

In addition to the classical and modern exegeses referred to above, I also present and analyse other secondary sources by modern Muslim and non-Muslim scholars from various backgrounds.

Although the selected exegeses present the main understanding of how Qur'anic topics such as jihad and brigandage (*ḥirābah*) can be understood, their handling of terrorism-related issues remains difficult to relate to our modern context without being accompanied by the views of modern scholars who are witnesses of today's terrorist acts and are, therefore, better able to assess whether or not they are in conformity with the Qur'an. These supplementary non-exegetical references are secondary sources written in Arabic and English by modern Muslim and non-Muslim scholars from the last quarter of the nineteenth century up to the present. Of these secondary sources, only mainstream Muslim and Western literature has been selected; I have tried my best to avoid what might be classed as "hate literature" and extremist writing. However, clearly it has been necessary to examine in detail certain extremist writings, such as some of the core ideologies of al-Qaeda regarding jihad in the Qur'an and their support for killing innocents, for the purposes of critique and refutation.

The main and secondary sources on the Muslim side constitute the insider approach, while the non-Muslim side constitutes the outsider approach, as will be explained in the methodology below. As far as the insider approach is concerned, this study is confined to Sunni exegesis and literature, as is the case with the juristic sources consulted to define legal terms that are not discussed in the selected Qur'an commentaries. In this regard, only the four Sunni schools of jurisprudence – namely the Ḥanafī, Mālikī, Shāfiʿī and Ḥanbalī schools – are consulted, except for the views of Ibn Ḥazm (d. 456/1064), who belongs to the Ẓāhirī school, in a few instances.

The main method I use to analyse the literature consulted is content analysis. This is because of its importance in examining "historical artefacts".[55] Given that this study is based on the views of selected classical and modern exegetes and those of contemporary scholars, I use a comparative method for the selected exegeses, so far as the Qur'anic terms and selected verses are concerned. I juxtapose the views of modern scholars with those of the exegetes to give a more comprehensive understanding of terrorism from a Qur'anic perspective. With both content analysis and comparison,

I employ an insider/outsider approach.[56] For the purposes of this study, I take as read the grounds of fundamental beliefs and the positions advocated for by both insiders and outsiders. The diversity found in the exegetical selection and the variations in the ideological inclinations of modern scholars makes the adoption of these methods of content analysis, comparison and an insider/outsider approach logical in my view. While they help to define the aims and scope of my study, they remain relative in their application, making objectivity, especially in the field of religious studies, an aim that is very difficult to achieve even though it is still a helpful and essential ideal.[57] Finally, I have made linguistic analysis central to my discussion of the literal and technical meanings of the main terms discussed, such as terrorism, jihad, martyrdom, and *ḥirābah*.[58]

In Chapter 1, I present the various definitions of terrorism from both Islamic and Western perspectives and attempt to arrive at a comprehensive definition of this issue. As discussed above, a thematic exegetical approach in English on the verses relevant to the study of terrorism from a Qur'anic perspective, at a time when modern Muslim scholars are trying to explore the importance of writing a complete thematic exegesis of the Qur'an in Arabic, will, it is hoped, make this study not only timely but strategically important. Therefore, in Chapter 1, I propose a comprehensive definition of terrorism in order to make it applicable to the field of Qur'anic exegeses, with special reference to existing major Western and Islamic organizational definitions, and it is necessary to address the fundamental question as to whether the Qur'an actually addresses terrorism and related issues or not. In fact, I ask if there are direct or implied (or indirect) references applicable to the modern issue of terrorism in the Qur'an or not? In considering this fundamental question, I attempt to trace and examine the occurrences of the term itself (and especially its cognates) in both Qur'anic and extra-Qur'anic sources.

In much of the literature published after the 11 September attacks, jihad is used as a synonym for terrorism. Therefore, in Chapter 2, I attempt to examine and define both terms and explore whether or not there is a relationship between the two from a

Qur'anic perspective. For my argument, much hinges upon whether it can be ascertained that the two terms are distinguished in the Qur'an exegetical genre, as an essential step in refuting their conflation as synonyms. Chapter 2 examines this issue by way of a thorough examination of a Qur'anic verse key to this whole debate, 8: 60, which is misinterpreted by extremists to allow for aggressive action as opposed to armed deterrence, and is an essential part of mislabelling terrorism as jihad. Therefore, the examination of the Qur'anic notion of deterrence is essential to reclaiming jihad from terrorism. My finding is that the Muslim adoption of armed deterrence for strategic defence purposes has strong and persuasive backing in the Qur'an exegetical tradition, and is unaffected by the prohibition of terrorism.

The next two chapters build further on my case to reclaim jihad from terrorism. Chapter 3 examines whether or not there is a relationship between terrorism and military jihad in respect of the *tafsīr* literature, both classical and modern. Central to this question is how relations between Muslims and non-Muslims are construed: is either peace or conflict the norm? Chapter 4 considers the same debate in the context of two extremist groups, al-Qaeda and Egyptian Islamic Jihad. Understood through the Sunni exegetical tradition and indeed the arguments of the *ulema* in general, the attacks of 9/11 are analysed to show that these are terrorist actions and cannot plausibly be construed and justified as jihad. In the book as a whole, but particularly in Chapters 1 and 4, I address moral and ethical responses to terrorism at length. As well as my own attempt here to distinguish terrorism from jihad, I also survey in detail the mobilization of Sunni orthodoxy after 9/11, and its central role in rebutting terrorism, through restating the ethical and moral heart of the Islamic tradition with respect to war, deterrence, and jihad. I also examine the place of repentance and recantation, an integral part of Islamic applied ethics, in examining the case of Egyptian Islamic Jihad, a terrorist group that renounced violence in 1997. Finally, I turn from moral and ethical responses to terrorism to consider legal sanctions against it in Islam. Chapter 5 discusses the possibility of identifying a Qur'anic punishment for terrorism by exploring whether or not the punishment for *ḥirābah* should be applied to terrorism as well.

On technical matters, all translations of Qur'anic verses are quoted from M.A.S. Abdel Haleem's *The Qur'an: A New Translation* unless stated otherwise, any interpolations in them are denoted in square brackets, and Qur'an referencing follows the commonly circulated Egyptian edition.[59] All the translations of the hadiths and all Arabic terms and phrases are mine unless indicated otherwise. I employ the standard Arabic transliteration system normally used in Anglo-American academia, but have preferred Anglicized forms where they have become widely used and accepted. Finally, where both calendars are used, I mention the Hijrī date before the Gregorian one; otherwise, in singular instances only the latter is used.

To preface all of my acknowledgements, this book would not have been possible without the guidance of Allah. The personal motivation for me to study terrorism through the lens of the Qur'an began very early on when I enrolled in secondary religious education at the Azhar. In that period, I witnessed the extent to which Qur'anic verses were sometimes quoted out of context to fulfil the whims of those who, in the guise and attire of religious authorities, lacked basic training in Islamic learning. An inner desire arose in me to challenge such misguided interpretations. Later on, when the Qur'an was "hijacked" to justify the terrorist attacks of 11 September, I became passionate to write about how jihad was presented in electronic media with reference to both the Qur'an and the Sunnah; a more feasible and slimmed-down version of that original aim emerged first as a thesis and now as this book.

Special acknowledgement here is due to my late father Muhammad, who took from life's necessities to fund my religious education as a young boy at the Azhar, my mother Zaynab Ali, who taught me the meaning of love and sacrifice, my wife Magdah Hassan, whose habitual endurance is always a source of inspiration, support and encouragement, and my son Ziyad Amin, whose coming to the world has made all the difference to me.

I am very grateful to Professor Muḥammad M. Abū Laylah, former chair of the Department of English and Islamic Studies in

English at the Azhar University in Cairo, whose profound knowledge of Islam inspired me as a young undergraduate. His commitment and dedication to Islam inspired a generation of seekers of knowledge.

I would also like to express my deep appreciation to all those who aided me with reading parts of my book, provided me with references and contributed in various scholarly discussions. It would take many pages and much space to thank them all. They include Professor Samīr al-Shaykh, Dr Ahmad Mohsen Al-Dawoody, Muataz al-Abd from al-Azhar University in Cairo, Dr Jabal Buaben, Dr Bustami Khir, Dr Sigvard von Sicard, Dr Ian Draper, Dr Haifaa Jawad, Professor Gordon Woodman, and Dr Christopher Finlay from the University of Birmingham. I am also grateful to Dr Khalid El-Awaisi from Aberdeen University, Datuk Professor Osman Baker, Director and Chair of SOASCIS, Universiti Brunei Darussalam, Dr Heba Raouf Ezzat from Cairo University and Professor David Cook from Rice University, Professor Kuṭb Muṣṭaphā Sano, Minister of International Co-operation in Guinea, the late Dr Hānī ʿAṭiyyah from Qatar University, and Dr ʿAbd al-Raḥmān Spīndārī from Iraq. I thank them all for their scholarly comments and critical insights.

Much appreciation is due to Yahya Birt of Kube Publishing for his editorial comments, spiritual support and patience, Carol A. Rowe for editing earlier versions of this book and Dr Daniel Jackson for editing most of the chapters in the first two-and-a-half years of my research in the UK. Appreciation is also due to Fiona Breckenridge and Selma Cook who edited some parts of the original book.

Finally, I am indebted to the Egyptian Ministry of Higher Education for funding this research during my study at the University of Birmingham, UK, and am also grateful to the Universiti Brunei Darussalam (UBD) in the Sultanate of Brunei for funding this research in its final stages.

1

DEFINING TERRORISM: SECULAR AND ISLAMIC PERSPECTIVES

NO ATTEMPT TO REACH a common definition of terrorism is easy, as finding necessary shared ground between two quarrelling parties may entail agreement and compromise that is detrimental to each party's strategic goals and interests, and it might, perhaps, even be a question of survival. I present and criticize definitions of terrorism from both Western and Muslim-majority countries in this chapter. However, the inhibiting elements in these definitions from both official and non-official sources necessitate a compromise for both Western and Muslim-majority countries to stand firmly together to be able to fight the roots of terrorism threatening our modern world.

It has been commonplace in recent times to find many Muslims and non-Muslims abhorring terrorism and dismissing any link between it and Islam. Very few, however, attempt to define terrorism comprehensively, and this has left the door open for different interpretations and personal justifications at a time when references to terrorism from Islamic and Qur'anic perspectives have dominated the headlines. In the present chapter, I set out to investigate the various definitions of terrorism from an Islamic perspective, while considering its major and minor definitional problems and highlighting the efforts made by both Muslim and non-Muslim researchers in this regard.[1] I also evaluate those definitions by presenting a workable definition of my own.

In this regard, I will examine in detail the Qur'anic references to various forms of corruption, and the Qur'an's attitude towards them, and how classical and modern exegetes regarded them. As a term, "terrorism", as understood in its various current international definitions, is not explicitly mentioned in the Qur'an, but it is important for Muslims themselves to ascertain the attitude of the Qur'an towards it. Unfortunately, terrorism is promoted today by some extremist Muslims who falsely attribute it to Islam and more specifically to the Qur'an. They depend on some superficial and ideologically-driven readings of some classical and modern Qur'anic interpretations, as will be explained later in this book. It is my aim also that this exercise will enhance mutual understanding between Muslims and non-Muslims, who are often confused about links made between Islam, the Qur'an and terrorism. The centrality of the Qur'anic term "corruption" in its different forms to my analysis emanates from the fact that it has certain commonalities with "terrorism", as I will explore in this chapter.

The Struggle to Define Terrorism

There is almost a consensus among contemporary scholars and researchers in various fields that defining terrorism presents a number of difficulties.[2] Such difficulties tempt scholars who study terrorism to discuss issues arising from it without first attempting to define the term,[3] and this is also the case with even the major nation-states and institutions in the modern world. According to Amir Taheri, "It is surprising that, although the West in general and the United States in particular are prime targets of most forms of contemporary terrorism, these countries have done so little to define and understand the danger."[4] This attitude apparently reflects a state of despair[5] because of the number of problems arising from the inability to reach a convincing and agreed-upon definition of terrorism.[6] Therefore, before attempting to discuss the important aspects of terrorism from a Qur'anic perspective, it is essential first of all to define this term. Although it is difficult to arrive at a definition that will please all scholars,[7] the Saudi researcher

ʿAbd al-Raḥmān Sulaymān al-Maṭrūdī states that it is necessary for Muslim scholars, law-makers and official bodies to reach a unified, precise and measurable definition of terrorism.[8] However, this definition, he continues, is surrounded by numerous definitional problems to which many scholars and researchers refer.[9] Thus, it is important to discuss such definitional problems before presenting and evaluating the definitions themselves.

Indeed, the inability of the international community to agree upon a unified definition of terrorism is the major problem that poses the greatest obstacle to defining this term.[10] According to Walter Gary Sharp, "Although the international community began a concerted effort to control international terrorism in the late 1920s, it has never been able to agree on a definition of international terrorism."[11] Almost all members of the international community, particularly those concerned with the study of terrorism, condemn it but unfortunately without exerting much effort to define it.

Another serious obstacle to defining terrorism is relativism. This is highly stressed by both Muslim and non-Muslim scholars.[12] For al-Maṭrūdī, both the definition of terrorism and the acts of terror are "relativistic", i.e. they vary from one society to another and from one culture to another. What is seen as terrorism by one society may not be so by another. Al-Maṭrūdī further states that what a given country views as a legal right may not be so in other countries.[13] As a Muslim researcher, his view of relativism is also shared by his non-Muslim counterparts such as Perlmutter, who refers to two well-known sceptical statements which assert that relativism is a major problem in defining terrorism: "One man's God is another man's devil" and "One man's terrorist is another man's freedom fighter."[14] This latter is also reiterated by Turner, who states that the promulgation of this cliché constitutes a major problem in defining terrorism.[15] It should be noted here that these pessimistic clichés are very popular among other specialized theorists concerned with defining terrorism such as Javaid Rehman.[16] In addition, scholars such as Teichman, who cites the first cliché to refer to the same definitional problem, acknowledges that "terrorism is a disputed term".[17] Stressing how big the problem is, Asma Barlas adds that "if one person's freedom fighter is another's terrorist, then on what basis can we distinguish between them?"[18] This challenging question put forward by Barlas indicates the seriousness of the issue of "relativism" because of which researchers in the field are faced with a tough definitional challenge.[19]

Dynamism can be identified as a third problem in defining terrorism. Most of those who tackle the action admit that terrorism is a "dynamic" term whose types, forms and motives, according to the Muslim researcher Haytham ʿAbd al-Salām Muḥammad, vary according to time and place.[20] However the factor of dynamism is more or less related to the issue of relativism discussed above. Here, Haytham is not adding a problem that can be considered significant, but is referring to dynamism as a simple problematic element that overlaps with relativism. He identifies specific problems faced by those dealing with terrorism from an Islamic perspective, stating that every objective explanation of terrorism becomes a condemnation of it.

Haytham also refers to the Western media as a major factor behind the hazy definition of terrorism, stating that the Western media campaign launched under the banner of *mukāfaḥat al-irhāb* (combating terrorism)[21] does not distinguish between different forms of terrorism, some forms of which some may regard as legitimate, arguing that the aim of this Western campaign is to tarnish the image of Islam.[22] However, Haytham's views here seem to be vague and unrealistic. He himself mentions what he considers "legal and illegal terrorism" without defining the difference between the two, leaving his reader in utter confusion.

Looking at the major definitional problems identified above, it can be observed that they reflect the deplorable reality that all attempts to decry terrorism and acts of terror fail to reach a universally acceptable definition of the action. However, according to Jörg Friedrichs, reaching such a definition is essential to help the fight against terrorism.[23]

In addition to the major definitional problems identified above, there are other minor definitional problems, such as lack of objectivity, which leads to a tendency to apply the label "terrorist" to enemies while turning a blind eye to equally terrorist acts carried out by friends or allies pursuing congenial goals.[24] Moreover, the lack of "precision and certainty demanded by legal discourse" are, according to Ben Saul, problems that are likely to be encountered when an attempt is made to define terrorism, especially in the field of international law.[25] Saul further states that determining whether the struggle for national liberation or self-determination is a form of terrorism or not is a difficult issue, which adds more complexity to the debate about the definition of terrorism. Thus, mixing the term "terrorism" with both jihad and resistance creates a problem for those attempting to define all these terms. Furthermore, seeing some Muslims contending that terrorism is a basic Islamic term adds to the complexity of the issue and creates a state of uncertainty about the sincere efforts exerted by Muslims and non-Muslim scholars who are attempting to define it.[26] Finally, it can be said that the limitation in almost all the definitions of terrorism is a relatively minor problem which challenges the comprehensive understanding of this thorny issue.[27]

It appears that it is because of the above major and minor definitional problems that scholars find the term "exceedingly difficult to define mainly because of the ideological and political aspects" it involves.[28] Susan Tiefenbrun, Professor of Law at Thomas Jefferson School of Law, states:

> It is hard to believe that a word like "terrorism," which is used so frequently these days in different contexts and in casual, colloquial, political, and legal discourses, does not have a universally-accepted definition. It is not enough to say, as United States Supreme Court Justice Potter Stewart once said of pornography, "we know it when we see it." Terrorism must be deconstructed to distinguish between domestic and international terrorism, state-sponsored and non-state sponsored terrorism, and terrorism per se and legal revolutionary violence that falls within the law of war.[29]

More importantly, in light of the current media campaign in which violence is unjustly attached to Islam, it is of paramount importance for Muslims to reach a comprehensive definition of terrorism, particularly from an Islamic perspective, for the following reasons. Firstly, the absence of a clear understanding of what constitutes terrorism is a stumbling block that adds more uncertainty and complexity for those who study terrorism from an Islamic perspective in general and a Qur'anic perspective in particular. Secondly, terrorism poses a challenge to our daily activities if it is left without a precise definition. According to Roberta Senechal de la Roche, "Without a useful definition of terrorism, a theory of the subject [i.e. terrorism] is not even possible. How do we identify a case of terrorism? What characteristics distinguish it from other collective violence?"[30] Thirdly, defining what constitutes terrorism is of extreme importance in order to evaluate whether or not it is a punishable crime according to the Qur'an. It is worth noting here that there is much controversy about whether or not modern terrorist acts are equal to *ḥirābah* (brigandage, armed robbery) referred to in the Qur'an (5: 33–38).[31] Fourthly, attempting to define terrorism in clear terms will make it possible for Muslims and non-Muslims to understand where terrorism stands in relation to Islam, and whether or not the Qur'an, as a Divine book, prescribes severe punishments for terrorists.[32] Fifthly, the definition of terrorism sought in this chapter is intended to enable researchers in the field of Qur'anic studies to become better able to put the views of both traditional and modern Qur'an exegetes in their true contexts. Sixthly, the terms terrorism and jihad are mistakenly used interchangeably by some modern researchers. That is why defining terrorism and explaining the difference between it and jihad will clarify many of the misconceptions related to both.[33] Indeed, equating jihad with both holy war and terrorism as some have done causes a great deal of confusion.[34]

There are two important issues worth considering before embarking on defining terrorism. The first is the fact that there is vast amount of literature dealing with the definitions of terrorism from "as early as 1920s" with up to "109 different official and academic definitions of terrorism" from differing religious, political, legal, economic and sociological perspectives.[35] It is of great importance here to state clearly that the focus of this chapter will be on the definitions of terrorism from an Islamic perspective, whilst drawing on other definitions where relevant. Thus, a special focus will be given to definitions of religious-based terrorism in general and from an Islamic perspective in particular.

The second issue to be highlighted here is the following:

> Terrorism inspired by religious goals is by no means confined to Muslims or the Muslim world for that matter. In recent decades, Sikh groups in the Punjab section of India; Jewish settlers who live on the West Bank (in territory Israel occupied during the 1967 war); and extremist Christians who hope to accelerate the coming of the Millennium ... have all carried out terrorist attacks in order to further their goals.[36]

Thus, the "terrorism" being discussed here is not restricted to a specific nation or religion.[37] It is, therefore, clear that current media claims in many parts of the world that terrorism is attached to Islam and Muslims are unjust. The "correlations" between "Muslim terrorists" and "Muslim terrorism"[38] make terrorism, according to Mahathir Mohamad, look as though it is a "Muslim monopoly". It is similarly questionable, according to Mahathir, to attribute every wrongdoing done by Muslims to the religion (i.e. to Islam), regarding all Muslims as one monolithic group. This leads to painting a whole religion with the brush of a few criminals within it. He further states that "every terrorist act is attributed to Muslims until proven otherwise".[39] Indeed, this view is shared by many other Muslim scholars.[40]

Terrorism in Classical Arabic

Before presenting the legal definitions of terrorism, it is important to track the term itself in both Arabic and English lexicons, with special reference to the occurrence or otherwise of the term in the Qur'an. As far as the Arabic language is concerned, the words *irhāb* and *irhābī* ("terrorism" and "terrorist" respectively) occur neither in the Qur'an nor in the old Arabic lexicons. Muslim scholars such as Muḥammad al-'Ulamā' argue that the reason behind this non-occurrence can be attributed to the fact that these two terms are products of the modern age.[41] This view is stressed by another contemporary scholar, Kuṭb Muṣṭafā Sano, who supports this view with an even deeper insight stating:

> With an in-depth look into the intellectual, creedal, political, and juristic literature, it can be easily seen that no one of the classical Muslim scholars in those different fields has ever attempted to define terrorism. Terrorism is a modern issue that has not been referred to let alone been tackled by the classical jurists or exegetes.[42]

Indeed, the above view of Sano constitutes a landmark in exploring the history of modern terrorism in the Muslim intellectual, juristic and exegetical literature. On the one hand, it proves to a great extent the falsehood of those who propose "hawkish interpretations", who believe in having carte blanche to strike terror into the hearts of their imaginary enemies.[43] On the other hand, it undeniably rebuts the allegation of researchers such as Haytham Muḥammad who claim that al-Rāzī is the "ideologue of the philosophy of terrorism".[44] The baselessness of Haytham's allegation here is self-evident, especially when the scholarly statements laid down by the two prominent scholars mentioned above are taken into consideration. Thus, it is unfounded to claim that there is a necessary link between the Qur'anic lexeme *rahaba* (to fear), along with its derivatives, and the term "terrorism", which lexically refers to the use of violence for political aims.[45] What clearly establishes the above view is that the Cairo-based Academy of Arabic Language endorses the use of the word *irhāb* (terrorism) as a newly-introduced word in the Arabic language with the root *rahaba*. The Academy states that terrorists are those who adopt violence and terrorism to achieve their political objectives.[46] This definition of the academy is the same as that adopted by the authors of *al-Mu'jam al-Wajīz*.[47]

From the above, it can be observed that some researchers and lexicographers believe that the term "terrorism" has its roots both in the Arabic language and in the Qur'an. However, they admit that there is a yawning gap between the "positive" fear that denotes respect inherent in the lexeme *rahaba*, and the word *irhāb*, which refers to the "negative" fear occurring as a result of threats arising from using different material force. Thus, according to them, *irhāb* in its negative sense is equal to *ru'b* (fright) or *zu'r* (horror), and both meanings have nothing in common with the "reverent fear" understood by the Arabic word *rahaba*.[48]

Other researchers argue that terrorism has been wrongly translated into Arabic as *irhāb*, stating that the precise translation of the word should instead be *ir'āb*. Therefore, it is of great importance, as far as the issue in question is concerned, to make such differing viewpoints known because this paves the way towards enhancing awareness of the serious repercussions that surface as a result of mixing linguistically different terms together (i.e. *ir'āb* and *irhāb*), when seeking to define terrorism. When, for example, the word *rahab*, *rahaba* and *irhāb* are all said to mean "reverent fear" or "awe", they are, according to Scott C. Alexander, all primarily directed to God alone (e.g. 2: 40), though misdirected toward other issues (59: 13),[49] then such interchanging adds more confusion to what are already confusing concepts. Here, it can be stated that unlike *rahab*, which has an almost exclusively positive connotation, *irhāb* carries an exclusively negative connotation. On the one hand, while *ir'āb* can be considered as a very accurate Arabic translation of the English term "terrorism", it is infrequently used. *Irhāb*, on the other hand, is more common, even though it expresses the true meaning less accurately.

Terrorism in the English Language

The term "terrorism" is not originally an English word but rather an adopted one, which found its way into the English language only at the time of the French Revolution.[50] The word "terror" itself, according to Charles Tilly, also entered the West's political vocabulary to describe the actions of French revolutionaries in 1793–1794.[51] Viewing the aims of the French Revolution, which according to Bruce Hoffman were adopted to establish order during the anarchic period that followed the uprising of 1789, it can be easily observed that the word "terrorism", when studied in its original context, carries a positive meaning.[52] Thus, when it comes to the meaning of the term "terrorism", it can be claimed that it was originally positive but the word acquired negative connotations later on. It was after World War Two, according to Hoffman, that the meaning of terrorism gained the revolutionary connotations with which it is most commonly associated today. He also states that in the late 1960s and 1970s, the word terrorism continued to possess its positive revolutionary context whereas in the 1980s and 1990s the word came to be regarded as referring to means to destabilize the West.[53] Thus, it is only recently that the term begins to acquire a negative meaning, although writers such as Whittaker would argue that the English word "terrorism" has long had a negative meaning.[54]

Looking at some of the reputable English dictionaries, it can be easily noticed that most of the definitions either trace the origin of the word to the French Revolution[55] or else limit its lexical definition to the use of violence for political rather than ideological or religiously-motivated aims, making the attempt to define terrorism from this perspective difficult.[56]

It appears from the above that there is a similarity between the words *irhāb* and "terrorism" in that neither is found in classical dictionaries. Rather, these words were introduced into both Arabic and English as a result of particular contextual and historical circumstances. In both languages, they mostly carry similarly negative connotations, and especially in recent times, as is vividly demonstrated by the historical origin of the English word and its relation to the *régime de la terreur*, and the recent introduction of the word *irhāb* into modern Arabic lexicons. However, this similarity in terms of the etymological aspect of both words does not rule out the fact that both words are wrongly translated. When *irhāb* is translated as "terrorism" and vice versa, a great deal of confusion arises from the implicit claim that they are bilingual synonyms. Yet, as stated above, it is *irʿāb* and not *irhāb* that is the most accurate Arabic equivalent of the word "terrorism". Therefore, the differences in perception and usage between *irʿāb* and "terrorism" in Arabic and English contributes to widening the gap in understanding that exists because of failing to reach a common bilateral lexical definition of both words. A general evaluation of the dictionary definitions of both words leads to the conclusion that, while useful to a certain extent, they are of little help, which is why attempting to tackle the legal definitions of terrorism should be seen as essential.

Legal Definitions of Terrorism

Legal definitions of terrorism include economic, social, and religious types among others. This last type of terrorism is perhaps the most vivid of all. It has various internal subcategories, such as the internal terrorist strife between Protestants and Catholics within Christianity, or between Sunnis and Shi'ites within Islam. Thus, even within a single religion, "intra-religious terrorism" between followers of the same faith can be clearly seen, with a dissenting group emerging and claiming that their path is the correct one, and are prepared to back the political ramifications of that claim with violence. There are also sorts of other definitional "layers" within each type of terrorism, for example, academic, individual, governmental, non-governmental, international, national etc. While I focus on definitions of religious-based terrorism within Sunni Islam that are given by official and unofficial organizations, where relevant, I discuss some non-Muslim definitions to explore their similarities or dissimilarities. The reason for my selective approach is the lack of definitions of terrorism from a religious perspective, even academic ones.[57] I have also chosen to narrow this discussion of legal definitions of terrorism further to organizational definitions in view of their wide public promulgation and the legislative effectiveness of such official organizations.

The first legal organizational definition to be cited here is the official definition formulated in Cairo on 22 April 1998 by the Arab Convention for the Suppression of Terrorism, which was adopted by the Council of Arab Ministers of the Interior and the Council of Arab Ministers of Justice in their final declaration. According to Article 1.2, the definition runs as follows:

> Terrorism is any act or threat of violence, whatever its motives or purposes, which occurs in the advancement of an individual or collective criminal agenda. Its aim is to disseminate panic among people, causing fright by harming them, or by exposing their lives, freedom or security to danger, or attempting to cause damage to the environment or to public or private installations or property or occupying or seizing them, or attempting to jeopardize any of the national resources.[58]

The second definition appears in a statement issued by the Islamic Research Academy at al-Azhar on 1 November 2001:

> Terrorism is the act of frightening the secured, destroying their public interests, life essentials and human dignity for the purpose of sowing aggression and corruption on earth.[59]

The third definition was issued in a resolution published by al-Majmaʿ al-Fiqhī al-Islāmī (Islamic Fiqh Academy), which is affiliated to the Muslim World League (MWL) in Saudi Arabia, at its sixteenth session, held in Mecca 5–10 January 2002. The text of the resolution, with special focus on the definition, states:

> Terrorism is the aggression perpetrated by individuals, groups or states[60] with the purpose of infringing against people's religion, life, intellect, property, and honour. It includes all types of disseminating panic, harm, threat or killing unjustly, including armed burglary, striking terror among travellers and highway robbery. It also includes all acts of violence or threats to implement any individual or group crimes for the sake of striking terror among people or terrifying them through threats of causing harm to them or endangering their lives, freedom, security or general

> conditions. It also includes causing harm to the environment, public utilities or public or private properties.[61]

The fourth definition was issued by Majmaʿ al-Fiqh al-Islāmī al-Dawlī (International Islamic Fiqh Academy), which is affiliated to the Organization of the Islamic Conference (OIC), at its seventeenth session, held 24–28 June 2006:

> Terrorism is aggression or the dissemination of panic or threat materially or immaterially carried out unjustly by states, groups or individuals against people's religion, self, honour, intellect and property. It comprises all types of aggression and corruption.[62]

Definitions of Terrorism Evaluated

A close examination of the above four definitions discloses the seemingly biased approach in them, because they apparently give a judgmental view of terrorism, considering it a form of aggression, and hence unlawful (haram), as far as Islam is concerned, instead of giving the reader the opportunity to have a full perception of the essential nature of terrorism. The above definitions, with the exception of the second one, attributed to the Islamic Research Academy at al-Azhar, share the view that "threat" is a tool of terrorism, as well as the act of aggression which is its main component. All the definitions agree that terrorism needs to be necessarily related to political objectives, which is a common perception of the terrorist act, particularly in the non-Muslim context, but also refer to aggression against man or nature, whether the objective is political, religious or economic, etc. In addition, these definitions agree that terrorism is not restricted to a specific nation or religion. They consider the threat or use of violence against innocent people or public or private property to be the aspect of terrorism that is criminalized and prohibited in Islam.

None of the four definitions refer specifically to the targets of terrorism. All focus on the "terrorist" but do not refer to *al-murhab* (the one who is terrorized), whether or not he is violable or inviolable in the Islamic sense, or the source of his *'iṣmah* (inviolability).[63] According to Sano, the inviolability (or violability) of *al-murhab* has its source in either religion or in the place where he lives.[64] For him, these two sources are the only criteria upon which *al-murhab* is either granted or denied security.[65] He further states that it is essential for any definition of terrorism to include a clear reference to these two factors, because both of them affect the permissibility or impermissibility of terrorist acts.[66]

Moreover, another unmistakable element in the MWL and the OIC definitions is the emphasis on terrorism being "unjust" aggression or killing. This may be seen indirectly to consider as alien to terrorism violence that furthers a just cause, such as in the case of freedom fighters who unilaterally consider themselves to be fighting for a legal right or in self-defence. Boaz Ganor considers that the MWL's definition cited above implies that acts committed in a just cause are permissible. In a tone apparently critical of the MWL's definition and definitions similar to it, Ganor argues that these definitions cause a great deal of confusion, thwarting any attempt to reach a consensus definition of terrorism.[67]

Indeed, Ganor's evaluative approach is one of the very few attempts that have recently begun to surface in international conferences concerned with the study of terrorism. His view is also expressed in many other conference papers submitted to the fifth three-day Worldwide Security Conference (WSC5) organized by the EastWest Institute (EWI) on 19–21 February 2008. Interestingly, this conference attracted more than 750 security experts, government officials and concerned Muslim and non-Muslim scholars, who gathered from different parts of the globe to discuss terrorism-related issues with especial focus on its relation to jihad. The major topics for WSC5 occupied the front pages of many well-known websites in both Muslim and non-Muslim countries.[68]

All the above-cited four definitions were all referred to throughout a three-day international conference entitled "Islam's Stance on Terrorism" organized by Al-Imam Muhammad Ibn Saud Islamic University in Riyadh, Saudi Arabia on 20–22 April 2004. The conference brought together more than 120 Muslim scholars and researchers from places as diverse as Asia and North America to discuss terrorism.[69]

With these two examples of international attempts to define terrorism, among many others, it can be safely asserted that, after 11 September 2001, there have been ever-increasing attempts to study terrorism from a religious perspective, with special reference to definitional issues. The attempts made by the Muslim scholars at the Saudi-based conference, as well as the definition put forward by the Islamic Research Academy at al-Azhar, may be called a "semi-collective" effort by modern Muslim jurists to explore terrorism, something hardly imaginable for the classical exegetes whose opinions are considered throughout this book.

The four definitions mentioned above reflect the most prominent efforts by Arab Muslims to define terrorism. Of all these definitions, the least comprehensive is the Azhar's, while the apparently most comprehensive is the Islamic Fiqh Academy's. The Azhar's definition emerged a few weeks after 11 September 2001, and it looks like a hasty response to condemn the attacks and reject any link between the teachings of Islam and terrorism. It is clear from the statement issued by the Azhar that this was not done solely to define terrorism, but also to express its view as a leading Islamic institution about the 11 September attacks, after which terrorism was often (wrongly) linked to Islam and Muslims. In addition, the first and the second definitions refer neither to the causes of terrorism nor to state terrorism.[70]

Those of the Arab Ministers and al-Azhar represent the official Arab definition of terrorism and that of the highest seat of Islamic learning in the Sunni world, but despite their official status the definitions themselves are apparently vague. Both have been widely quoted, but researchers such as Ganor have regarded the definition of the MWL in Saudi Arabia as representing the Islamic view of defining terrorism, which is not entirely accurate.

There are certain weaknesses in Ganor's analysis of the MWL's definition, which devalue his criticism of the definition. The first is the ambiguity of the source from which Ganor obtains his definition. Although he states straight after his quotation that the

"Muslim World League, 2001" is his source, he refers neither to the original source of his quoted definition nor to the website of the MWL, even as a secondary source.[71] The second is that, given that the original language of the definition is Arabic, Ganor's quoted version is imprecise and he does not state whether he is quoting from another source or has translated it himself from Arabic into English. The definition as he quotes omits, for example, some of the forms of terrorism mentioned in the original, such as "armed burglary, striking terror among travellers and highway robbery". The third is that Ganor selectively chooses the phrase "outrageous attack" as a translation of the Arabic word *'udwān* although the precise English equivalent is "aggression".[72] The final weakness is that Ganor overemphasizes the "killing without a just cause" in his quotation, considering it a major stumbling block to reaching a consensus definition of terrorism, while he pays comparatively little or no attention to the "terrorized", or to "state terrorism", whose perpetrators commit acts of terror, whether justifiable or not.

In spite of these reservations about Ganor's criticism of the MWL's definition, his apparent interest as a non-Muslim researcher in examining and evaluating the definitional attempts by the scholars of the MWL is in itself remarkable in view of the small attention non-Muslim scholars paid by to definitions put forward by their Muslim counterparts. However, the attempts made by non-Muslim scholars themselves to define religious-based terrorism are worth stressing here in order to see how similar or dissimilar their definitions are, and whether or not both worlds may reach a consensus definition in the foreseeable future.

Definitions of Terrorism in the non-Muslim Context

Non-Muslim scholars concerned with investigating religiously-based terrorism argue that religious motives, whether Jewish, Christian or Islamic, are the most important defining characteristics of modern-day terrorism.[73] Hoffman stresses this view, stating that religiously-based terrorism leads to a considerably higher level of casualties if compared, for example, with secular terrorism. He further argues that, between 1998 and 2004, religious-based terrorism—although it led to only 6% of recorded incidents—was responsible for 30% of the total number of fatalities.[74] Such appalling statistics lead Hoffman to declare that religious-based terrorism is more striking in what he dubs as "Muslim terrorism" than that in any other religion. This is the core of Hoffman's argument, despite the fact that he occasionally mentions that religious-based terrorism is not exclusively confined to Islam.[75] Yet despite this tendency to consider Islam as mainly responsible for terrorism, it is rare to find scholars such as Hoffman and his peers simply defining what is meant by religious terrorism or even Muslim terrorism. Even the definitions they adopt, such as that of the Federal Bureau of Investigation (FBI), contain religious along with ideological and political components.[76]

Given the above, it can be generally observed that many of the non-Muslim researchers on terrorism resort to commenting on the given definitions of terrorism formulated by Muslim scholars, as in the case of Ganor above. Researchers such as Aref al-Khattar would argue, therefore, that there is no satisfactory religious-based definition of terrorism, and there is a pressing need to search for a meaningful definition while admitting that there is a general lack of literature on terrorism in this regard.[77] Given this situation, it is of great importance to discuss the very few definitions that are apparently considered relevant to the religious realm of the definition of terrorism in general and the Islamic concept of terrorism in particular, according to those who adopt them, in order to bridge the gap that exists between the two.

Here, it can be argued that non-Muslim terrorism writers such as Hoffman and Perlmutter give special importance to the FBI's definition of terrorism, claiming that it constitutes the base upon which a religious definition of terrorism can be formulated.[78] Given that the US sets the political agenda globally, and it has been dominating such debate on terrorism for more than a decade, it is highly salient to discuss this apparently influential American definition, which runs as follows:

> [Terrorism is] the unlawful use of force or violence against persons or property to intimidate or coerce a government, the civilian population, or any segment thereof, in furtherance of political or social objectives.[79]

The second definition to be presented here is that of the US Department of Defense which defines terrorism as:

> The calculated use of unlawful violence or threat of unlawful violence to inculcate fear; intended to coerce or to intimidate governments or societies in the pursuit of goals that are generally political, religious, or ideological.[80]

The third definition to be mentioned here is what Dawn Perlmutter named the "Definition of Religious Terrorism", which goes as follows:

> Religious terrorism is defined as any act of violence or threatened use of violence by a group or individual with the intent of intimidating individuals, citizens or governments in the furtherance of religious objectives. Religious terrorism is frequently characterized by the imposed or self-imposed infliction of either physical, psychological, symbolic or spiritual assaults in order to achieve the group's and/or individual's objectives.[81]

Now what is motivation behind this selective list of three quotations? It can be observed that American definitions of terrorism in general and the FBI's definition in particular have been cited in almost all discussions about this issue, especially since the tragic events of 11 September 2001. This interest is noticeably shared by both Muslim and non-Muslim researchers in the field. Modern Muslim scholars such as Sano, for example, discuss the FBI definition of terrorism, arguing that it "gains weight by virtue of carrying the influential American brand represented in the FBI".[82] Other Muslim researchers even cite the FBI definition without mentioning the reason, and deal with this definition at face value.[83]

American definitions of terrorism are arguably the most cited in comparison with others by both Muslim and non-Muslim researchers. The latter place much emphasis on the FBI's definition and consider it, along with the State Department's definition, as the basis from which a definition of religious terrorism can be derived.[84] Perlmutter's individual definition of terrorism cited above provides an example of this derivation. Thus, this wide citation among specialists and the apparent interlinkage between these official definitions and the ideological and religious elements stressed in derived definitions may be considered sufficient reasons to analyse them here. Al-Maṭrūdī, for example, is one of the modern Muslim researchers who refer to the State Department's definition of terrorism even without commenting on it, even though he considers it as the American definition of terrorism.[85]

A critical tone is noticeably absent in the writings of Muslim researchers about these definitions. For example, a considerable number of the papers submitted to the 2004 Saudi-based conference referred to earlier mention several definitions in general along with the FBI's. The FBI's definition is frequently referred to without contextualization, comment or analysis. An exception is Sano's scholarly critique of the definition. Sano's selection of the FBI's definition is far more deliberate, as he evaluates it in juristic terms in comparison with other Islamic definitions.[86] So the fact that both Muslim and non-Muslim researchers give special attention to the FBI's definition is a point worthy of discussion.

Both Sano and Hoffman discuss the FBI's definition in detail. Both refer to the international scholarly status of those who formulated this definition, stating that it reflects certain priorities and interests of the FBI as an international organization, although, in contrast to Hoffman, Sano does not allude to this latter point clearly.[87] Moreover, they refer to the generalization of political and social objectives in the definition. Although Hoffman does not consider this to be a weakness in the definition, Sano opines that the definition not only limits the objectives to political and social ones but that it is silent concerning whether the action committed is lawful or unlawful from an Islamic perspective. This, according to him, is a crucial point in determining the nature of, and hence the ruling concerning, a given terrorist act.[88] Hoffman's approach is analytical, while Sano's approach is juristic, applying the tools of a Muslim jurist whose main objective is to determine whether actions are permissible or prohibited. Finally, as the FBI's definition refers neither to religious nor ideological objectives – a fact acknowledged by Hoffman – Sano attempts to criticize in Islamic terms the seemingly "un-Islamic" definition by citing three main reservations. These include the absence of scientific objectivity about formulating the definition, generalizing the position of the terrorized, and generalizing the aims of terrorism.[89] For Sano, the FBI's definition is neither a religious definition with complete or semi-complete characteristics nor, according to Hoffman, is it a comprehensive general definition, as it overstresses political and social objectives while neglecting others.

These shortcomings in the FBI's definition mean that a religious or an Islamic definition of terrorism cannot be based on it. It is void of any reference to religious objectives. The US Department of Defense's definition, on the other hand, significantly refers to religious, ideological, and political objectives, although it omits the social objectives mentioned in the FBI's definition. The numerous elements in the Department of Defense's definition lead Hoffman to declare that it is arguably the most comprehensive among the other definitions he cites.[90] This makes Perlmutter argue that both definitions constitute the basis for a religious definition of terrorism,[91] and this may explain why Perlmutter's definition is mentioned above as the only scholarly definition that omits any reference to state terrorism, although it does refer to "psychological, symbolic or spiritual assaults", which the official American definitions cited above do not refer to. Perlmutter's definition also refers to religious terrorism in general without going into details about each religion's definition of terrorism. Although she dedicates a whole chapter to discussing Islamic beliefs and Islamic religious sects in particular,[92] she neither names nor articulates an Islamic definition of terrorism in her book.

Synthesizing a Definition of Terrorism

The above analysis of non-Muslim definitions of terrorism reveals that they do not provide the basis for a single comprehensive Islamic definition of terrorism. Sherman A. Jackson has argued that this is because Muslim and non-Muslim scholars alike devote little attention to the Islamic definition of terrorism.[93] The definitional attempts presented so far in this chapter refer to religious terrorism rather than singling out the Islamic definition of terrorism per se, although the non-Muslim organizations and authors whose "religious" definitions of terrorism are presented in this chapter also provide a rich resource for condemning what they call "Muslim terrorism".

Moreover, the lack of consideration of Islamic definitions of terrorism by non-Muslim scholarship is paralleled by the paucity of Muslim scholarly definitions having Qur'anic interpretations as their basis. Although modern Muslim scholars have made concerted efforts to disassociate terrorism from the teachings of Islam in general and even from the Qur'an, their efforts to formulate a comprehensive definition of terrorism from a Qur'anic perspective are still very rare. In the rich literature by modern Muslim scholars who discuss the definition of terrorism, it is still unusual to find a scholarly attempt to put forward a Qur'anic definition of terrorism. I could find no definition of terrorism from a Qur'anic perspective by a Muslim researcher except for that formulated by Aḥmad ʿĪsāwī. Yet while his definition[94] makes reference to a Qur'anic "approach", it uses a generalized Islamic methodology.

A Proposed Islamic Definition

Based upon a critical evaluation of the various definitions cited earlier in this chapter, and especially those from an Islamic perspective, I would propose that an Islamic definition of terrorism could be deduced as follows:

> Terrorism is the premeditated, physical or non-physical attempt by individuals, groups or states to infringe upon the

> religion, life, intellect, property or honour of innocent people, regardless of their faith, race or nationality. It consists of all types of unjust dissemination of panic, harm, threat or killing, including brigandage, striking terror among travellers, and causing harm to the environment and public utilities, carried out for non-Islamic and illegitimate causes.

Having now proposed a definition of terrorism from an Islamic perspective, I would like to further propose that, on its basis, terrorism could be classed as a crime in Islam.[95] In the reminder of this chapter, I would like to explore briefly the history of this crime within Islam, and to assess whether or not the Qur'an has referred to any aspect of terrorism as stipulated in my proposed definition.

Two Attitudes in the History of Muslim Terrorism

Many contemporary studies either associate or disassociate modern terrorist actions with the eleventh-century Assassins in Islamic history.[96] In this regard, it can be observed that there are two main attitudes, of which the major dominant one links modern 'Muslim terrorism' historically to the Assassins. This dominant attitude can be widely seen in the works of some non-Muslim authors such as Bernard Lewis and J.P. Larsson.[97] The other attitude is less powerful and hence its supporters are far fewer in number. Olivier Roy is supposedly the champion of this attitude. He states that there has almost never been an example in Muslim history to parallel today's terrorist acts, claiming that Lewis – being a champion of the proponents of the first attitude by virtue of concerning himself with the etymological aspects of the Assassins – established the opposite while trying to link present-day terrorism to the Assassins.[98] To back his argument, Roy states that the Assassins themselves constitute a marginalized heresy and so they are an exception in Islamic history.[99] However, Larsson counters Roy's argument, declaring that, although much of the information available about the Assassins is derived from sources that are historically unreliable, or deliberately misleading, and is mentioned in passing in the absence of a comprehensive and objective study dedicated to the Assassins as a subject in their own right, there are nevertheless still some authoritative writings solely dedicated to unravelling the real history of the Assassins.[100] Moreover, he argues that there are similarities between contemporary religious terrorists and the Assassins, stating that the strong belief in martyrdom, as well the intention not to escape or survive their mission of assassination, are the main elements that link modern-day terrorists to the 'first terrorists' (i.e. the Assassins).[101] Indeed, the Assassins, as a perverted sect in Islam, are seemingly the most controversial for modern non-Muslim researchers who trace the history of "Muslim terrorism". Compared with other sects that engaged in various forms of killing and assassination in Islamic history, such as al-Azāriqah, the Khārijites, al-Khannāqah or al-Raḍḍākhūn, and al-Qarāmiṭah (Karmathians), the Assassins remain one of the most radical sects in Islamic history, although the "Assassins" who survive today, according to Larsson, are far removed from modern-day terrorism.[102] Having now briefly dealt with the historical aspect of terrorism in Islam and the polemics surrounding it, it is time to discuss the Qur'anic references to various aspects of terrorism.

The Qur'an and Various Forms of Corruption

A careful consideration of the components of the proposed definition of terrorism above, as well as most of the other definitions discussed in this chapter, makes it apparent that killing and other forms of corruption are the major aspects of terrorism that are clearly presented.[103] Indeed, the Qur'an has much to say about these elements. *Fasād* (causing corruption) and its various lexemes such as *fasada* (to become corrupt), *afsada* (to act corruptly), *mufsid* and its plural form *mufsidūn* (corrupting person(s)) occur fifty times in the Qur'an.[104] Those fifty occurrences have many forms that can be categorized as general and specific so as far as terrorism is concerned.[105] General references to *fasād* in the Qur'an include reference to declaring disbelief in Allah, hypocrisy, extravagance, magic, etc., whereas the specific references to *fasād* and its derivatives that are thought to have a direct relationship to various forms of modern-day terrorism include unjust killing, acting corruptly, and causing corruption (i.e. *fasād* and *ifsād*) in the land by destroying crops, livestock and other public utilities.[106]

According to Khalid Abou El Fadl, the Qur'an refers to various forms of corrupting the earth, such as terrorizing residents and wayfarers, as well as other attacks in which non-combatants are targeted.[107] However, the main form of corruption that is directly related to terrorism from a Qur'anic perspective is unjustly taking the life of a human being, irrespective of his or her faith, race or geographical location.[108] Such action is strongly prohibited in the Qur'an: *Do not take life, which God has made sacred, except by right...* (17: 33).[109]

Al-Rāzī states that this verse indicates that taking the life of a human being without a just cause is the greatest sin after associating partners with Allah. He stresses that strong prohibition (*al-ḥurmah al-mughallaẓah*) is the original ruling that governs killing others unjustly, affirming that killing can only be legitimate if clear reasons are established.[110] Here, al-Rāzī gives an outstanding explanation for his inference from the verse, especially when he discusses the main reasons behind the prohibition of murder, arguing that taking the lives of others unjustly constitutes an irreparable harm that runs counter to the main spirit of Islam, as a religion that states that there should be neither harm nor reciprocating harm. Moreover, al-Suyūṭī stresses that the above verse was the first Qur'anic verse to be revealed prohibiting the killing of others unjustly.[111]

In this respect, modern exegetes, such as al-Shaʿrāwī, assert that taking the life of a single soul unjustly renders the whole society responsible and not just the killer himself.[112] However, holding the whole society responsible for the crime committed by a single individual, as described by al-Shaʿrāwī here, is an unnecessary overemphasis on the prohibition of such a crime at a time when the Qur'an is decisive in declaring that *no soul shall bear the burden of another* (53: 38).[113] This Qur'anic concept of personal responsibility for one's actions is reiterated five times in the Qur'an, leaving no doubt that the collective responsibility of society should not be asserted unnecessarily.[114] The society itself is a group of individuals and accepting al-Shaʿrāwī's opinion here without question is a form of injustice against innocent people who neither commit nor share in the criminal act of killing. The fact that murder is a horrible crime is not a pretext for declaring that once it is committed by a single individual, the society becomes responsible or shares in the responsibility. The Qur'an, according to Abou El Fadl, "reminds Muslims that no one should be made to suffer for the sins of another".[115] Unlike al-Shaʿrāwī, Quṭb gives a very balanced explanation of 53: 38 by stating that each human life has a sanctity that cannot be violated, arguing that Allah is the Giver of life and none other than Him can take life away without His permission and within the limits He has allowed.[116] Furthermore, Quṭb quotes a hadith narrated by Bukhārī and Muslim, which, according to him, contains the only three legal justifications for killing. The hadith, reported by ʿAbdullāh ibn Masʿūd, goes as follows:

> No Muslim person who bears witness that there is no deity other than God and that Muhammad is God's Messenger may be killed except for one of three reasons: a life for life, a married adulterer and a rebel who renounces his faith and abandons his community.[117]

Although Quṭb quotes this hadith as evidence for specifically stating that killing is only permissible in these three cases, Ibn Kathīr considers it to be major evidence for the prohibition of taking the life of others unjustly.[118] Moreover, a careful investigation into both Ibn al-ʿArabī and Darwazah's interpretations of the above verse reveals that the two exegetes look at the verse from two different angles. Although Ibn al-ʿArabī gives much attention to the second half of the verse and talks about the rulings pertaining to *qiṣāṣ*[119] (retribution), Darwazah focuses on the first half of the verse while only citing two hadiths to support the view that the Qur'an prohibits such heinous acts of killing.[120] The first hadith he cites is narrated by Ibn ʿUmar, who reported the Prophet as saying, "A believer remains within the scope of his religion as long as he does not kill another person illegally."[121] The second hadith is reported on the authority of ʿAbdullāh ibn ʿAmr ibn al-ʿĀṣ in which the Prophet is reported to have said, "The destruction of the whole world is less enormous in Allah's sight than killing a Muslim."[122] Indeed, "killing a Muslim" in this hadith is not meant on its own. Al-Jaṣṣāṣ states that 17: 33 is evidence for the prohibition of the unjust killing of a Muslim or a non-Muslim, with no distinction between the two.[123]

It has now become clear that the classical and modern exegetes give special emphasis to the seriousness of taking the lives of others unjustly. No one accepts that such a horrible thing can be legalized, and so it can be argued that the Qur'an forbids unjust killing – something that is almost inseparably linked to modern-day terrorism.

Moreover, when telling the stories of ancient nations, the Qur'an refers to what may be termed "state terrorism", in which the tyrannical ruler(s) or those in authority mercilessly torture and kill their subjects unjustly. ʿAbd al-Raḥmān Spīndārī cites 2: 49 and 7: 141 as clear examples of this.[124] Moreover, it can also be added that 28: 4 directly refers to the Pharaoh, the king of Egypt, as an example of a tyrannical ruler who terrorizes his subjects and spreads corruption among them by slaughtering their male children at birth, and sparing their female offspring.[125] The reason for this, according to Quṭb, was to ensure that their women outnumbered their men, and hence weakened them.[126] The approach of the exegetes towards all these verses is linked to the historical context and the occasions of revelations related to them. Noticeably, the modern exegetes follow the line of the classical ones: the approaches of al-Shaʿrāwī, Quṭb and Darwazah in their interpretations are very similar to those of classical exegetes such as al-Ṭabarī.[127] Therefore, it can be said that the idea of linking today's modern terrorist actions with something similar within the Qur'anic context is a meretricious aspect of personal interpretation exercised by modern Muslim researchers. Spīndārī, al-Maṭrūdī and Zakī Abū Ghaḍḍah are three modern Muslim researchers whose efforts in this regard should be highlighted due to their laudable contribution on this particular point.

Spīndārī argues that the Qur'an talks about what may be termed "religious terrorism" practised by the followers of a certain religion against those who have a different faith. He cites the story of *aṣḥāb al-ukhdūd* (the trench-makers) mentioned in 85: 4–10 as a clear Qur'anic example of persecution and oppression against those who refused to adopt the religion of the oppressors, and as a result they were buried alive and burned in mass graves.[128] Another form of "terrorism" according to Spīndārī is the "terrorism of the upper class" in society against the weak. He gives the example of the Quraysh's plot against the Prophet to capture, kill or expel him - to which there is a reference in 8: 30 - as an example of this.[129] With all the forms of terrorism Spīndārī refers to, he attempts to take the Qur'anic discourse beyond its historical and occasional contexts to relate it to the modern-day terrorism.

With the above definition of terrorism in mind, it can be said that Spīndārī's attempts here should be credited as being the product of modern scholarly reasoning carried out with an eye on current-day realities, in those cases where the Qur'anic discourse has many historical and circumstantial verses and chapters. It is through applying and making use of modern tools that these verses and chapters need to be unravelled in order to pave the way towards an insight into the Qur'anic text and context not only with regard to terrorism-related issues but also other challenging issues of modernity.

Al-Maṭrūdī is the second Muslim researcher whose effort to relate some forms of modern-day terrorism with the Qur'anic text cannot be overlooked. He declares that, as far as the Qur'an is concerned, the destructive act of killing is as old as the presence of humanity on earth. To back his view, al-Maṭrūdī states that the God–angels dialogue in 2: 30 is a reference to that.[130] He cites this verse to argue that terrorism is deeply rooted in human history, and that human suffering from it is ancient too.[131] Al-Maṭrūdī's inference here may be a personal understanding of the Qur'anic text in a modern context, although he apparently derives his argument from many classical exegeses such as those of al-Ṭabarī, al-Qurṭubī, and Ibn Kathīr. They state that the angels' dialogue with God is no more than inquiry (*istifhām*) on their part after they know that the jinn have corrupted the earth before the creation of Adam, and thus they inquire whether the new *khalīfah* (viceroy) will be like the jinn who corrupted the earth and shed blood or whether he will be an obedient *khalīfah*.[132] Unlike classical interpreters, modern ones such as al-Shaʿrāwī, Riḍā, and Mawdūdī, for example, do not pay much attention to the God-angels dialogue regarding the corruption of human beings on earth, but rather focus more on the nature of man's *khilāfah* and his creation, as well as why Allah honours Adam and his children over other creatures through knowledge.[133]

Following al-Maṭrūdī's line of thinking, Abū Ghaḍḍah states that there is a reference in the Qur'an to the first story of "religious terrorism" in human history.[134] Abū Ghaḍḍah further states that 5: 27–31 is a clear reference to this where Cain, the eldest son of Adam and Eve, murders his brother Abel. He further states that this act of unjust killing should be considered a terrorist act because Cain, the killer, does not have a legally-acceptable right to kill Abel. According to Abū Ghaḍḍah, his primary motives for killing him are envy and jealousy arising from his brother's supposed marriage to his beautiful sister.[135] It should be added here that classical interpreters such as al-Qurṭubī and modern ones such as al-Shaʿrāwī clearly point out that the murder to which 5: 27–31 refers is evidence that killing is a very old act, stating that Abel is the first victim of murder in human history.[136] However, Abū Ghaḍḍah's argument is not very well-founded because he attempts to impose 5: 27–31 as a main reference within the context of modern-day terrorism while divorcing these verses from their contextual and historical circumstances. The murder of Abel is not motivated by "religious terrorism" as Abū Ghaḍḍah claims, but rather by envy and jealousy, which he himself admits. It may be reasonable here to accept the fact that Abel is the first victim of murder in human history, as argued by the exegetes above, but not claim that he was the first human victim of "religious terrorism".

The second issue that deals with terrorism-related forms within the Qur'anic discourse on *fasād* refers to its domains, causes and effects. And not only that, but it also clearly states its judgment concerning *fasād*[137] and the *mufsidūn*, as well as their punishment in clear terms.[138]

As far as Qur'anic references to *fasād* are concerned, there are five main passages which can be said to have direct links to terrorism-related forms. These are 2: 30–51, 5: 34, 18: 94, 27: 34, and 30: 41. It is also worth noting that in these five passages different lexemes of *fasād* also occur, such as *fasada* (to become corrupt), *afsada* (to act corruptly, to cause damage), *fasād* (causing corruption, physical damage), and *mufsid* (someone who spreads corruption).[139]

Most of the classical and modern interpretations cited above show that *fasād* and its lexemes in the above five passages refer to killing, the destruction of crops and livestock, polytheism, various moral sins such as adultery and theft, and natural disasters. Human beings in all these occurrences are the primary cause of *fasād* through their irresponsible act of killing and of lapsing into sin, leading to moral decline. The domains of *fasād* include aggression against human beings through killing and other acts such as adultery, theft and destruction of fauna and flora. Al-Rāzī, as an example, commenting on 2: 251, states that *fasād* in this verse refers to killing and committing sins. He backs his argument by citing references from the Qur'an in confirmation, such as 30: 41 and 40: 26.[140] This is the case with al-Suyūṭī when he interprets 5: 34, and al-Alūsī's interpretation of 18: 94 and 30: 41.[141] It can thus be stated that the Qur'an is concerned with the elements of modern-day terrorism through the various examples it mentions. The opinions of the classical and modern interpreters on this issue, although not directly related to this statement, still constitute a guide to modern Muslim researchers who try to formulate a link between some elements of modern-day terrorism and the Qur'an in terms of how the latter deals with such elements, and whether its attitude is generally supportive or otherwise.

The Qur'an prohibits outright causing corruption in the land. Frederick Denny states that *fasād* is very frequently paired with the phrase "in the land/earth" in the Qur'an citing 5: 30 as an example.[142] Out of the 114 surahs (chapters) in the whole Qur'an, five surahs clearly refer to the prohibition of causing corruption or acting mischievously in many of their verses.[143] In nine passages, the Qur'anic attitude is very clear in prohibiting corruption in all its forms where the prohibitions *lā tufsidū* (*Do not cause corruption*) and *lā ta'thaw* (*Do not act mischievously*) are used interchangeably, although the latter (i.e. *lā ta'thaw)* occurs five times and the former occurs only four times.[144] *'Ithiyy* (mischief), which occurs once, is the absolute form of corruption according to al-Alūsī.[145]

A careful consideration of the contexts of the nine occurrences reveals that two of them refer to individuals who are prohibited from committing corruption. In 28: 77, Allah orders Qārūn *not to seek to spread corruption in the land, for God does not love those who do this.*[146] In 7: 142, the Prophet Moses orders his brother Aaron to *act rightly* and *not to follow the way of those who spread corruption.*[147] The Qur'an further addresses specific communities such as the Children of Israel (Banū Isrā'īl) in 2: 60, the People of 'Ād in 7: 56, the People of Thamūd in 7: 74, the People of Madyan in 11: 85, and the People of Shu'ayb in 26: 183, prohibiting them all from causing corruption on earth.

A close reading of both classical and modern interpretations of these occurrences shows that those communities were involved in committing acts of killing and robbery; a reason behind the Qur'anic prohibition of corruption and all its forms. Such acts, prohibited by the Qur'an, are still committed by perverted individuals against their fellow human beings and by countries against other countries in our modern world.

Importantly, it can be argued that the Qur'anic call for the cessation of all forms of corruption is a nostrum from which modern societies can greatly benefit. Of all the Qur'anic passages concerning corruption, the following verse may be considered comprehensive: *Do not corrupt the earth after it has been set right – call on him fearing and hoping...* (7: 56).[148] It addresses a wider audience that transcends individuals and small community groups to include all human beings in every age and clime. Mawdūdī noticeably adopts this attitude by considering that human beings are the main reason behind the spread of corruption on earth as they succumb to base desires and alter the light of Divine Guidance.[149] 'Abd al-Fattāḥ

Idrīs further opines on the basis of this verse that attacking human beings, animals and the environment is a criminal act according to the law-giver.[150] This can also be easily discerned from the way classical and modern exegetes, especially al-Qurṭubī and al-Alūsī, deal with this verse. Al-Qurṭubī states that Allah prohibits people from committing any form of corruption in the land whether it is of lesser or greater effect. He quotes al-Qushayrī (d. 465/1072) as saying that this verse is a call to avoid associating partners with Allah, shedding blood and causing disorder on earth.[151] Unlike al-Qurṭubī, al-Alūsī derives a more generalized implication from 7: 56, stating that it prohibits all forms of corruption whether done against individuals, properties, intellect, honour and religion.[152] Indeed, al-Alūsī's explanation here is inextricably linked to the definition of terrorism I proposed above as he deals with the verse uniquely as if he were a twenty-first-century exegete applying his hermeneutical tools while witnessing modern-day terrorism in which the religion, life, intellect, property and honour of civilians are targeted.

Conclusion

The discussion in this chapter has raised a number of central difficulties surrounding the definition of terrorism, with particular attention being paid to Islamic perspectives. It is clearly the case that reaching a comprehensive definition that will satisfy all scholars is highly unlikely, due to certain major and minor definitional problems among which "relativism" and "dynamism" are major contributing factors. However, I would argue that reaching a "semi-collective" definition, while difficult, is still possible.

I have traced the lexical origin of the Arabic word *irhāb* and the English word "terrorism", showing how these words were introduced and then used in both languages. They have conflicting meanings, at least with regard to their lexical origins. More importantly for my purpose here, the Arabic word *irhāb* neither occurs in the Qur'an nor in the old Arabic lexicons. After evaluating the organizational definitions of terrorism, with a special focus on Islamic institutions, as well as Islamic scholarly opinions, I offered a definition which, it is to be hoped, avoids many of the weak points in the definitions surveyed above. Another goal of this proposed definition is to help bridge the gap between non-Muslim and Muslim scholarship in attempting to understand and define terrorism from an Islamic perspective, or who attempt to define it with respect to religions.

While I have shown that modern-day terrorism is not tackled in Qur'an exegesis in either ancient or modern times, the Qur'an nevertheless refers to many of its elements by discussing various types of corruption that may be linked to modern terrorism, and I concluded that the Qur'an takes a very decisive attitude in prohibiting and condemning all types of corruption committed against human beings and their property, intellect, honour and religion, as well as other forms, such as destroying the environment.

Overall, the Qur'an exegetical tradition concerning killing and other forms of corruption leads to the conclusion that while the Qur'an itself does not explicitly define or tackle modern terrorism, it refers to certain elements that are essential in almost all general definitions of terrorism as well as Islamic ones. While defining terrorism is important, in and of itself a definitional exercise is insufficient. This is because a great deal of confusion and perplexity in the understanding of both terrorism and jihad that exists in the minds of many non-Muslims as well as some Muslims. In the next chapter, I will attempt to remove such perplexity by focusing on 8: 60 as my main case study because this particular Qur'anic verse has been widely misunderstood with respect to the debate on jihad and terrorism, in which it has played a central role.

2

ARMING FOR DETERRENCE IN THE QUR'AN

MANY QUR'ANIC VERSES are sometimes used, or more accurately abused, to suit certain extremist ideological inclinations and to satisfy the unfounded intellectual thirst of some Muslims and non-Muslims. Each partisan group tries its best to promote its cause but with little care or attention to how the text of the Qur'an itself is understood by its mainstream classical and modern interpreters. In this chapter, I attempt to fill this lacuna by presenting the interpretation based on mainstream readings of the Qur'an. Away from the old-new debate about the so-called "verse of the sword", I present a thematic analysis of one of the most contentious verses in the Qur'an, which is 8: 60. Some Muslims and non-Muslims see this verse as a call for terrorism, which, I want to argue, stems from their lack of understanding that it calls Muslims to prepare for defensive purposes sufficient forces to deter their enemies. The verse reads:

> Prepare whatever forces you [believers] can muster, including warhorses, to frighten off God's enemies and yours, and warn others unknown to you but known to God. Whatever you give in God's cause will be repaid to you in full, and you will not be wronged.[1]

There are various reasons why this verse is of central importance in any discussion of the contemporary debate on Islam and terrorism. Firstly, the verse has been widely quoted by some extremist groups and I want to focus in particular upon one example, that of al-Jamāʿah al-Islāmiyyah (Islamic Group) in Egypt.[2] In this chapter, I will look at the Group before its initiative to reject violence (although I will look at this initiative in detail in Chapter 4). In its violent phase, the Group used 8: 60 as a pretext for subduing non-Muslims to Muslim rule as well as killing unbelievers. A statement quoting the verse attributed to Sayyid Imām al-Sharīf (better known as Dr Faḍl), the reformed ideologue of the Group, reads, "Terrorism is part of Islam and whoever denies that has indeed become an unbeliever (*al-irhāb min al-Islām wa man ankara dhālika faqad kafara*)."[3] While Egypt's Islamic Group turned away from the path of terrorism, movements such as al-Qaeda still embrace the same extremist interpretation.[4] Secondly, this verse was quoted worldwide in the media after originally being given in Arabic and was inaccurately translated into English in order to justify a fierce campaign in which the Qur'an was falsely portrayed as a "fascist book" calling for the killing of all unbelievers, e.g. in the film *Fitna* by the right-wing Dutch MP Geert Wilders.[5] The Muslim response to *Fitna* ranged from similarly counterproductive, reactionary accusations in which certain biblical verses were unfortunately taken out of context to various other media responses.[6] Lamentably, Wilders' political party is on the rise in the Netherlands, perhaps because of such Islamophobic campaigns.[7] Despite an exhaustive search, I did not find any detailed academic responses either to the Group's or Wilders' misuse of 8: 60. Thirdly, 8: 60 is apparently the only verse in which, according to Jørgen S. Nielsen, "the Qur'anic term that provides the modern Arabic word for terrorism, *irhab* ... can be – and actually is – used as a justification for terrorism."[8] Therefore, in light of this misrepresentation from both within and without the Islamic tradition, it is vitally important to understand the above verse in its true context.

Quwwah in the Qur'an

In Arabic, the word *quwwah* (power, strength) along with its derivatives occurs forty-two times in the Qur'an taking different lexical forms such as *qawiyy* (mighty) and *quwā* (mighty powers).[9] Interestingly, *quwwah* (pl. *quwā*), according to Elsaid M. Badawi and Muhammad Abdel Haleem, carries five meanings in the Qur'an: (1) power (81: 20); (2) affluence and prosperity (11: 52); (3) strength (30: 54); (4) resolution (19: 12); and (5) firmness (16: 92).[10] Noticeably, *quwwah* is referred to as having both material and immaterial aspects. In 2: 63, for example, the Qur'an refers to exerting effort to apply the teachings of the Torah when addressing the Children of Israel. The same is the case when Allah addresses the Prophet John in 19: 12.[11] In addition, the Qur'an refers to various forms of material and physical power, whether related to groups representing different nations (28: 78; 30: 9; 40: 22), or individuals such as the Prophet Moses, who is described in 28: 26 as "strong, trustworthy".[12] Allah is also referred to as the All-Powerful (*al-Qawiyy*) in 11: 66, and the Lord of Power (*Dhū al-Quwwah*) in 51: 58.[13] Having referred to some of the main usages and general meanings of *quwwah* in the Qur'an, it is important to focus on an aspect of *quwwah* that is essential to understand its use in 8: 60.

Quwwah according to Classical Exegetes

In their discussion of 8: 60, the classical exegetes al-Qurṭubī, al-Suyūṭī, Ibn Kathīr and al-Jaṣṣāṣ consider that the *quwwah* Muslims are ordered to prepare is mainly archery.[14] They all quote the following hadith to support their view: On the authority of 'Uqbah ibn 'Āmir al-Juhaniyy, who said: "I heard the Prophet saying while standing on the pulpit: 'Prepare whatever *quwwah* you [believers] can muster,' and then he said, '*Quwwah* is but archery, *quwwah* is but archery, *quwwah* is but archery.'"[15]

Al-Rāzī, however, broadens the concept of *quwwah* when he states that no specific *quwwah* is indicated in this verse, arguing that what constitutes *quwwah* is considered *quwwah* in itself, citing weapons and fortresses as examples. He also goes on to state that although *quwwah* is explained by many exegetes as meaning archery, this does not rule out other forms such as mastering horsemanship, adding that learning how to shoot arrows, use weapons, and ride horses is a communal obligation (*farḍ kifāyah*).[16] The apparently broad understanding of *quwwah* held by al-Rāzī is shared by al-Ṭabarī, who states that Allah orders the believers in the above verse to prepare for combat against their enemies in jihad by using all available means that might eventually lead to their victory. Such means include weapons, archery, warhorses and other means. He further adds that the concept of *quwwah* in this verse is general in its application, stressing that, while the Prophet explained *quwwah* in the hadith cited above to mean archery, there is no indication in the text that archery is the only meaning intended. Al-Ṭabarī even argues that the above hadith is weak (*ḍa'īf*),[17] although there is no clear evidence for this, given that this hadith is included in Abū Dāwūd's *Sunan* and classified as authentic in this reliable hadith collection.

Furthermore, some other classical exegetes, such as al-Suyūṭī give an unusual explanation of the word *quwwah* in the above verse. *Quwwah*, according to him, refers to stallions, whereas "warhorses" (i.e. *ribāṭ al-khayl*) refers to mares. What makes this explanation unusual is that it is neither supported by the Prophetic hadiths nor by the Arabic language itself. Other classical exegetes, such as Ibn al-'Arabī leave the word *quwwah* unexplained, while referring in detail to the various advantages of having mares on the battlefield compared to stallions. To support his view, he cites several sayings of the Companions of the Prophet, who argued that mares were preferred to stallions because the horse of the Angel Gabriel was a mare. This even leads him to argue that it is praiseworthy (*mustaḥabb*) to have mares rather than stallions on the battlefield. Ibn al-'Arabī's view here lacks even lexical support, because a reference to the meaning of the Arabic word *khayl* (horses) in Arabic lexicons proves otherwise.[18]

An in-depth look into the classical exegeses cited above shows that a seemingly limited concept of *quwwah* is encouraged, and followed by classical exegetes in their explanations. This concept, which mostly limits *quwwah* to archery and sometimes leaves the word unexplained, is related to the explanations derived from the well-known hadith of the Prophet cited above. Only al-Rāzī and al-Ṭabarī broaden the concept of *quwwah* to include different types of weapons, fortresses, and horsemanship.[19] Importantly, the occasion of the revelation of the verse - which is strongly linked to the two preceding verses (8: 58–59) - refers, according to al-Alūsī, to the Prophet's intention to confront the people of Makkah because he knew they were collaborating with Banū Khuzā'ah against him and his Companions.[20]

Thus, the context of the revelation of 8: 60 refers to an imminent war between the Muslims and the unbelievers, which naturally necessitated that Muslims arm themselves in order to be able to repel an impending attack by their enemy. The classical exegetical understanding of the verse remains linked to this warring situation, and therefore implicitly rejects the absolute use of *quwwah* beyond this context, especially when innocents are targeted in terrorist acts.

Quwwah According to Modern Exegetes and Scholars

One of the foremost modern exegetes who discussed the issue of *quwwah* in detail was Quṭb. Commenting on 8: 60, he discusses the concept of *quwwah* and its purposes as follows:

> The first purpose that this *quwwah* serves is to establish peace and security for those who choose to accept Islam so they do not suffer any persecution as a result of this choice. Second, it deters the enemies of Islam from contemplating any form of aggression against the land of Islam. Third, such enemies would be sufficiently intimidated that they would not ever entertain any thought of trying to check the tide of Islam as it fulfils its mission of liberation. Finally, this *quwwah* is to be used to break any force that claims the attributes of the Almighty Allah and enforces its laws and legislation on human beings and refuses to accept that all sovereignty belongs to the Creator alone.[21]

The four purposes of *quwwah* referred to in the above quotation show the range of meanings Quṭb perceives in *quwwah*. According to him, it is a comprehensive and all-embracing concept; a view that is not shared by either modern or classical exegetes. *Quwwah*, according to him, has both constructive and destructive aspects. The first and the second purposes above indicate that *quwwah* has an apparently positive and constructive nature. Its aim is to establish peace and security and save Muslims from persecution at the hands of their enemies. According to the third and fourth purposes, however, it is perceived as something negative and destructive because its aim, in Quṭb's understanding, is to intimidate those who may think of stemming the tide of Islamic liberation. In this case, *quwwah* is to be used to break those who refuse to surrender to the Sovereignty of Allah (*ḥākimiyyat Allāh*), a controversial concept widely discussed in some of Quṭb's writings.[22] Importantly, Quṭb also perceives *quwwah* as something limitless, which Muslims are ordered to secure to the best of their ability.

Having discussed these four purposes, Quṭb also refers to the importance of acquiring resources as a conditional element in attaining *quwwah*, stressing that the *quwwah* Muslims are ordered to establish should strike fear and disseminate terror in the hearts of the enemies of Allah. According to him, there are two kinds of enemies: those who are open and hostile and therefore known to the entire Muslim community, and others who hide their animosity and hostility towards Islam.[23] In addition to embracing such constructive and destructive forms of *quwwah*, it can be inferred that Quṭb strongly propounds the offensive use of force; an attitude for which he has been severely criticized. This criticism has been pointed out by Mohd Shah Bin Jani who states that the source of criticism of Quṭb lies with liberal critics and Western observers, who tend to find a direct link between Quṭb's understanding of jihad and the widespread violence and political turbulence that significantly characterized so-called "Islamic" radicalism in Middle Eastern politics throughout the 1970s and early 1980s. Although Bin Jani argues that the influence of Quṭb on many extremist or radical groups in Egypt and in other Arab countries has been exaggerated, there are elements of truth in the analysis of these liberal and Western critics.[24]

Undoubtedly, these extremist views of Quṭb – in which *quwwah* shifts from being mere military preparedness for the purposes of deterrence to being an offensive tool whose purpose is to subdue others – have had their impact in shaping the understanding and attitudes of some extremist groups such as the Islamic Group in Egypt, as well as al-Qaeda and its affiliated groups internationally.[25]

The second important interpretation of 8: 60 is that of al-Shaʿrāwī, who focuses mainly on three central issues related to *quwwah*: (1) its aspects; (2) its arrangement; and (3) its means. Al-Shaʿrāwī refers to two aspects of *quwwah*: (1) its internal aspect, which he sees as the innate driving force that entirely equips one's mind and body with courage to face the enemy, and (2) the external aspect, which is the possession of modern, sophisticated and long-range weapons as well as all the means that can lead to the real possession of *quwwah*. A close look at al-Shaʿrāwī's interpretation of *quwwah* in the above verse shows that he agrees with Quṭb on the necessity of acquiring and possessing it. Furthermore, he views *quwwah* as something Muslims are ordered to acquire and exert to the best of their abilities. Once they have done their utmost, they are sure to be supported by Allah, the Omnipotent. To establish this concept, al-Shaʿrāwī compared the Muslims, who are supported by Allah, with their enemies, who have no source of support at all.[26]

Indeed, a thorough analysis of al- Shaʿrāwī's view of the internal and external aspects of *quwwah* may reveal that his interpretation is unique among traditional and modern exegetes. This is because having "internal" courage acts as a psychological shield that is as important and vital as taking all possible safety measures when entering the actual battlefield.

Discussing the arrangement of *quwwah*, al-Shaʿrāwī states that the development of *quwwah* is a preliminary step to war. War, according to him, begins with air missile strikes that are supposed to weaken the enemy before ground forces march forward. He considers this successive arrangement of *quwwah* as an inimitable (*muʿjiz*) aspect of the Qur'anic style, insisting that war has never begun with a ground invasion followed by air strikes; it is always air strikes that precede ground invasion, and not vice versa.[27]

This strict successive arrangement of *quwwah* argued for by al-Shaʿrāwī is not, however, the only method in modern warfare. While the successive arrangement of *quwwah* he referred to is quite common, it is not strictly followed in the way he mentions. Interestingly, al-Shaʿrāwī's interpretation of acquiring and possessing *quwwah* remains within the positive aspect of the term, in both its internal and external domains, which further confirms the connection of this thematic component of the verse (i.e. *quwwah*) with an imminent war situation, linked to launching deterrent strikes based on military preparedness. This does not rule out the idea of Muslims, both collectively and individually, being required to be militarily prepared to repel possible attacks. However, they are in no way allowed to turn their possession of *quwwah* into a destructive tool to harm civilians beyond a situation where hostilities are launched on a defensive basis, because peace is the norm of the relationship between Muslims and non-Muslims, as explained fully in Chapter 3 of this book. Although al-Shaʿrāwī explains *quwwah* in a broader sense, he does not clearly describe the mechanism for using it, or how it could be attained. This point, however, is clearly outlined by Riḍā. He associates the preparation of *quwwah* with war, stating that such preparation can be achieved in two ways: firstly, by preparing as well as possible all means that lead to *quwwah*; and secondly, by equipping Muslim soldiers to be ready to defend the community of Muslims worldwide (*ummah*) in case of attack. Riḍā states that the preparation of *quwwah* referred to in the verse under discussion differs according to time and place. Although he agrees with the classical exegetes that *quwwah* here refers mainly to archery, as stated in the Prophetic hadith above, he nevertheless maintains that the wording of the verse is general, and so it is obligatory upon Muslims in this age to spare no efforts in manufacturing various weapons such as tanks, warships and warplanes. He also states that mastery and excellence in developing the range of military industries is a communal obligation (*farḍ kifāyah*) upon Muslims.[28]

Moreover, Mawdūdī stresses that Muslims should have their

"standing army" on the alert whenever needed in order for them not to be caught unawares and then hurriedly have to look around to build their defences when it is too late. Falling short in carrying out this communal duty is, according to Darwazah, a heinous sin because it runs counter to the general Divine order in the verse and, as a result, exposes Muslim countries to physical and psychological harm.[29]

So according to the modern exegetes, *quwwah*, it turns out, is a broad concept. Although its interpretation is influenced by the way it was explained by classical exegetes, the verse is still seen as being applicable to modern-day military developments. With the exception of Quṭb's seemingly extreme view of *quwwah* being used as a "backbreaking tool", other modern exegetes observe that it is vital to apply *quwwah* in times of war and peace.

It may also be noted that modern exegetes do not refer to the Muslim state as the body responsible for the preparation of *quwwah*. Rather, they highlight the role of individual Muslims as if it were they to whom the verse is mainly addressed. The failure to develop the necessary means of *quwwah*, which is a communal obligation, according to them, is a heinous sin. Again, the role of the Muslim state is clearly marginalized, and it is only the individual's role that is stressed. Having discussed the purposes of the preparation of *quwwah* – its aspects, conditions and diversity according to time and place – according to modern Qur'anic exegetes, we now move to a broader and more comprehensive view, which is presented by some modern scholars.

The study of the concept and aspects of the preparation of *quwwah* in modern Muslim scholarship reveals that there is no significant difference concerning the importance and necessity of such preparation and the classical and modern exegetes. They all agree that the preparation of *quwwah* is necessary for Muslims; however, with respect to 8: 60, modern Muslim scholars have diverse opinions about the concept of *quwwah* itself.

Modern scholars agree that *quwwah* in this verse is not strictly limited to the physical aspect of military *quwwah* alone, and that it encompasses economic, educational, technical, administrative, moral, intellectual, psychological, financial and medical *quwwah* as well, which differs according to time and circumstance.[30]

One of the many modern scholars who discuss the preparation of *quwwah* in 8: 60 in great detail is Aḥmad Nār. He surveys various concepts of the preparation of *quwwah* in more than seventy pages in his *Al-Qitāl fī al-Islām*.[31] In Nār's view, the preparation of *quwwah* has five main categories: (1) theoretical, (2) material, (3) managerial, (4) technical, and (5) financial preparation. Nār goes on to mention the subcategories of each kind and their importance. He, for example, divides theoretical preparation into two main subcategories: (1) scientific, which includes ideas, principles and ideology; and (2) moral, which includes the behaviour to be followed by both leaders and soldiers. He also states that material preparation includes three sub-categories preparing: (1) individuals for the battlefield, (2) military supplies, and (3) the necessary ammunition.[32]

Although Nār's view of the concept of *quwwah* is detailed, it is mostly related to military preparation, especially when he discusses technical preparation.[33] Laudably, Nār has broadened the concept of the preparation of *quwwah* in a unique way in terms of the categories and subcategories he outlines in detail. However, Nār's continual linkage to achieving excellence in the battlefield limits his seemingly detailed concept of the preparation of *quwwah*. It is also noteworthy that only Nār's detailed discussion about the preparation of *quwwah* seems to be highlighted in only some of the modern English-written literature concerned with the issue.[34] It has not, as of yet, gained the wider popularity it deserves among Western academics. Furthermore, Nār is not the only scholar whose view about *quwwah* in 8: 60 is limited to military preparedness.

The well-known contemporary scholar Yūsuf al-Qaraḍāwī considers that military *quwwah* is the most important aspect of preparation in this verse, although such *quwwah*, in his understanding, is not sufficient by itself. Nevertheless, being self-sufficient in acquiring it – as opposed to acquiring it from others – for possible future use on the battlefield may become inevitable for Muslims. Referring to modern ways of possessing *quwwah*, al-Qaraḍāwī also draws a clear line between possessing and using weapons of mass destruction (WMDs). According to him, the Muslim *ummah* is obliged to possess these kinds of weapons. At the same time, he considers it strictly forbidden in Islam to use these weapons against others. He argues that Islam forbids killing non-combatants – women, children, the aged, farmers, and monks – let alone killing thousands or even millions at the same time by using WMDs.[35]

This last view of al-Qaraḍāwī is supported by the Azhar Institute of Fatwa in Egypt. A fatwa (or legal opinion), which first appeared in Arabic on www.islamonline.net on 23 December 2002 and was updated on 10 April 2007, states that manufacturing and possessing WMDs is an obligation upon Muslims in order to deter the enemies of Islam and defend Muslims, provided that this does not lead to transgression against non-combatants. It is even obligatory, according to the Azhar House of Fatwa, for Muslim countries to use any weapon that they deem suitable to defend themselves if using such weapons is necessary for self-defence.[36] This fatwa by the Azhar has been condemned by some Western authors, such as Anne-Marie Delcambre who claims on its basis that "the Islamic university of al-Azhar, in Egypt, preaches war ... [so] why should we expect Al-Azhar to speak the same language of peace as Pope John-Paul II?"[37] Delcambre's claim is baseless because she quotes selectively that part of the fatwa that serves her claim, while ignoring the restrictions stipulated in it that limit legitimate use of these weapons to defensive purposes. This selective approach could be erroneously applied to any other religious authority, e.g. the speeches and statements of the Catholic Popes. Delcambre also mistakenly refers to "the Islamic university of al-Azhar" as the source of the legal opinion rather than the Institute of Fatwa, which is an institution affiliated to the Azhar. However, some modern scholars, such as the well-known American scholar Muzammil Siddiqi, have opposed the opinion of al-Qaraḍāwī and that of the Azhar Institute of Fatwa, declaring that Islam is against all forms of WMDs. In his critique, Siddiqi does not distinguish between the possession and the use of WMDs, but it is clear from the context that he is against both, especially towards the end of his fatwa, where he calls for a universal ban on the testing, development and possession of all weapons of mass destruction and nuclear weapons.[38]

Thus, the differences between modern scholars regarding the possession and use of WMDs by Muslim countries reflect opposing attitudes. All that has been written so far about this issue, according to the best of my knowledge, does not amount to a comprehensive-enough deliberation on the issue. Therefore, it is necessary that individual and collective exertion of intellectual reasoning in understanding laws (*ijtihād*) be applied in order to study this important topic in the light of 8: 60.[39] Notwithstanding the need for further research, my preliminary view is that the possession of WMDs by Muslim countries may constitute a necessity in the contemporary age in order for Muslims to achieve the required deterrence that is clearly envisaged in 8: 60.

All in all, none of the modern scholars above have referred to any negative aspect of using *quwwah* against non-Muslims while employing violent means that may lead to killing. To the contrary, their discussion generally applies in times of both war and peace.[40] On those occasions when military conflict between Muslims and non-Muslims becomes inevitable, preparation for the use of *quwwah* is still limited to an enemy who either shows animosity or who could be judged to have the serious intent to attack Muslims. It is significant also to note the absence of any interpretations by modern or classical scholars – with the exception of Quṭb – that call for the "abuse" of *quwwah* in a way that is harmful to others. As shown above, this broad and continuous Sunni consensus justifies the rejection of marginal and extremist interpretations of 8: 60 both by terrorist groups and by some non-Muslims whose understanding of the verse proves to be highly selective.

Warhorses in the Qur'an 8: 60

Ribāṭ, which is originally derived from the root *r-b-ṭ* (to tie or bind), literally refers to the place where horses are usually tethered to protect the frontiers, but also to the horses themselves, and to the accommodation historically used by poor Sufis.[41] According to al-Aṣfahānī, *ribāṭ* in the Qur'an has two meanings: (1) "warhorses" (*ribāṭ al-khayl*), as in 3: 200 and 8: 60; and (2) "self-control" (*ribāṭ al-nafs*), as in 8: 11; 18: 14; and 28: 10. Al-Raḥmānī states that the word *ribāṭ*, like jihad, carries various meanings, although it is widely attached to *ribāṭ al-khayl*. Quṭb opines that *ribāṭ al-khayl*, which is one of the main aspects of *quwwah* in 8: 60, is not literally restricted to horses, but includes other forms of *quwwah*. He argues that Allah mentions warhorses in the verse because they were the most prominent means of fighting when the Qur'an was revealed.[42]

According to al-Qaraḍāwī, the *khayl* of our modern age are tanks, armoured vehicles, warships, submarines, gunboats, rockets and air missiles, as well as other sophisticated weapons used on land, sea and air. For him, *khayl* is just a tool in jihad that is subject to change according to time, place and circumstance. He further stresses that the real power is the human element and that any state-of-the-art weaponry is useless unless wielded by capable and well-trained soldiers. As stated above about the preparation of *quwwah*, *ribāṭ al-khayl* in its modern sense should be understood as a tool of defensive war, and its use as a tool of disseminating fear and terror into the hearts of non-Muslims who do not have an issue with Muslims is not permitted. Rather, it is a tool whose legitimate objective is to make the enemies of Muslims think twice before attacking their frontiers.[43]

The Arabic root *r-h-b*, which generally refers to 'fear', and its lexemes - such as *turhibūna* (to frighten off), *ruhbān* (monks), *istarhaba* (to seek to frighten) - occur thirteen times in the Qur'an in ten chapters (surahs).[44] The lexemes of this root word appear in three main lexical forms in the Qur'an; verbal form, verbal noun form, and active participle form. These three word forms do not convey identical meanings, although they are easily noticed in the Qur'an.[45] The thirteen occurrences refer to meanings such as: fearing Allah and being grateful for His favours (2: 40), according to al-Ṭabarī; fearing His punishment and being aware that one must not worship or associate partners along with Him (16: 51); disseminating fear among people through the use of magic tricks used by the magicians of Pharaoh in his challenge to the Prophet Moses (7: 116); those who fear Allah especially when they commit sins (7: 154);

the hypocrites being very fearful of Muslims (59: 13); monks (9: 31–34), and monasticism (57: 154). These meanings mentioned by al-Ṭabarī are also cited by al-Aṣfahānī (d. 502/1108), who adds that the Arabic word *irhāb* originally refers to terrifying camels. The textual meanings mentioned by al-Ṭabarī and al-Aṣfahānī are consonant with those mentioned by other classical Arab lexicographers.[46]

The above lexical and contextual meanings of *r-h-b* and its lexemes reveal that *al-rahab* (fear) and *irhabūnī* ("fear Me", i.e. Allah) are contextually associated with worshipping Allah and obeying Him. The two lexemes usually address unbelievers and the hypocrites. The word *al-rahab* and *istarhabūhum* (to seek to frighten them) occur in the contexts of magicians and the baseless imaginative thoughts that occur in people's minds. This is in addition to other meanings denoting lying and deceit. *Al-rahb* (awe or fear) refers to an extreme fear of Allah due to the miracles with which the Prophet Moses was supported. The word *rahaban* denotes fear of the punishment of Allah.[47]

Almost all the meanings of *r-h-b* and its lexemes refer to a two-way relationship. Firstly, they signify the human being's relationship with Allah, which entails fearing His punishment after hoping for His reward. Secondly, they denote the relationship between human beings, e.g. the above-mentioned fear the hypocrites feel about Muslims. Zakī Abū Ghaḍḍah goes so far as to state that *r-h-b* and all its derivatives in the Qur'an denote positive meanings indicative of a total abhorrence of killing, destruction, spreading injustice and occupying the lands of others.[48]

Turhibūna in the Qur'an 8: 60

As has been argued, the failure of some Muslims and non-Muslims to understand the context of 8: 60 and the word *turhibūna* (to frighten off) has led them to argue that Islam is a religion that supports terrorism, extremism and violence. The contemporary Saudi researcher al-Maṭrūdī notes that some writers not only claim that the teachings of Islam, as well as some verses and rulings in the Qur'an including 8: 60, justify terrorism but even justify calling for its adoption. Although he does not name any of these writers, some non-Muslim examples from the 2000s include Schwartz-Barcott, Dobrot and Grinstein, although they do not represent mainstream Western scholarship.[49] Al-Maṭrūdī describes such claims as baseless,[50] and stresses the importance of refuting this claim, arguing that a study of the lexical connotations of all the Qur'anic verses containing the word *irhāb* and its lexemes is necessary to dismiss such claims.[51] He does not undertake this himself but does deal with 8: 60 in detail. In view of the widespread false claims about this, the views of classical and modern exegetes concerning the word *turhibūna* in 8: 60 is extremely important.

Turhibūna in Classical and Modern Exegeses

Although researchers like al-Maṭrūdī state that the word *rahaba* and its derivatives refer solely to fear in the Qur'an, according to the collective views of the exegetes, a meticulous tracing of the meanings of the word in the Qur'an shows otherwise.[52] Although the meanings generally refer to fear, the absolute generalization of al-Maṭrūdī loses validity when the views of the classical exegetes are examined, not only with regard to the word and its derivatives, as he says, but also the word *turhibūna* itself.

Al-Ṭabarī, for example, states that the word *turhibūna* refers to bringing humiliation (*khizy*) to the enemies of Allah and the enemies of the Muslims. There is, however, a significant difference between fear (*khawf*) and *khizy*, even though the latter may refer to some physical and psychological aspects of the former. Ibn Kathīr and al-Rāzī also interpret *turhibūna* to mean fear.[53] However, al-Rāzī adds that *turhibūna* in this verse is intended to achieve five main objectives: (1) to prevent the unbelievers from invading the land of Islam; (2) to make them committed to paying the poll tax (*jizyah*);[54] (3) to make them embrace Islam; (4) to prevent them from supporting other unbelievers against Muslims; and (5) to increase the pride of Muslims.[55] These objectives have not been stated by other traditional exegetes in the way classified by al-Rāzī, and it may be said that some of them are unsubstantiated because, to take an example, there are no recorded historical instances in which non-Muslims paid the poll-tax in advance for fear of the overwhelming *quwwah* of the Muslims. In addition, being fearful of the power of others may lead people to leave their homeland, but it seems far-fetched to assume that it will as a matter of course affect their belief or make them change their religious convictions. Of course there is a reference in the Qur'an (16: 106–107) to declaring disbelief under coercion for fear of persecution, but again one may be compelled by physical fear to deny belief, while one's heart remains true.

Moreover, when Muslims demonstrate before people of other faiths that they are strong and powerful, it does not mean that they are doing so out of pride and ostentation. On the contrary, the true Muslim is the one who expresses more humility towards His Lord when his *quwwah* increases by showing more mercy towards all creatures, and not just his fellow human beings. Furthermore, al-Rāzī's first objective, which concerns preventing the unbelievers from invading the land of Islam as a result of seeing the *quwwah* of the Muslims, is an indirect call to peace. Unlike the other objectives, it can be assumed that this one may lead to peaceful co-existence among nations and therefore help to prevent war from breaking out.

Given the above, it should be made clear that the "collective" view of the exegetes asserted by al-Maṭrūdī is not as "complete" as he assumes. Importantly, the aims of fear mentioned by al-Rāzī cannot be absolutely followed or adopted in the way to which he refers. Equally important is to consider the views of modern exegetes regarding the aim of *turhibūna* in this verse, so as to discern the difference between what al-Rāzī and modern exegetes have stated.

Modern exegetes vary in how much they emphasize the objective(s) of *turhibūna* in 8: 60. Riḍā's interpretation virtually repeats those stated by al-Rāzī, while Darwazah does not refer to the objective of *turhibūna* or its centrality in the verse at all.[56] Al-Sha'rāwī, however, refers to "peaceful equilibrium" (*al-tawāzun al-silmī*) – an apparently different yet almost identical objective. For him, this peaceful equilibrium can be achieved when fear is disseminated in the other party by a country displaying its various military, economic and communicative powers. Its show of *quwwah* can be viewed as an effective way of preventing war from breaking out. As a result, an enemy of Muslims would think twice before attacking them.[57] Thus, according to al-Sha'rāwī, *turhibūna* encompasses peaceful, positive and comprehensive meanings. It is a means to peace because it helps prevent war, positive because its aim is not just to disseminate negative fear that leads to the outbreak of war but uses *quwwah* for a legally acceptable objective, and comprehensive because it refers to the importance of achieving excellence not only in military fields, but also in the economy and mass communications as well.

Moreover, the known enemy, according to al-Sha'rāwī, originally refers to the unbelievers of Quraysh, as well as the Jews and the hypocrites, during the Prophet's time. The unknown enemy of the Muslims refers to those who may not appear on the battlefield but harbour animosity towards Muslims.[58] This view of al-Sha'rāwī, which considers hypocrites to be part of the known enemy, seems inaccurate because hypocrites by nature being secretive about their true affiliation are more akin to unknown enemies. His understanding of *al-tawāzun al-silmī* is almost the same as Riḍā's coinage "armed peace" (*al-silm al-musallaḥ*), who argues that in this context it refers to the fear that exists in the hearts of the Muslims' enemies as a result of seeing the Muslims' *quwwah* on the increase, which will eventually help to prevent war. On the other hand, if Muslims did not show that they were powerful, or if they lagged behind in equipping themselves with the necessary *quwwah*, they would fail to achieve the objectives of *turhibūna* and, as a result, would become vulnerable to attack by their enemies.[59]

The two interrelated concepts of *al-tawāzun al-silmī* and *al-silm al-musallaḥ* are also acknowledged by the Egyptian scholar Muṣṭafā Zayd (1917–78) as taken from other exegetes. Zayd states that the aim of *al-silm al-musallaḥ* is to strike fear into the hearts of the enemies of Muslims, especially the polytheists, the Jews, and other enemies unknown to them. Zayd criticizes al-Rāzī for claiming that one of the meanings of *turhibūna* in the verse is to strike fear into the hearts of those Muslims who may harbour animosity towards fellow Muslims.[60] For Zayd, al-Rāzī's view cannot be accepted unless the Muslims who are thinking of attacking their fellow Muslims consider them as rebels (*bughāh*). Thus, according to Zayd, Muslims in this case would only be targeting rebels.[61] However, both al-Rāzī's claim and its refutation by Zayd are unsupported by the context of the verse or by logic. Careful scrutiny of the verses preceding and following 8: 60 shows that the context and the occasion of revelation of the verse refer to the relationship between Muslims and the unbelievers. There is no reference to *bughāh* in *Sūrah al-Anfāl* in general or to the context of 8: 60 in particular. Moreover, al-Rāzī's claim is far from being logically acceptable, as Muslims cannot be ordered to prepare the necessary *quwwah* to strike fear into the hearts of fellow Muslims, unless the latter are hypocrites known to the Muslim community. However, common sense dictates that the *quwwah* being prepared by Muslims would be in anticipation of attack by non-Muslim enemies. If there were to be animosity between Muslim factions, then reconciliation and not fighting, according to 49: 9, should be given priority.

In further explanation of the objectives of *turhibūna*, Quṭb clearly states that the first and main objective behind the preparation of *quwwah* is to strike terror into the hearts of the enemies of Allah, who may either be openly hostile or discreet in their feelings of enmity towards Muslims. Quṭb makes the case that the *quwwah* of Muslims is intended to intimidate their enemies even though the latter may not directly suffer the consequences.[62] Thus, Quṭb's view of *turhibūna* goes beyond the case for positive dissemination of fear that al-Shaʿrāwī and Riḍā make. He highlights the necessity of intimidation, which is a close equivalent to the Arabic word *ruʿb*, as an integral element in achieving the objective of *turhibūna*. Quṭb advocates a relatively extreme view that supports both fear, as a simple equivalent of *turhibūna*, and intimidation or *ruʿb*. What particularly makes Quṭb's view relatively extreme is that he seeks to equate *irhāb* with *irʿāb*. Yet, even though both words carry similar lexical connotations in Arabic by virtue of the fact that they both refer to fear, *irʿāb* refers specifically to panic, an aspect denoting physical intimidation, which is not a connotation of the lexical

Arabic word *irhāb*.[63]

Turhibūna in a Modern Scholarly Context

ʿAbdullāh al-Najjār argues that the word *turhibūna* in 8: 60 should be restricted to existing or imminent military confrontation between two armies, and that such confrontation should have a legal cause and objective. Al-Najjār also contends that it is not part of the legitimate causes or objectives to use *turhibūna* to deter those who are not at war with Muslims. Neither should it be used to cause destruction or unjust killing. He reluctantly declares that the apparent meaning of *turhibūna* in the verse refers to threatening the use of *quwwah*, and that it does not refer to inflicting actual harm.

Al-Najjār stresses that *turhibūna* should not be directed towards those who are not at war with Muslims.[64] In this context, he does not refer to a deterrent *quwwah* that is supposed to protect Muslims from being attacked, a point clearly highlighted by modern exegetes. Rather, he gives precedence to an apparently apologetic approach, while attempting to condemn international terrorism and reject any link between the latter and Islam. By stating that *turhibūna* is not directed towards those who are not at war with Muslims, al-Najjār is following a defeatist approach at odds with that of modern exegetes. Stating that *turhibūna* can only be applied at times of conflict between warring factions is a very limited explanation of a comprehensive concept as expounded upon by traditional and modern exegetes. This comprehensive concept is a permanent principle both in times of war and peace. It is a positive approach propounded by many other modern scholars such as al-Maṭrūdī who states that *turhibūna* lexically carries both positive and negative meanings. Al-Maṭrūdī adds that what is meant in the verse is the positive meaning, which prohibits killing, corruption and destruction and eventually leads to a permanent state of peace.[65] Unlike al-Najjār, al-Maṭrūdī views *turhibūna* as being equally directed towards those who are at war and those who live in peace with Muslims, because its aim is to stop war if it breaks out or to prevent it from happening in the first place. Thus, it can be argued that al-Maṭrūdī's explanation here is more convincing and balanced compared to that of al-Najjār.

In addition to the defeatist and the balanced approaches championed by al-Najjār and al-Maṭrūdī respectively, another extreme explanation of *turhibūna* can be clearly seen in the emotional writings and fiery statements issued by some Muslims and non-Muslims who adopt violence as a basis for relations between Muslims and non-Muslims. The proponents of this extreme view do injustice to 8: 60, especially the word *turhibūna*, by quoting it out of context.

Decontextualizing Qur'an 8: 60

Certain extreme views of 8: 60 are widespread and can be found in the many written statements made by those who champion violence as a basic norm in Muslim–non-Muslim relations. In a harsh criticism of one of these statements, ʿAbdul-Raḥmān Spīndārī lashed out against those who twist the meaning of the word *turhibūna* in 8: 60, naming them "terrorism theorists".[66] Spīndārī argues that their claim is baseless and their only share of Islam is in name only. He refers to one of the widely-propagated slogans: "Terrorism is part of Islam and whoever denies that has, indeed, become an unbeliever." As mentioned above, this statement is attributed to Sayyid Imām al-Sharīf who quotes 8: 60, claiming that terrorizing unbelieving enemies is a religious obligation dictated by this verse. Al-Sharīf claims further that those who deny this are unbelievers, also quoting 29: 47 in support of his view.[67]

Yet Spīndārī's harsh criticism of the "terrorism theorists" lacks a firm foundation. Although his *Al-Irhāb min Manẓūr Qur'ānī* was published in 2006, he seems not to have noticed that al-Sharīf and other members of the Islamic Group in Egypt had renounced violence some years prior to the publication of his book. Al-Sharīf and the leaders of the Group, which had taken a violent path in the early 1970s, announced their turn to non-violence on 5 July 1997 in a statement read by Muḥammad al-Amīn ʿAbd al-ʿAlīm, one of their members. This culminated in the publication of several books condemning violence and the clarification of various issues related to jihad. Although I could not identify a specific discussion of 8: 60, it can be readily observed from the Group's publications about jihad that it has forsaken its original notion of violence and now condemns killing or terrorizing non-Muslim civilians.[68]

While the Group has renounced violence, there remain other misguided groups that continue their advocacy of a unilateral war against non-Muslims, targeting both civilians and military personnel alike, and take 8: 60 out of context to justify their actions. According to al-Najjār, These groups harm Islam although they imagine that they are serving it. Their line of thinking is short-sighted and they have distanced themselves from the current realities of life, choosing a peculiar lifestyle in which they blindly imitate the eating habits, way of dressing, and line of thinking of the early days of Islam.[69] While al-Najjār focuses on the outward appearance of these misguided groups, other scholars, such as al-Qaraḍāwī, argue that their main problem lies in their minds, not in their consciences. For al-Qaraḍāwī, the majority of them seek to serve Islam sincerely, but good intentions do not justify illegal actions.[70] Al-Qaraḍāwī is far more balanced in his judgment than al-Najjār, who puts too much emphasis on the outward appearance and lifestyle of these groups rather than on their ideology or intentions. In this discussion, it should be borne in mind that most of the "terrorism theorists" as well as the misguided groups have not had a religious training capable of giving them scholarly insight. Their misguided views about Muslim–non-Muslim relations, and about 8: 60 as "the verse of terrorism", are neither scholarly nor authoritative.

The Enemy in the Qur'ān 8: 60

Of the forty-two occurrences of the Arabic word *'aduww* (enemy) in the Qur'an, two are mentioned in 8: 60, and enmity is also referred to indirectly.[71] The verse under discussion thus mentions three types of enemies in succession: the enemy of Allah, the enemy of Muslims, and other unknown enemies of Muslims who are only known to Allah. Compared with the details given in the other main themes of the verse, there is less emphasis on clarifying who the known enemies are (i.e. the enemy of Allah and the enemy of Muslims). Al-Ṭabarī states that the known enemy in the verse refers to the polytheists, while the hidden enemy refers either to hypocrites or to the jinn, giving precedence to the jinn because, at the time the verse under discussion was revealed, the hypocrites were not fearful of the might of the Muslims or their weapons.[72] Al-Ṭabarī's explanation is unsubstantiated by either contextual or historical analysis of the verse. The reason why he interprets the hidden enemy in the verse as referring to the jinn might be because the jinn belong to the realm of the unseen (*ghayb*) while the context of the verse mainly suggests a hidden human enemy.

Furthermore, Darwazah asserts that the unknown enemy in the verse cannot refer to the jinn. According to him, those who take this view refer to a hadith in which the Prophet gives this explanation, but Darwazah stresses that it is not mentioned in any of the collections of authentic hadiths, so it cannot be considered authentic. Darwazah's argument is reasonable and supported by evidence. Although he rejects the jinn as a possible interpretation, he adds that it is better to desist from attempting to discover the identity of the unknown enemy in the verse. What is more important is to prepare *quwwah* in order to face any known or unknown enemies who may attack the Muslim community.[73]

Moreover, the interpretation that considers the unknown enemy to be human is supported by many modern exegetes such as Riḍā, who follows and confirms the opinion of al-Rāzī who states that the hypocrites are the unknown enemy, and that only when the hypocrites see the might of Muslims would they be persuaded to forsake the hidden unbelief in their hearts and become sincere believers in Islam. He further adds that the hypocrites, who customarily seek to spread corruption and chaos within the Muslim community, will cease to do so when they see the might of Muslims on the increase.[74] Riḍā rejects al-Rāzī's first argument, which maintains that it is better to say that the hypocrites will try to adapt themselves to the teachings of Islam in order to become sincere believers. For Riḍā, a person has no control over his heart, so changing one's attitude comes first and foremost from adapting one's outward behaviour rather than one's heart.[75]

Al-Shaʿrāwī adopts what may be termed a "futuristic vision" concerning the unknown enemy when he states that it goes beyond the combatants in the battlefield to include all those enemies outside it who declare war against Allah, His Prophet and the Muslim community. He further argues that this "futuristic vision" confirms the accuracy of the Qur'anic style, adding that the general meanings of the verse under discussion, and the meaning of the unknown enemies in particular, are revealed day by day. With the passing of time, many unknown enemies will appear whom Muslims did not know much about, but they are known to Allah.[76]

The views of al-Shaʿrāwī and Darwazah are more reasonable in generalizing the identity of the unknown enemy. Had Allah wished to specify the unknown enemy, He would have mentioned it and saved the exegetes the agony of attempting to unravel its secrets. Making the enemy unknown acts as a motivating factor for Muslims to be on the alert against unexpected attack. Such generalization acts as a warning sign for Muslims to achieve the level of preparation necessary in various military and non-military fields, which is the main requirement set out 8: 60.

Concluding Qur'ān 8: 60

It is difficult to find a strong link between the explanations of classical exegetes of the end of 8: 60, namely *Whatever you give in God's cause will be repaid to you in full, and you will not be wronged*, and its main components discussed above. They do not provide any explanation for the last part of the verse, which refers to spending in the cause of Allah, e.g. in Ibn al-ʿArabī's exegesis.[77] This maybe because Ibn al-ʿArabī generally prioritizes verses that contain legislative rulings, so he left the last part of the verse unexplained. Other classical exegetes adopt a general explanation, namely that Allah is encouraging Muslims to spend in His cause, who are assured of His generous rewards in this world and in the Hereafter. However, there is hardly any reference to the importance of spending in the process of preparation of *quwwah* that is the subject of the first part of the verse.[78]

On the other hand, it is clear that modern exegetes, such as al-Shaʿrāwī, Quṭb and Riḍā, link the end of the verse to its beginning, stating that good preparation of *quwwah* entails generous giving.[79] However, the nature of the link is described in various ways. For example, al-Shaʿrāwī strongly urges Muslims to spend generously so as to prepare to face their enemies in case of attack, although this preparation and spending should lead them to justice and not to transgression. Al-Shaʿrāwī refers to 8: 60 in support of his argument.[80] Quṭb stresses that the encouragement to spend in the verse means that Muslims should have mutual support (*takāful*) to be able to carry out jihad in the cause of Allah.[81] Quṭb's focus on solidarity is also emphasized by Riḍā, who stresses that it is incumbent upon the *ummah* to spend in Allah's cause to make the necessary preparations. If Muslims are miserly and refuse to spend, the Muslim ruler has the right to order the rich to spend according to their ability in order to protect the *ummah* from its enemies. Riḍā uniquely links spending in the cause of Allah in 8: 60 to what he calls protective jihad (*al-jihād al-wāqī*), in which those who have been wronged launch an attack to resist the wrongdoers. He states that there is a very strong link between the verse under discussion and 22: 39–40.[82] Compared with what other traditional and modern exegetes have said, Riḍā provides an in-depth and straightforward explanation of the last part of the verse. His view concerning "protective jihad" is difficult to trace in the explanations given by both the classical and the modern exegetes surveyed in this chapter.

Conclusion

From the foregoing discussion, it would appear that the meaning of the text of the Qur'an, like any other divine text, can be easily altered if studied without giving due importance to its original context. This decontextualization provides the rationale for the survey of classical and modern exegesis of 8: 60, as well as other modern scholarship, the context of which originally related to the strong possibility of war between Muslims and non-Muslims. The verse calls for Muslims to be well prepared for possible or imminent military attacks against them. The various themes highlighted in this chapter – including the preparation of *quwwah*, the warhorses, *turhibūna*, and spending in the cause of Allah – are all means that should serve Muslim causes in times of war and peace. It emerged that *quwwah* should not be understood only in the sense of physical and military preparation. Rather, it is a comprehensive concept that encompasses economic, educational, intellectual, psychological and other domains. Moreover, the use of military *quwwah* should be directed against an enemy whose animosity is known to Muslims or is known to be on the verge of attacking them. While classical exegetes, especially al-Rāzī and al-Ṭabarī, broadened the understanding of military *quwwah* to include various weapons, fortresses and horsemanship, their interpretations reveal that the use of *quwwah* is limited to self-defence. This is also the view expressed by modern exegetes with the exception of Quṭb.

Quṭb's extremist understanding of the use of *quwwah* in the verse under discussion has contributed to a large degree of misunderstanding about verses discussing military confrontation within the Qur'an in general, and particularly with respect to 8: 60. This misunderstanding is exemplified by some extremist Muslim groups who embrace Quṭb's views and attempt to apply them by giving themselves the authority to kill people of other faiths, lamentably in the name of Islam. This misunderstanding gives some non-Muslims, who already have biased attitudes towards Muslims, the justification to attack the Qur'an as a fascist book preaching hatred and animosity, as has been carefully orchestrated by right-wing opportunists such as Geert Wilders, whose "abuse" of the verse under discussion cannot be denied. The "abuse" demonstrated by erroneously naming 8: 60 "the verse of terrorism" is not limited to Wilders and other right-wing politicians, but also encompasses a few Muslims who, while apparently not known for harbouring extremist views about the Qur'an, are unprepared to act according to its teachings.

Although the vitally important comprehensive understanding of this Qur'anic verse has been surveyed in this chapter, it remains essential to widen out the discussion further, beyond the relatively narrow issue of military preparedness for the purposes of deterrence. This can be achieved by attempting to understand the Qur'anic discourse on the wider concept of jihad, according to the classical and modern exegetical tradition and how it can be misunderstood by modern terrorist groups such as al-Qaeda. This and other jihad-related issues will be dealt with in the next chapter.

3

JIHAD VERSUS TERRORISM IN THE QUR'AN

JIHAD IS ONE of the most widely-invoked terms in modern writing on Islam. Lamentably, Jihad is commonly associated with terrorism in much contemporary writing or discussion too. Yet few scholarly studies on the subject seriously attempt to question the easy link made between jihad and terrorism using the Qur'an as a criterion. Therefore I aim in this chapter to address this political, intellectual and academic lacuna. I also highlight the various stages of jihad in the Qur'an and how far these stages are employed by classical and modern Qur'an interpreters to shape the what might be called international relations theory of the Muslim state in both the classical and contemporary periods.[1] I go on to criticize some prominent modern writers on jihad in light of the contexts from which they emerged in order to provide more understanding of the deployment of the concept of jihad in modern times and the related discussion of its connection to terrorism.

JIHAD AND ITS RELATED TERMS IN THE QUR'AN

The Arabic word "jihad" generally refers to "striving" or "exerting one's utmost effort to do something". The Qur'an refers to these two meanings in 9: 79 and 24: 53.[2] In both of these Qur'anic verses, "striving" (*juhd*) and "doing one's utmost" (*jahd*) are used respectively to denote these two lexical meanings. A review of Qur'an usage of jihad and its derivatives shows that there are five forms (*jāhada, jahd, juhd, jihād* and *mujāhidūn*) occurring forty-one times in eighteen chapters (surahs).[3]

Haykal – after citing various lexical definitions of the term jihad – defines the term as "exerting the utmost effort in one's struggle between two aspects: physical and non-physical".[4] These two aspects, as understood from Haykal's explanations, are good and evil inclinations within the human soul. Therefore, the one who exercises jihad struggles to overcome his evil inclinations, whether fighting the enemy on the battlefield, verbally by enjoining good and forbidding evil in society, or controlling one's illicit wants and desires.

Jihad can also be against the self (*jihād al-nafs*), the devil, sinful and immoral people (*al-fussāq*) and unbelievers.[5] Although the above types of jihad are commonly discussed in both classical and modern texts, the meaning of the term is not confined to them. There are other modern lexical meanings that have surfaced as a result of globalization, "jihad" now being a global term. Al-Qaraḍāwī contends that the modern concept of jihad includes the struggle to communicate the message of Islam by using all sophisticated means, such as radio, satellite channels and the Internet.[6] This means that the meaning of jihad goes far beyond its apparently limited scope, especially in the modern context. It seems that al-Qaraḍāwī is not alone in holding this view. Gary R. Bunt discusses e-jihad as a modern activity integral to cyber Islamic environments.[7] With this broad vision of the linguistic meanings of jihad, it is hardly surprising to find some modern researchers citing up to twenty-four meanings of jihad that can be identified if its shades of meaning are tracked and analysed.[8]

Contrary to these broad linguistic meanings, the technical meaning of jihad is mainly limited to one aspect: the armed struggle against non-Muslims. Although this meaning is enshrined in almost all classical and modern exegeses of the Qur'an, it is very difficult to find an exegete who defines it. This may be because

Qur'an exegetes see no benefit in defining a term whose meaning they assume is very clear. Sunni jurists, however, made great efforts to define the term. For the sake of brevity, I only cite the Ḥanafī definition of jihad here, "To exert one's utmost effort in fighting for Allah's cause by increasing the number of fighters or by assisting them with one's own money, advice or any other means."[9] This Ḥanafī definition is a telling example of how the meaning of jihad moves from its broad linguistic definition to the limited sense of armed struggle against non-Muslims, at least in Islamic jurisprudence. Haykal stresses this view and adds that it is espoused not only by jurists but also by the scholars of hadith, Qur'an exegetes, and biographers of the Prophet.[10] Furthermore, this definition, as well as other technical ones, reveals two important points about jihad. The first is that jihad should be "for Allah's sake" (*fī sabīlillāh*); the second is the fact that jihad is defined as "fighting" (*qitāl*). *Qitāl* – along with other related terms such as "war" (*ḥarb*) – merit careful consideration in their own right, as they both occur in the Qur'an and are frequently used by exegetes and jurists. There is also growing interest in these three terms related to jihad – *fī sabīlillāh*, *qitāl* and *ḥarb* – among modern researchers looking at "human conflict" in the Qur'an, which, in many instances, is subjected to "torturous interpretations" in order to defend certain ideological views, which I assess later on in this chapter.[11] Finally, I want to explain the various meanings of jihad and its related terms with the aim of removing the ambiguity that dominates some academic discussions.[12]

To begin with the first point, the phrase *fī sabīlillāh* is connected with jihad thirteen times in the Qur'an (2: 218; 4: 95; 5: 35, 54; 9: 19, 20, 41, 88; 29: 6, 69; 49: 15; 60: 1; 61: 11).[13] In these occurrences, different forms are used such as "they strive for Allah's sake" (*yujāhidūna fī sabīlillāh*) in 5: 54 and "they strive for Our cause" (*jāhadū fīnā*) in 29: 69. Clearly the number of verses that convey this meaning, as well as the ways they have been interpreted, the dominant meaning of *fī sabīlillāh*, when annexed to the word "jihad", is fighting non-Muslims. Although this is emphasized in the Qur'an, other occurrences of *jāhada, yujāhidu, jāhadū* (for example, in 29: 6, 69) refer to something different.[14] Al-Alūsī states that the meaning of the phrase in the first of these two verses refers to striving one's utmost in obeying Allah, whilst in the second verse it alludes to striving to please Him, whether the struggle is military or otherwise.[15] Thus, the Qur'anic term *fī sabīlillāh* is not as widely attached to military jihad as sometimes depicted by some modern researchers, such as Randall, Firestone and others, who attempt to interpret jihad and *jihād fī sabīlillāh* in the same way. Al-Hāshimī attempts to assert that the great majority of exegetes would favour the military-based meaning for both jihad and *jihād fī sabīlillāh*.[16] However, a close examination of the occurrence of these two phrases in the exegetical literature proves otherwise, as explained by al-Alūsī. What further weakens al-Hāshimī's argument is that he neither cites any exegetical views to support his claim nor admits that the military meaning of jihad cannot be taken as general.

On the other hand, Robert D. Crane maintains that the Qur'an refers to jihad only in the sense of intellectual effort.[17] A very similar view is maintained by Khaled Abou El Fadl, who states that "the Qur'an does not use the word jihad to refer to warfare or fighting."[18] The views of Crane and Abou El Fadl are questionable because the Qur'an does use the word jihad and some of its lexemes in the context of fighting in 2: 218; 4: 95; 8: 72, 74–75; 9: 16, 20, 41, 86; 47: 31; 61: 11.[19]

As explained, in the Qur'an *jihād fī sabīlillāh* carries various military and non-military meanings. Riḍā's explanation of 2: 207 is a clear example. He states that *fī sabīlillāh* generally refers to the way in which a believer chooses to live in order to please Allah.[20] Even when the phrase is used in the context of fighting, it seeks to distinguish jihad from other wars, such as those that took place during the times of pre-Islamic ignorance (*jāhiliyyah*).[21] Within the Qur'anic context, it generally refers to the "way of truth and justice, including all the teachings it gives on the justifications and conditions for the conduct of war and peace".[22]

Unlike jihad, *qitāl*, to which the phrase *fī sabīlillāh* is also annexed in the Qur'an, carries an exclusively military meaning. The phrase *fī sabīlillāh* is mentioned along with *qitāl* only thirteen times in the Qur'an (2: 154, 190, 244; 3: 157, 169; 4: 74, 75, 76, 84; 9: 111; 47: 4;

61: 4; 73: 20).[23] However, *fī sabīlillāh* carries different shades of meaning and is frequently annexed to other concepts, such as spending in the cause of Allah (2: 195, 261, 262), and emigrating for fear of persecution (4: 100).[24] Moreover, the word *qatala* (to kill) and its various lexemes such as *qutila* (to be killed), *qātala* (to fight against), and *taqtīl* (intense killing) occur 170 times in the Qur'an.[25]

Alsumaih argues that the words "jihad" and *qitāl* are used with the same meaning in the Qur'an.[26] This view, however, is unsupported by solid evidence, as can be understood from our previous discussion, where jihad was shown to be a much broader term than *qitāl* in the Qur'an. Al-Khalafī considers that there is what may be termed a "general-specific" (*'umūm wa khuṣūṣ*) relationship between the two terms, arguing that every *qitāl* is jihad, but not every jihad is *qitāl*.[27] Darwazah stresses this view, arguing that there are verses in the Qur'an (22: 78; 25: 52 and 29: 69) that support this approach. Whenever fighting is specified, Darwazah argues that the Qur'an uses the word *qitāl* or one of its lexemes (2: 190; 4: 73, 84). He also argues that there are other verses (4: 94 and 9: 86) where jihad means fighting.[28]

Ḥarb is the general word for "war".[29] As explained in Chapter 5 of this book, in Qur'anic usage this term carries various meanings such as enmity, killing, and disobedience and occurs "far less frequently in the Qur'an" than jihad and *qitāl* – eleven times in four lexical forms.[30] The verb *ḥāraba* (to fight) occurs twice (5: 33 and 9: 107). The noun *ḥarb* occurs four times, in 2: 279; 5: 64; 8: 57; and 47: 4, the last three of which mean fighting.[31] Ibn al-Khūjah apologetically tries to disassociate the involvement of Muslims in war in the Qur'anic narrative. He claims that *ḥarb* is only mentioned to demonstrate how vicious the enemies are in their mischievous machinations against Muslims. Ibn al-Khūjah quotes 5: 64 to support his argument, but this is the only verse where his argument applies.[32] Consideration of the interpretation of *ḥarb* in 8: 57, for example, shows that *ḥarb* is something in which both Muslims and their enemies are mutually involved.[33] A careful study of these occurrences gives rise to two main observations. First, unlike jihad and *qitāl*, the term *ḥarb* is not followed by the phrase *fī sabīlillāh*.

Second, the expression "holy war", which is "a Western concept referring to war that is fought for religion, against adherents of other religions, often in order to promote religion through conversion, and with no specific geographic limitation" does not occur in the Qur'an, even literally.[34] Johnson, concludes, "The term 'holy war' itself is problematic, since it is relatively late in Western usage and since it does not directly translate any of the regularly used Muslim terms, including the central term 'jihad'."[35]

Johnson proves that *al-ḥarb al-muqaddasah*, which is the Arabic phrase commonly used to translate the English term "holy war", is not an honest translation, whether from an Islamic or a Qur'anic perspective, for two reasons: (1) the phrase neither occurs in the Qur'an nor in its classical interpretations;[36] and (2) it is originally a Western term that finds no parallel in Islamic jurisprudence.[37] Intentionally or otherwise, the term has even been used to tarnish the image of jihad in the Qur'an in both Western academic literature and the Western media.[38] Although prominent Western authors such as Bernard Lewis attempt to convince readers that as the words *ḥarb* and *muqaddas* are mentioned in the Qur'an separately, there is no problem in using them together, their arguments are not convincing. Lewis admits that the term "holy war ... does not occur in classical Islamic texts", adding that it has only recently been introduced into Arabic.[39] This is reason enough to cast doubt on his argument, as his deduction clearly decontextualizes the Qur'an. Undoubtedly, such views obscure the way jihad is portrayed in the Qur'an and as part of the Islamic tradition.[40] Moreover, Peters ascribes the widespread occurrence of such erroneous translation to the *prima facie* "influence of Western languages".[41]

Thus as a Qur'anic term, jihad cannot in theory or practice be defined as "holy war". It is a term whose linguistic connotations encompass many aspects and, although this chapter is mainly concerned with the military aspect of jihad in the Qur'an, it is still unjust to link even this aspect to the theory of "holy war" or to translate military jihad itself, which is an intrinsically Qur'anic concept, as "holy war", an expression alien to Islamic history and Qur'anic usage.

In order to reach a sound understanding of the Qur'anic passages frequently cited by "radical Islamists",[42] which–according to them–justify killing non-Muslims, jihad and the other Qur'anic terms related to it require an in-depth examination of the interpretation of the verses in which they occur.[43] This will begin with tracing the origin of such "interpretations", which is a vital element in our discussion. More important, however, is to discuss the different legislative stages of military jihad in the Qur'an in order to be better able to analyse and assess whether certain Qur'anic verses constitute legally valid evidence or not.

In presenting these various stages of military jihad, it is important to clarify something that is often overlooked in Western scholarship, which is the Makkan period when Muslims were prohibited from fighting despite being oppressed. Instead, they start with the Madinan verses when the legalization of jihad was clearly established.[44] In fact, most classical and modern exegetes consulted for this study omit to clarify this point also, but al-Qurṭubī addresses this important gap. He states that fighting had been banned before the Prophet's emigration to Medina in 622.[45] He argues that a consistent message, instructing Muslims to repulse aggression with forgiveness and to respond to oppression with patience, can be deduced from the verses revealed during the Makkan period. These include Qur'anic verses such as 41: 34; 23: 96; 73: 10; and 88: 22, which were all revealed in Mecca.[46] A further look into the Qur'an shows that there are also other verses that can be cited in this context, such as 96: 1–5; 109: 1–6; 53: 29; 7: 199–200; 25: 30–31; 35: 18–26; 20: 130; 26: 216; 27: 70, 78, 81, 91–93; 28: 56, 87–88.

Although persecution of the nascent Muslim community in Makkah continued for over ten years, and fundamentally threatened its well-being, Muslims were ordered not to fight, even in retaliation. This clearly indicates that the Makkan period, as far as the Qur'an is concerned, was marked by non-violence and non-aggression from the early Muslim community.[47] Al-Daqs argues persuasively that a careful study of the Qur'an undoubtedly leads to the conclusion that all the jihad verses and legislative rulings related to them were revealed during the Madinan period. Based on this, al-Daqs contends that jihad during the Makkan period can be termed as "peaceful jihad" (*al-jihād al-silmī*) whereas in the Madinan period it can be designated as "military jihad" (*al-jihād al-ḥarbī*).[48]

Thus, peace dominates the Makkan revelations in the Qur'an. However, this peaceful character of the Makkan period does have a caveat: 42: 39–42, according to Darwazah, refers indirectly to the principle of defending oneself by fighting in case of oppression, although while these verses were revealed during the Makkan period, they are the foundation for the Madinan revelations which permit fighting.[49] The reason why 42: 39–42 did not directly command fighting is that it was revealed at a time when Muslims were persecuted. When the situation changed in Madinah, Darwazah argues, Qur'anic legislation changed to adapt to the new environment.[50] With regard to this change, Quṭb contends that the peace that existed in the Makkan period was an exception to the established rule Muslims had to follow after migrating to Madinah, which was to defend themselves when they were oppressed.[51] The seemingly opposed arguments of Darwazah and Quṭb do not rule out the fact that a non-fighting strategy was the basic rule to which all Muslims adhered during the Makkan period, regardless of whether or not 42: 39–42 indirectly refers to repelling aggression during the Makkan period.

According to al-Ṭabarī, 42: 41 carries a direct meaning that calls for the forgiving of wrongdoers.[52] Thus, the exceptional interpretations of Darwazah and Quṭb fail to rule out the basic rule of non-combat which the overwhelming majority of Makkan verses lay down. Accepting this, however, does not necessarily mean that peace predominates when Muslims are weak and that, once they gain in strength, they start an open military campaign against all non-Muslims. An examination of the legislation regarding jihad during the Madinan period will aid us in understanding the issue better.

The Stages of Military Jihad

Apart from a few exceptions, discussion of the various stages of military jihad in the Qur'an is not given due consideration in the vast amount of Western academic literature studies over the last two decades.[53] An examination of the Qur'an itself, however, reveals what can be called a "carefully orchestrated theory" of jihad, in which the relationship between Muslims and non-Muslims is established. This theory, in our view, merits close consideration, in view of the fact that all the military jihad-related verses in the Qur'an can easily be manipulated into reductionist and exclusivist interpretations by forcibly altering their original contexts.[54] This decontextualization has led to the hijacking of the Qur'anic text by terrorists from Muslim backgrounds and some non-Muslims who may lack understanding of the gradual sequence of Qur'anic legislation on military jihad. This gradualness in the legislation of jihad is marked by three different stages.

The first stage began, according to Ibn al-ʿArabī, after the Prophet established his rule in Madinah, when Allah permitted him to fight in retaliation after he and his Companions were oppressed and tortured.[55] The attempt to belittle the amount of torture to which Muslims were subjected in this period with the claim that it was "individual rather than institutional in nature" is not substantiated by the evidence. When persecution and torture directly affected the head of the nascent state (i.e. the Prophet), it clearly indicates the extent to which it was systematically and institutionally orchestrated. The verses 29: 2–3 and 68: 51 clearly establish this argument. Thus, attempting to argue that Muslims in the Makkan period were subjected to a "minor level"[56] of persecution is a questionable statement, as 22: 39 was revealed because of the on-going unbearable level of persecution at that time.[57]

In this regard, 22: 39–40 is widely known as the oldest reference to jihad in the Qur'an.[58] When interpreting these two verses, al-Shaʿrāwī refers to the different stages of the legislation on jihad, stressing that 22: 39 marks the beginning of the first stage.[59] Al-Shaʿrāwī's interpretation is apparently a leading contribution because classical exegetes such as al-Qurṭubī and al-Ṭabarī do not refer clearly to this gradual approach, although it can easily be inferred from their interpretations.[60] However, Firestone's discussion of the stages of military jihad in the Qur'an and the way he classifies them may lead the reader to believe that he has come up with an original classification, but a critical analysis suggests otherwise, as shown by his indirect reference to the classical exegetes and direct citation of modern exegetes.[61]

Furthermore, Firestone marks the Makkan period of non-combat earlier discussed as the first stage, although a detailed examination shows that the great majority of Muslim researchers and exegetes do not consider the Makkan period as a stage of military jihad in the Qur'an. The question that should be posed to Firestone then is: How can we consider "non-confrontation" as a stage in fighting when the Qur'an itself does not mention it during the Makkan period? Thus, the first stage that marks the beginning of the legislation on military jihad in the Qur'an starts with the revelation of Qur'an 22: 39–40 in Madinah.

However, 22: 39–40 is not the only Qur'anic reference to the first stage.[62] Another verse, 2: 190, also constitutes the Qur'anic basis for fighting. Although al-Ṭabarī and Ibn Kathīr cite an interpretation to the effect that 2: 190 is the first verse commanding Muslims to fight in self-defence, al-Nīsābūrī and al-Suyūṭī argue otherwise, indicating that it is the second verse in this stage of defensive combat.[63] Thus the classical exegetes differ on whether 2: 190 was the first verse to be revealed in this regard. However, it may be more appropriate to consider that as 22: 39 preceded 2: 190 the former constitutes permission to engage in fighting that was prohibited *ab initio*, whereas the latter clearly ordains fighting in self-defence. It seems more logical to conclude that the permission to fight precedes fighting in self-defence.

Indeed, Qur'an 22: 39 and 2: 190 provide two important principles: (1) fighting can only be launched by Muslims in self-defence when they are oppressed; and (2) although Muslims are allowed to fight, they are not allowed to initiate hostilities, to fight noncombatants or to respond to aggression disproportionately. This is confirmed by all classical and modern exegetes who interpret 2: 190. They state that the prohibition in the verse includes all noncombatants such as women, children, the infirm, the aged, monks, rabbis, the sick, and all who conclude peace agreements with Muslims and those who proffer peace.[64] Ibn Kathīr also adds that killing animals and burning trees that do not benefit the enemy is also forbidden.[65] Notably, Riḍā argues that 2: 190 does not restrict non-aggression to fighting on the battlefield, but includes a prohibition on initiating fighting without being attacked. Muslims are also not allowed to resort to other forms of destruction, such as demolishing infrastructure, uprooting trees, etc.[66]

The second stage of military jihad in the Qur'an is usually marked by verses that directly order Muslims to fight those who fight them. Compared with other stages, this stage - according to Firestone - is referred to by the greatest number of verses, and the sake of brevity, I only refer here to 2: 191 and 194, and 9: 36 as clear examples.[67] As in the first stage, Muslims are to fight in "fending off aggression" (*dafʿ al-ʿudwān*) directed against themselves or their lands.[68] Haykal states that such aggression must have been launched by non-Muslims against Muslims, arguing that 2: 190, 194; 4: 91; 9: 36; and 22: 39 anchor this concept.[69] Here, it can also be argued that this stage is a continuation of defensive fighting in the Qur'an.[70] Haykal also considers that pre-emptive fighting is permitted for Muslims too according to 4: 75 and 8: 58.

Indeed, little or no criticism would be directed against Muslims if they resorted to defensive or even pre-emptive fighting, especially if their motives were to defend themselves. However, Muslims have faced and will continue to face harsh criticism as a result of the various interpretations of the last stage of military jihad in the Qur'an. As there is no unified view concerning this final stage, the need arises to identify the individual approaches of classical and modern exegetes in order to discover their impact on the modern conception of military jihad in the Qur'an.

According to the classical jihad theory, all unbelievers are seen as the avowed enemies of Muslims, and Muslims are therefore obliged to fight them until they embrace Islam or pay the poll-tax (*jizyah*). According to the classic theory, the enmity of non-Muslims towards Muslims arises as a result of their disbelief (*kufr*), due to which they are to be fought against.[71] The following Qur'anic verse constitutes the main criterion upon which the above judgment is based: *Fight them until there is no more persecution [fitnah], and that worship is devoted to God. If they cease hostilities, there can be no [further] hostility, except towards aggressors* (2: 193).[72]

In their commentaries on 2: 193, al-Ṭabarī, al-Qurṭubī, Ibn al-ʿArabī, al-Suyūṭī, al-Jaṣṣāṣ, al-Rāzī and al-Alūsī are united in maintaining that *fitnah* in this verse means unbelief (*kufr*).[73] However, Ibn Kathīr does not seemingly express his view concerning persecution here.[74] Schleifer maintains that Ibn Kathīr interprets persecution as idolatry or polytheism, following al-Qurṭubī's interpretation, but al-Qurṭubī maintains his interpretation without reference to Ibn Kathīr's, which is reason enough to cast doubt on Schleifer's argument.[75]

Of the classical exegetes, al-Ṭabarī and al-Qurṭubī provide detailed explanations for their attitudes on the Qur'anic *casus belli*. Al-Ṭabarī emphasizes that 2: 193 is a Divine instruction to the Prophet to fight the unbelievers until there is no more persecution, i.e. until there is no more polytheism (*shirk*).[76] Al-Qurṭubī stresses this hostile attitude towards non-Muslims. He states that authoritative figures such as Ibn ʿAbbās (d. 68/687), Qatādah (d. 118/736) and others interpreted persecution in this verse to mean "polytheism and all forms of persecution done by the unbelievers against Muslims".[77] Moreover, abrogation (*naskh*) plays a central role in this classical theory.[78]

The proponents of the theory of abrogation consider 2: 106 and 16: 101 as the main evidence upon which this theory is built.[79] The classical exegetes view 9: 5 as constituting the underlying principle of Muslim external relations and as abrogating approximately 113 verses.[80] While rejecting this view, al-Qaraḍāwī states that the classical exegetes differ on identifying which Qur'anic verse is "the verse of the sword" (*āyat al-sayf*). Simply put, he throws doubt on citing 9: 5, 36, and 41 as representative verses.[81] This may explain why Bin Jani prefers the plural form, i.e. "the *verses* of the sword" (my emphasis).[82] Moreover, the members of the International Union for Muslim Scholars (IUMS) remark that early scholars and exegetes did not agree on which Qur'anic verse is the "verse of the sword", and on this basis they argue that it is neither reasonable nor legitimate to render null and void the definitive Qur'anic verses that call for peace, given this disagreement.[83]

Clearly classical theory took the view that polytheism and unbelief are the main causes behind the hostile attitude of Muslims towards non-Muslims. The essence of this classical exegetical theory is based on the assumption that Muslims have to launch all-out war against non-Muslims because of the latter's unbelief. To them, military jihad is the overriding principle (*al-aṣl*) upon which the norm of external relations between Muslims and non-Muslims is based.

In his interpretation of persecution in 2: 193, Riḍā clearly sets out his view concerning the final stage of military jihad. He considers that persecution in this verse refers to the attempt of the unbelievers to oppress, torture and expel Muslims from their homeland, as well as to confiscate their property. He argues that no greater affliction can befall a human being than being oppressed and tortured for adopting a creed that has already permeated his soul and intellect.[84] Riḍā quotes ʿAbduh as saying that interpreting persecution in this verse to mean unbelief takes the interpretation of the verse out of its original context. ʿAbduh also maintains that the insistence of the classicists on considering military jihad as the basic norm of external relations between Muslims and non-Muslims prevented them from saying that permission to fight is conditional on a prior attack from the side of the unbelievers.[85] In a bid to demonstrate how the safety of believers with regard to their creed is vital, ʿAbduh argues, the classical exegetes insist on making military jihad the basic principle *stricto sensu*. He adds that this verse was revealed to establish the same defensive purpose of military jihad that was previously established by 22: 39–40.[86] It is clear that ʿAbduh and Riḍā are strong adherents of the defensive jihad theory, and so their view contrasts sharply with that of the classical exegetes.

As far as "the verse of the sword" is concerned, Riḍā maintains that there are different opinions as to whether it is Qur'an 9: 5 or 9: 36 or both.[87] He argues that the insistence of the classical exegetes that the verses pertaining to patience, coexistence and tolerance were abrogated by "the verse of the sword" carries no weight as far as abrogation is concerned; Riḍā's view is apparently in favour of discounting any link between the two verses. He tries to back his opinion by citing al-Alūsī's view, which follows a similar pattern.[88] However, an examination of al-Alūsī's interpretation of the verse may reveal that his viewpoint is not exactly that of 'Abduh's and Riḍā's, albeit that he too does incline towards defensive jihad theory.[89]

Moreover, al-Sha'rāwī states that persecution (*fitnah*) in Qur'an 2: 134 and 193 refers to the trials and tribulations that befell Muslims at the hands of the unbelievers in the early days of Islam. These arbitrary actions, according to him, are worse than killing, and so it is justified for Muslims to resort to fighting in self-defence.[90] Like Riḍā, al-Sha'rāwī is a staunch advocate of defensive combat, but he broadens its scope to encompass lifting the yoke of oppression from the subjects of some tyrant non-Muslim rulers – at the time when Islam was in its nascent stage – who oppress the masses and block their way to the religion of Islam.[91] For al-Sha'rāwī, this latter objective of military jihad is still defensive, even though launched without prior aggression. He takes the view that defence entails fighting to remove the obstacles that may hinder Islam from reaching the oppressed masses. However, as a result of the information revolution, the wide and easy accessibility of modern communication no longer necessitates applying this method of propagating Islam to non-Muslims. The use of this tool may have been a necessary justification for Muslims in certain historical periods, such that this method of calling others to Islam was viewed as the main, if not the only, effective tool at that time. However, the non-Muslim masses living within the modern nation-state system find it easy to choose between Islam and other religions, thanks to the more than adequate available means of propagating the message of Islam to others. Interestingly too, the Qur'an has established the freedom to choose one's religion in many of its verses, such as Qur'an 2: 256, 272; 3: 20; 16: 82; 25: 43; 88: 21–22.

Moreover, there is almost no discussion in al-Sha'rāwī's interpretation of "the verse of the sword" and whether or not it abrogates other verses.[92] Although his explanation of 2: 106 shows that he gives due regard to "abrogation", his handling of this theory within the context of military jihad is clearly very limited.

Darwazah is a modern exegete whose view stands in total opposition to classical interpretative theory. In his commentary of 9: 5, he states that the classical interpretation of this verse contradicts the definitive [Qur'anic] rulings (*aḥkām muḥkamah*) which not only ordain refraining from fighting non-hostile entities, but also entail dealing with them kindly and justly. For Darwazah, the definitive Qur'anic rulings further include but are not limited to prohibiting compulsion in religion (2: 256), calling others to Islam with wisdom and fair exhortation and only arguing in the best way (16: 125), and applying a just and fair foreign policy towards non-Muslims who do not fight against Muslims or drive them from their homes (60: 8–9). Darwazah also considers that taking "the verse of the sword" as abrogating all these definitive Qur'anic rulings is simply a contradictory interpretation. Furthermore, he states that the verses following "the verse of the sword" (i.e. 9: 6–7) clearly order Muslims to honour their agreements with non-Muslims so long as the latter remain committed to their peaceful agreements. All these arguments, according to Darwazah, strengthen this interpretation.[93]

Darwazah is the last of the modern exegetes we shall consider here who maintain that peace (*al-silm*) is the underlying principle upon which foreign relations between Muslims and non-Muslims are established. However, another important trend among modern exegetes needs to be explored, which is the view of Mawdūdī and Quṭb, and the extent to which they are in harmony with or contradict both classical interpretative theory and modern exegeses.

Mawdūdī is a leading modern exegete who sees military jihad as "a perpetual revolutionary struggle" whose aim is to bring the whole world into conformity with the ideals of Islam.[94] He states that for the persecution (*fitnah*) referred to in 2: 191, 193; 4: 91; 8: 73 and 9: 48 to be eliminated, there is no option but to use the sword.[95] He also takes the view that eliminating all governments that are contradictory to this ideology is the assured way of uprooting and putting an end to evil powers.[96]

Moreover, Mawdūdī states that what is famously known as "offensive" and "defensive" fighting have nothing to do with jihad in Islam. For him, these two terms can only be used to describe national wars. Viewing military jihad as a permanent ideology for all Muslims, Mawdūdī argues, that jihad is both "offensive" and "defensive" at one and the same time. On the one hand, it is "offensive" because it aims to dislodge all systems whose aims contravene the ideals of Islam, even though military power is used to achieve this aim. On the other hand, it is "defensive" because part of securing the eternity of the religion of Islam is to defend it against its enemies in order to enable Muslim rule to remain uninterrupted by external threats.[97] However, he adds that this should not necessarily lead us to think that military jihad in Islam is confined to a specific "abode" that is limited to a certain geographical location. This view, according to him, does not entail converting unbelievers to Islam, but to dethroning those who believe in principles and lead ideological systems that run counter to those of Islam. The exercise of military jihad in this case is a necessary procedure to establish Islam and hence eliminate persecution.[98] Mawdūdī's revolutionary concept of jihad sees no point in dividing military jihad into defensive or offensive modes. In fact, for Mawdūdī, the classical dichotomous classification of the world into what is famously known as the territory of Islam (*dār al-Islām*) and the territory of war (*dār al-ḥarb*), does not make sense either.[99]

It is worth adding here that this bipolar classification is not Qur'anic.[100] The only "hadith"[101] narration cited in reference to it is hard to find in the collections of authentic hadiths, which throws doubt on the authenticity of the classification, at least in its lack of grounding in the first two main sources of Islamic legislation.[102] It seems that this dichotomous classification is a product of the exertion of intellectual reasoning in understanding laws (*ijtihād*) mainly based on the attitude of the Muslim state towards its enemies and friends during the second Islamic century.[103] More interestingly, the geographical location of the Muslim state compared with other non-Muslim states at that time was certainly a determining factor in forming this dichotomous vision, as well as the binary division of jihad into defensive and offensive modalities.

Having briefly presented the "two abodes" and noted that forming legal rules with reference to them does not actually make sense in Mawdūdī's view, we must note, however, that another book by him indicates otherwise. Mawdūdī states the following:

> Islamic law divides all non-Muslim nations into two categories: First, a group who have concluded a *mu'āhadah* (pact) with Muslims. Second, a group who have not concluded a pact with Muslims. If the first group comply with the terms and conditions of the pact, then they are not to be fought against and this is what is known as the concept of "neutrality". However, those who have not concluded a pact with Muslims are considered in a state of war with them.[104]

The above statement by Mawdūdī shows that he is seemingly supportive of the classical dichotomous division of the world into two "abodes" referred to above, even though he does not say so in clear unequivocal terms. It can be observed that Mawdūdī puts much emphasis on both the doctrinal and political aspects of Islam and his view is therefore a synthesis of classical and modern interpretations.[105] Although Mawdūdī's view does not rely heavily on considering military jihad as defensive or offensive, his approach to this particular point remains sympathetic to the offensive approach, which helps us identify Mawdūdī's view as within the classical interpretive theory, even though he lived in modern times. His "fundamentalist" rather than "modernist" view of military jihad is more akin to the classical theory, even though it is cloaked in a contemporary robe. Of all modern exegetes, the final one whose view merits close consideration is certainly Quṭb's.

Quṭb's View of War and Peace in the Qur'an

Quṭb's view of jihad has been influential and continues to have a great impact on modern extremists. Moreover, Quṭb is apparently the only exegete who not only argues for his viewpoint as others do but also seeks to refute those who reject his interpretation.

Although there are similarities between Quṭb and Mawdūdī, Quṭb's views remain distinct because of his "aggressive overture of jihād" as reflected in his interpretation of the Qur'anic verses concerning war and peace.[106] Therefore, it is necessary to present his views as well as assessing his critique of other modern exegetes.[107]

Generally speaking, it is said that Quṭb's revolutionary view of jihad was influenced by two notable scholars, Ibn al-Qayyim (d. 751/1350), and Mawdūdī.[108] Like Mawdūdī, Quṭb's view of military jihad is also a synthesis of classical and modern exegeses.[109] Schleifer argues that Quṭb restated the traditional views of Mawdūdī using almost the same concepts, such as "Islamic movement", "ideology" and "revolution".[110] Moreover, Musallam adds that the wide circulation of the Arabic translations of Mawdūdī's works in Egypt in Quṭb's time had an impact on his understanding of jihad.[111] However, there is evidence that on this issue Quṭb was influenced by Ibn al-Qayyim too.

Ibn al-Qayyim's famous book *Zād al-Maʿād fī Hady Khayr al-ʿIbād* provides an overall analysis of the Prophet's struggle with the unbelievers and the hypocrites from the day he first received revelation until his death.[112] Quṭb was greatly influenced by Ibn al-Qayyim's synopsis of the various stages and methods employed by the Prophet in approaching the non-Muslims and the hypocrites during his lifetime.[113] After quoting from Ibn al-Qayyim's book at length, Quṭb deduced what he termed "the dynamic nature" of Islam as both a revolutionary movement and a system of life.[114] Quṭb closely follows Ibn al-Qayyim's sequence and analysis of the different stages of the legislation on jihad, which corresponds in its salient features to what is outlined above with the exception of the third stage. From Ibn Qayyim's analysis, Quṭb lays great emphasis on the final stage of jihad which, according to him, is marked by the revelation of the Qur'an's ninth chapter.[115]

Before the revelation of this chapter, Ibn al-Qayyim argues, non-Muslims were divided into three categories: (1) *ahl ṣulḥ wa hudnah*, who concluded a peaceful treaty with Muslims, displaying no enmity towards them; (2) *ahl ḥarb*, who were hostile towards Muslims; and (3) *ahl dhimmah*, who were the protected minority of non-Muslim citizens, comprising Jews and Christians, who reside within the "territory of Islam" (*dār al-Islām*), show no signs of animosity towards Muslims, and pay the poll-tax (*jizyah*) in return for protection by Muslims. After the revelation of the Qur'an's ninth chapter, Ibn al-Qayyim argues, these three categories were reduced to *ahl dhimmah* and *ahl ḥarb*. The Muslims were ordered to fight the latter category until they adopted Islam, were killed, or alternatively paid the poll-tax to Muslims and could thus be dealt with as *ahl dhimmah*.[116]

An in-depth look into Quṭb's citations from Ibn al-Qayyim, and a comparative study of their views of jihad might at first sight lead to the conclusion that the latter wholly affected the former. This is the case that Bin Jani did his best to establish,[117] but it seems that he might only have examined Quṭb's lengthy quotations from Ibn al-Qayyim's *Zād al-Ma'ād* to reach this conclusion. Indeed, at face value Quṭb's overemphasis on Ibn al-Qayyim's thesis of jihad makes this case tenable.

However, closer examination shows that both authors, along with Mawdūdī, were influenced by Ibn Taymiyyah (661–728/1263–1328).[118] This is supported by the following two quotations, which help us to understand Ibn Taymiyyah's view of jihad better:

> Anyone whom the call [*da'wah*] of the Messenger, peace be upon him, has reached but he refused to accept is an enemy of Allah and His Messenger. Therefore, he [or she] must be killed. Allah says, *[Believers], fight them until there is no more persecution [fitnah], and all worship is devoted to God alone* (Qur'an 8: 39).[119]

Ibn Taymiyyah adds that "The aim behind fighting is for the Religion [of Islam] to become dominant and for the Word of God to reign supreme. Whoever refuses to adopt Islam is to be fought against according to the consensus of Muslims."[120]

Thus, the claim that Ibn al-Qayyim and Mawdūdī were the inspirational figures behind Quṭb's hard-line view of jihad is unsubstantiated because the two quotations above clearly indicate that both Ibn al-Qayyim and Mawdūdī were themselves inspired by Ibn

Taymiyyah. This may be considered sufficient reason to argue that Ibn Taymiyyah was the original ideologue of this hard-line view.[121]

Heavily dependent on the Qur'an's ninth chapter in formulating his overall position about the final stage of jihad, Quṭb argues that the Qur'anic verses related to peace and war can be divided into two stages: "transitional texts" (*al-nuṣūṣ al-marḥaliyyah*) and "final texts" (*al-nuṣūṣ al-nihā'iyyah*). For him, the "transitional texts" include, for example, 3: 64; 8: 61 and 60: 8. These verses instruct Muslims to remain patient, even while under oppression. They are also asked to maintain peaceful co-existence and tolerance in their relations with non-Muslims. These verses and others similar to them in meaning, Quṭb argues, are limited to specific circumstances that have appeared and may reappear in the life of the Muslim *ummah*. However, he insists that while these "transitional texts" are applicable in certain periods of time, they do not constitute the definitive rulings upon which relations between Muslims and non-Muslims are established. The Muslim *ummah* is required to remove all obstacles to pave the way for the "final texts" to dominate the scene. By these "final texts" are meant 9: 1–5 and 9: 29 as the verses that ultimately determine the shape of the relationship between Muslims and polytheists on the one hand, and Muslims and the People of the Book on the other.

In an attempt to support his argument, Quṭb argues that as Muslims cannot put the "final texts" into effect in their contemporary lives, even temporarily, they should gradually apply the "transitional texts" until they reach the stage at which they can eventually apply the "final texts". He further argues that Muslims should not twist the contexts of the "final texts" to make them applicable to the "transitional texts".[122] He also adds:

> Only in the light of this explanation can we understand those verses of the Holy Qur'an which are concerned with the various stages of this movement. In reading these verses, we should always keep in mind that one of their meanings is related to the particular stages of the development of Islam, while there is another general meaning which is related to the unchangeable and eternal message of Islam. We should

not confuse these two aspects.[123]

The above quotation actually summarizes Quṭb's view of military jihad in the Qur'an. Although his view remains tied to the legacy of the classical exegetical jihad theory, it is distinct in maintaining that the "transitional texts" are not subject to the theory of abrogation, and cannot therefore be deemed effective after the revelation of the "final texts", especially in the Qur'an's ninth chapter.[124] Bin Jani tries to argue that Quṭb was not influenced by the classical interpretative theory that stands squarely behind the abrogation thesis.[125] However, Quṭb's insistence on jihad being a permanent obligation imposed upon Muslims strongly links his view to the classical theory, even though his focus remains on the "transitional texts" as opposed to the "final texts", paying less attention – unlike the classical exegetes – to the theory of abrogation.

Quṭb's binary division of the Qur'anic verses into "transitional" and "final" texts, as well as his view that the "transitional texts" are related to specific circumstances (*muqayyadah bi ḥālāt khāṣṣah*) whereas the "final texts" are absolute and unconditional guidance (*muṭlaqat al-dalālah*), confirms his adherence to the classical dichotomous classification.[126] Although Quṭb does not argue for abrogation, it can be deduced that he nevertheless introduces the idea of "transitional texts" as a viable solution to help solve the seeming "contradiction" between the war and peace verses in the Qur'an. Bin Jani insists that Quṭb's idea of transitional texts constitutes a modification of the classical theory whereby the "non-aggressive verses" are the "transitional texts" and the "verses of the sword" are the "final texts".[127] However, a more careful consideration reveals that Quṭb's view is seemingly different. He rejects abrogation, which is a common denominator in the classical theory, and comes up with a distinctive and revolutionary vision of jihad as a permanent struggle. While this view is not radically different from the classical theory, neither is it identical to or a modification of the latter, as Bin Jani argues. Quṭb does not rely on considering jihad as either "defensive" or "offensive", and like Mawdūdī he is more inclined to the "offensive" attitude.[128] This inclination of Quṭb's is supported by his categorical rejection of the "defensive jihad" theory and his insistence on naming its proponents "defeatists" (*al-mahzūmūn*), who succumb under the pressure of the miserable reality afflicting generations of Muslims whose share of Islam is nothing but its title.[129]

Quṭb's critique of the treatment of war and peace in the Qur'an by other modern exegetes can be illustrated by his refutation of the two main proponents of the modern "defensive jihad" theory and interpretation: Rashīd Riḍā and Darwazah. Riḍā is criticized by Quṭb for his advocacy of the "defensive jihad" theory and maintaining that the basic rule governing external relations between Muslims and non-Muslims is peace and not military jihad. After quoting Riḍā's view in the *Ẓilāl*, Quṭb refuses to accept that the "final texts" do not constitute the underlying principle, as Riḍā maintains, because he sees Riḍā's view as inconsistent with the revolutionary aims of jihad.[130]

Quṭb criticizes Darwazah for attempting to interpret 9: 5 as a "transitional text" to support the view that jihad does not constitute the underlying principle of external relations between Muslims and non-Muslims. Quṭb argues that Darwazah – like many other modern Qur'an exegetes and Muslim scholars who wrote during the apogee of European imperial and colonial rule in the Muslim world and its aftermath in the late nineteenth and early to mid-twentieth centuries – supports an apologetic interpretation that aims to present Islam as a religion of peace, is primarily concerned to secure peace within its boundaries and whose followers hasten to declare truces and sign peaceful treaties.

Quṭb criticizes Darwazah for limiting the scope of the military confrontation referred to in the "final texts" in his interpretation of 9: 5. Darwazah limits permission to fight only when the polytheists dishonour their temporary or permanent agreements with Muslims, as, in his view, the ninth chapter of the Qur'an stipulates that Muslims honour their agreements when the other party does so. Additionally, if the term of an agreement is brought to an end, Muslims are allowed to negotiate new agreements to maintain peace with them.[131] For Quṭb, Darwazah has, as Bin Jani puts it, "abandoned the orthodox classification of Qur'anic texts" concerning relations between Muslims and non-Muslims, and, as a result, has actually placed the final texts in the place of the transitional ones.[132]

Bin Jani states that Quṭb was "more severe" in his criticism of Darwazah than of Riḍā, accusing him of "intellectual incompetence", calling him an author of "apologetic" works, which represent the "epitome of the intellectual inferiority of the modernists as a whole".[133] However, as Bin Jani only refers to Qutb's *Ẓilāl* on this particular point, he fails to see that Quṭb criticizes modernists in general, calling them "defeatists" and "apologists", and does not single out Darwazah for these "scornful" remarks. On the contrary, Quṭb, despite his disagreement with Riḍā and Darwazah on the theory of jihad, remains committed to the ethics of scholarly criticism, according to which ideas not persons are rejected. In refuting their views, Quṭb addresses both men by their titles,[134] which indicates his deep personal respect for them despite their intellectual disagreement, for it would be unbecoming of an intellectual like Quṭb to criticize fellow exegetes harshly, no matter how different or contradictory their views were to his. Quṭb does criticize Riḍā and Darwazah implicitly when he calls modernists "defeatist", but not explicitly as he does not dub them defeatists by name. Bin Jani may have mistakenly applied Quṭb's criticism to them simply because Quṭb apparently singles them out from all other modernists by mentioning their names; however, Quṭb's *Ẓilāl* shows otherwise.[135]

Despite Quṭb's direct appeal to the classical theory in his interpretation of jihad, he notably introduces the concept of "transitional texts" and "final texts". In contrast to the common view that he was predominantly influenced by Mawdūdī, his position was shaped too by the medieval narrative of jihad linked to Ibn Taymiyyah.[136] Like the classical exegetes, Quṭb's interpretation of jihad favours its offensive aspect. He seemingly insists on disregarding modernist interpretations, which view peace – and not war – as the underlying principle of external relations between Muslims and non-Muslims. Quṭb's narrative of jihad reveals that there is no territory beyond the two dichotomous classifications of the world advocated by the classical theory. This is a reason why his detractors regard his narrative as reductionist, because its binary vision overrules those advocated by other exegetes.[137]

The historical and circumstantial contextualization which gave rise to Quṭb's view of jihad cannot be underestimated. Quṭb wrote most of the *Ẓilāl* in prison, and was later executed. Therefore, he may be excused as a result of his ideas being understood as "fairly general statements" that lack direct elaboration, since the straitened circumstances of his composition of *Ẓilāl* and his execution actually prevented him from expanding upon them.[138] While criticizing Quṭb's view of jihad as being selective, al-Qaraḍāwī sympathetically observes that if Quṭb had managed to lead a normal life outside the confines of prison, and had managed to exchange ideas with other scholars of his time in such a way that mutual interaction and constructive criticism were applied, he might have relinquished his radical views.[139] This is because Quṭb, according to al-Qaraḍāwī, was well-known as a staunch advocate of truth, who would never accept compromise in religion.[140] Here, the views of Kepel and al-Qaraḍawī on Quṭb may be deemed well-balanced because they do not overlook the harsh circumstances under which he lived, namely, under the shadow of a despotic regime prior to his execution.[141]

Having attempted to analyze Quṭb's view of jihad, it is equally important to study some later writings that may, to a greater or lesser extent, have been influenced by his interpretation. I will focus on the past and present understandings of jihad of the Islamic Group in Egypt and how far it influenced modern al-Qaeda members. These and other key issues, such as the case study of the Islamic view of the 11 September 2001 attacks, are dealt with in the next chapter.

4

THE MODERN DEBATE ON OFFENSIVE JIHAD

As JIHAD AND TERRORISM are sometimes seen as synonymous by the public, in this chapter I critically examine two key extremist groups – Egypt's Islamic Group and al-Qaeda. The first group has been influential in the shaping of the ideological outlook of the second, and I go on to present the attacks of 11 September 2001 as a case study to assess whether such terrorist attacks may be legitimately justified by the Qur'an.[1] The reason for singling out the 9/11 attacks is because of their immense international political, military and cultural impact on relations between Muslims and non-Muslims, even if there have been other massive-casualty terrorist attacks similar in style if not in scale. The cultural and intellectual legacy of the 11 September 2001 attacks means that various aspects of jihad and terrorism continue to give rise to controversy: moderate views are given less coverage than those of terrorists and extremists, which receive a disproportionate amount of exposure.[2] I shall attempt to address this imbalance first of all by presenting what may be termed the mainstream Sunni response to the notion of offensive jihad.

Having analysed Quṭb's view concerning jihad in Chapter 3, it is worth evaluating the writings that preceded or came after Quṭb's and that differ from his and from classical interpretative theory as well. In this regard, two diametrically opposed attitudes can be observed in modern Islamic literature on the theory of jihad. In this chapter, I analyse those who reject an offensive theory of jihad and then I examine those who advocate in favour of it. The advocates of each narrative marshal the same evidence and employ virtually the same tools used by classical and modern exegetes. And in the light of this polarized debate, modern Western scholarship remains in utter confusion about the image of jihad, caught as it is between perspectives such as Bernard Lewis's and those like John Esposito's.[3] To pave the way for a better understanding of this controversy, a concise analysis of both viewpoints is to be presented in a bid to identify which approach is to be adopted in this monograph. As it is impractical to cover all participants in this debate, I will focus upon the most prominent amongst them, because the objective is to explain the differences in attitudes rather than to provide an exhaustive accounting of all those who have taken part in this argument. To achieve a representative flavour of the debate, I will tackle the contributions of some modern scholars as well as referring to collective efforts that have taken the form of semi-collective *ijtihād* at international conferences.

Modern Rejectionists of the Offensive Jihad Narrative

Among the main rejectionists of the classical interpretative theory, whose view stands in contrast to that of Quṭb's, is Ḥasan al-Bannā (1906–1949), the founder of the Muslim Brotherhood (al-Ikhwān al-Muslimūn). While al-Bannā and Quṭb belonged to the same group, it was al-Bannā who set out his view of jihad first of all, as it was only in the late 1950s and early 1960s that Quṭb's controversial views of jihad were published.

In contrast to Quṭb, al-Bannā's view of jihad remains within the defensive attitude, according to which Muslim countries are envisioned as a monolithic and uniform entity that forms the Muslim *ummah*.[4] Consequently, he perceives that this uniformity necessitates that Muslims support each other by launching jihad against foreign aggression and occupation.[5] It is apparent that he developed this view as a result of the Western imperialism in the Middle East in his day. More specifically, he emphasizes the obligation of Muslims to support their fellow Muslim Palestinians by sacrificing their money and their lives to liberate their usurped land.[6]

Among the modern scholars who view peace as the basic principle which marks external relations between Muslims and non-Muslims is Abū Zahrah (1898–1974). According to him, military jihad is permitted only to remove aggression (*'udwān*) and religious persecution (*fitnah*) against Muslims. He further states that 4: 94 and 22: 39–40 establish this principle, adding that the scholars who state that military jihad is the basic principle between Muslims and non-Muslims derive their view from the reality they experienced rather than from the texts of the Qur'an and the Sunnah. The rulings arrived at by the classical scholars, Abū Zahrah argues, are related only to the historical period in which they lived, and therefore cannot be considered as definitive and binding rulings. Instead, military jihad is legislated to establish justice and fend off aggression. He considers the Qur'anic verses that call for peace as the basic norm in Muslim and non-Muslim external relations. For Abū Zahrah, the historical context cannot be underestimated, something which is uncommon in classical exegetical interpretations.[7]

Al-Būṭī (1929–2013) stresses, like Abū Zahrah, the intrinsic connection between peace and justice. He maintains that "any genuine call for peace necessitates a genuine call for justice", arguing that justice, which is one of the main causes behind the legislation of jihad, is the only principle that can lead to peace. If the equilibrium between peace and justice is evenly balanced, al-Būṭī maintains, then not only will Muslims and non-Muslims enjoy permanent peaceful relations (*ṣulḥ dā'im*), but all peoples will enjoy the same consequence regardless of their faith or ethnicity. However, al-Būṭī sets two conditions for this permanent peace to be achieved: (1) Muslims should be free to propagate their faith without restriction; and (2) there should be no occupation of *dār al-Islām*. Included in the meaning of occupation which may lead to fighting and put an end to peace, according to al-Būṭī, is when the enemies of Muslims confiscate, usurp and reside illegally in the land of *dār al-Islām*.[8]

On the unrestricted propagation of Islam, al-Būṭī does not identify the precise means of doing so that would help define and constitute it. His wording "without hindrance or restriction" (*dūna iḥrājin aw taḍyīqin*) refers to his belief in all possible options, including military action, if the propagation of Islam encounters restrictive measures that may stem its tide. Although al-Būṭī penned his *Al-Jihād fī al-Islām* in the late 1990s, his handling of the issue considers military jihad an option, even though the information revolution removes all obstacles to the propagation of any religion or ideology including the religion of Islam.[9] Contrary to what al-Būṭī's statement may indicate, Muslims nowadays enjoy full freedom to propagate their religion in majority non-Muslim countries, in contrast to the "restricted" freedom they enjoy in many majority-Muslim countries. Undoubtedly, modern technology has globalized many aspects of our lives, including the propagation of Islam, so the hindrance and restriction posited by al-Būtī is no longer the norm and if it does exist it does so in rare and limited circumstances. Moreover, al-Būtī's borrowing of *dār al-Islām*[10] from the classical jurists does not mean that he necessarily follows their lead. On the contrary, his support for maintaining permanent peace expressed above may indicate that the man is an outstanding pacifist. However, he remains adamant in his utter rejection of all forms of illegal confiscation and usurpation of Muslim lands.

The fourth modern scholar whose views stand in total contrast to the offensive jihad narrative is Wahbah al-Zuḥaylī, who strongly advocates that peace is the underlying principle of relations between Muslims and non-Muslims. Al-Zuḥaylī maintains that this view is supported by 8: 61, as well as 2: 208 and 4: 94 that establish the principle of international peace. For him, Muslims should be committed to peace and security (on the basis of 4: 90 and 60: 8).[11] Al-Zuḥaylī further argues that considering military jihad to be the norm in relations between Muslims and non-Muslims opposes what the jurists have actually agreed upon, which is that "permissibility is the underlying principle" (*al-aṣl fī al-ashyā' al-ibāḥāh*). He argues, if this legal maxim and others similar to it constitute basic principles, then why do some jurists not consider military jihad to be the original rule in Muslim–non-Muslim relations?[12] Consequently, al-Zuḥaylī takes the view that "the original rule in international relations is peace" (*al-aṣl fī al-ʿalāqāt al-dawliyyah al-silm*).[13]

Moreover, al-Zuḥaylī considers that the Qur'anic verses calling for permanent peace with non-Muslims do not include:

> The Jews who usurped the land of Palestine. Their residence in the territories of Muslims cannot be legally condoned. Therefore, it becomes incumbent upon Muslims to expel them, once they have the power [to do so]. Or to accept their stay provided that they submit themselves to the Muslim rule and Islamic legislations. The peaceful texts are directed to an external enemy outside the territory of Muslims living in his or her original country.[14]

While Islam maintains a permanent call for peace, this quotation indicates that it does not condone occupation. Thus, repelling aggression, self-defence, and vindication of the right to self-determination are all circumstances that make military jihad necessarily permissible. Al-Zuḥaylī's direct reference to the territory of Palestine and its usurpation by Israel strongly suggests that the Anglo-American led occupation of Iraq, Afghanistan and other parts of majority Muslim countries cannot be condoned either. According to al-Ḥifnī, "forced expulsion such as is the case in Palestine and Iraq and other parts of the world is a legal justification for Muslims to defend themselves on the basis of 22: 39–40."[15] Nevertheless, the mechanisms for reacting to this twenty-first century occupation cannot be left to the personal interpretations of individual Muslims, as will be clarified later in this chapter.

The above modern scholarly views considering peace as the norm in determining relations between Muslims and non-Muslims are not, however, limited to individual scholars, although the above discussion attempts to highlight the prominent examples among them.[16] Huge collective efforts have recently been made by Muslim scholars from places as diverse as Asia and North America in the eighth, fourteenth and sixteenth conferences of the Egyptian-based Supreme Council for Islamic Affairs from the 1990s onwards.

Looking at these three annual conferences collectively shows that an important turning point has been reached as to how modern Muslim scholarship evaluates the classical offensive theory of jihad, at least in its interpretative presentation as exemplified by classical and some modern exegetes, some of whom we have considered. Due to limitations of space it is impracticable to detail all the main papers presented, so an overview will be made of the three conferences with special reference to relations between Muslims and non-Muslims in light of the defensive and offensive understandings of jihad.

In a remarkable reaction to Samuel Huntington's hypothesis set out in his *The Clash of Civilizations and the Remaking of World Order*, the eighth conference held in 1998 chose "Islam and the Future Dialogue between Civilizations" as the title for its four-day proceedings.[17] Scholars from more than seventy countries representing various international organizations, some from European countries, considered the proposition that dialogue and not war is the way to solve modern international problems.[18] Mufīd Shihāb, the then-Chancellor of Cairo University, stated that war in Islam is defensive and Muslims resort to it once all other peaceful means are exhausted.[19] In a bid to explain the present-day attitude of Muslims towards non-Muslims with special reference to the 11 September attacks in 2001,[20] the fourteenth conference in 2003 directed a special focus on explaining the modern applications of jihad, its objectives and various rulings, and how it differs in meaning from other terms such as "fighting" (*qitāl*), "violence" (*'unf*) and "terrorism" (*irhāb*). Out of the fifty-two published research papers, around seventeen of them were dedicated to jihad alone. The scholars, who came from fifty-six countries, collectively agreed that peace was the underlying principle between Muslims and non-Muslims and that war was permitted only in self-defence.[21] It is a measure that could be likened to surgery carried out only when medicine is of no avail.[22] Some 153 scholars from all five continents attended the sixteenth conference in 2004 in which a special focus was given to terrorism from a Qur'anic perspective, the ethics of war in Islam, present-day attitudes in international relations between Muslims and non-Muslims, and tolerance as understood from the Qur'an and the Sunnah. It is clear from the almost seventy-five papers presented that war was considered by those present as an exception in relations between Muslims and non-Muslims.[23]

It is notable that the proceedings of these three conferences have received scant attention in modern Western scholarship, even though some of the papers were published in English. Moreover, while many of the participating scholars occupy leading positions among Muslim communities in the West, it is still rare to find a Western academic being fully involved in such serious collective discussions. In our view, this is a reason why authors such as Quṭb and his like-minded followers are widely discussed, and their views are sometimes mistakenly or intentionally represented as "mainstream" views of Islam. The absence of moderate voices, in their individual as well as collective forms, in modern Western scholarship adds to the blurred atmosphere. In addition, it should not be forgotten that some media outlets in the West have their own biases, shown by the way they selectively highlight extremist views of jihad by Quṭb and others.

Moreover, whether individual or collective, the modern views surveyed above are given by trained theologians and scholars well-versed in their fields, who have received solid theological training at reputable seminaries such as the Azhar University. While their views sometimes stand in total contrast to the classical interpretative theory, they apply convincing approaches in their criticisms.[24] The valuable efforts of such esteemed scholars, however, fade into the background - at least in modern Western scholarship - when the views of authors with hard-line attitudes dominate the foreground. In a bid to reach a comprehensive understanding, I will now proceed to examine the proponents of the use of violence between Muslims and non-Muslims, and then to assess whether or not the views of Quṭb have any influence on modern-day extremists and terrorists.

Quṭb's Influence on Proponents of Offensive Jihad

As far as military jihad is concerned, the radical and revolutionary views pioneered by Sayyid Quṭb have had their ideological impact on the proponents of offensive jihad from the second half of the twentieth century up to present times. This is widely acknowledged by many authoritative experts in the field.[25] Therefore, it is no wonder that Quṭb is regarded as the ideologue and the godfather of modern extremism.[26] His *Milestones* is considered the manifesto of modern radicalism. However, this view can easily be challenged if one undertakes a meticulous reading of the literature attributed to the Islamic Group in Egypt in the 1970s and early 1980s.[27] In this literature, it is easy to identify the huge influence of Ibn Taymiyyah, the same medieval thinker whose views influenced Quṭb.[28]

Although these various descriptions of Quṭb in Western academic literature have gained currency since 11 September 2001, an analysis of the extremist discourse in Egypt confirms this view.[29] A very clear example is *Al-Farīḍah al-Ghā'ibah* (*The Neglected Duty*), an important pamphlet of the Islamic Group in Egypt written by Muḥammad ʿAbd al-Salām Faraj (1954–1982).[30] The "neglected duty" refers to the duty of jihad, and its author was executed on 15 April 1982 along with the four assassins of the then Egyptian president, Anwar Sadat (1918–1981). Jansen, who translated the whole of the *Farīḍah*, is apparently the only Western scholar who has made an excellent presentation and analysis of this important document.[31] Jansen highlights the refutations of the pioneering Egyptian scholars of the time, such as the then Grand Sheikh of the Azhar Jād al-Ḥaqq ʿAlī Jād al-Ḥaqq (1917–1996), al-Shaʿrāwī, as well as Muḥammad ʿImārah (b. 1931). Before presenting the main refutations of the scholars who criticized the *Farīḍah*, it is of paramount importance to refer to the controversial views disseminated in this document with special reference to Muslim/non-Muslim relations. It is important, however, to have a general overview of the *Farīḍah* before attempting to highlight this specific point.

The *Farīḍah* asserts that "The State (of Egypt in which we live today) is ruled by the Laws of Unbelief although the majority of its inhabitants are Muslims."[32] As for the rulers of Muslims, the author of the *Farīḍah* declares that they "are in apostasy from Islam. They were raised at the tables of imperialism, be it Crusaderism, or Communism or Zionism. They carry nothing from Islam but their names, even though they pray and fast and claim (*idda'ā*) to be Muslim."[33] It is clear from these two quotations that the members of the Islamic Group at that time did not consider their fellow Muslim Egyptians as apostates although they did not hesitate to say that the ruler (i.e. Sadat) was *ipso facto* an apostate who should be killed.[34] Based on this extremist understanding, the author of the *Farīḍah* poses this challenging question: "Do we live in an Islamic state?"[35] To answer this question, he cites long quotations from the response of Ibn Taymiyyah who was asked about whether the people of Mardin were living in a territory of peace or war. The inhabitants of Mardin continued to follow the Yasa code of laws of Genghis Khan (1127–1167) instead of the Islamic law, even though they adopted Islam.[36] Ibn Taymiyyah declared that the people of Mardin were to be treated according to their beliefs: "The Muslim in this town should be treated according to what was due to him, whereas the one who rebelled against the laws of Islam should be treated according to what was due to him."[37]

In my view, Ibn Taymiyyah's answer cannot be justifiably transferred to a completely different context, as the author of the *Farīḍah* has done. Was Egypt's situation at the time Faraj authored his book the same as Mardin's? The answer is emphatically not. Interestingly, Ibn Taymiyyah's opinion on Mardin was recently highlighted at an international peace summit on the topic "Mardin: The Abode of Peace" convened at Artuklu University in the Turkish city of Mardin on 27–28 March 2010 to discuss the classification of the city of Mardin during Ibn Taymiyyah's lifetime.[38] The scholars attending came from countries as diverse as Bosnia, Iran, Morocco, Mauritania and Saudi Arabia, and concluded that:

> Ibn Taymiyya's fatwa concerning Mardin can under no circumstances be appropriated and used as evidence for levelling the charge of *kufr* (unbelief) against fellow Muslims, rebelling against rulers, deeming game their lives and

> property, terrorizing those who enjoy safety and security, acting treacherously towards those who live (in harmony) with fellow Muslims or with whom fellow Muslims live (in harmony) via the bond of citizenship and peace.... *Anyone who seeks support from this fatwa for killing Muslims or non-Muslims has erred in his interpretation and has misapplied the revealed texts* [emphasis theirs].[39]

Moreover, ʿImārah challenges Faraj's radical and unsubstantiated claim, doubting whether he had actually read the Yasa before expressing his view. He also adds that there is no evidence in the *Farīḍah* to support this claim. Thus, ʿImārah continues, Faraj's view cannot be accepted because claiming that the rulers of today are the same as the Tatars, are even more wicked than them, and therefore deserve to be killed is a false analogical deduction.[40]

The insistence on quoting Ibn Taymiyyah's views regarding this particular issue, as well as in various other parts of the pamphlet, reveals that Faraj and his like depend heavily on persons rather than texts in formulating their views, which is evidence of their inability to deduce rulings from their original sources.[41] ʿImārah consequently claims that Ibn Taymiyyah is the Group's first ideologue.[42] ʿImārah's claim is actually substantiated by solid evidence, but this is not to downplay the influence of Quṭb on this extremist group because, while Quṭb's name is hardly mentioned in the treatise, his radical views can easily be read in-between the lines.[43] Quṭb was undoubtedly a member of the Muslim Brotherhood and, towards the beginning of the 1970s, his group had, according to Salwā al-ʿAwwā, completely rejected violence, and started a process of gradual reform (*al-iṣlāḥ al-tadrījī*).[44] This may be a reason behind Faraj's vivid presentation of Ibn Taymiyyah, who is a more classical authority than Quṭb; while the latter belonged to an ideologically different group at that time, his views had an impact that remains hard to conceal. As explained earlier in this chapter, Ibn Taymiyyah's influence on Quṭb cannot be underestimated.

A consideration of the *Farīḍah* with specific reference to Muslim and non-Muslim relations shows that Faraj endorses the offensive jihad thesis. He states, "It is proper that we should refute those who say that *jihād* in Islam is defensive, and that Islam was not spread by the sword. This is a false view ... Islam spread by the sword" and "Most Koran [*sic*] commentators have said something about a certain verse from the Koran which they have named the Verse of the Sword (Qur'ān 9.5)."[45]

These two quotations promote the view that jihad is the underlying principle governing the external relations of Muslims and non-Muslims. The rulers, who are declared apostates by Faraj, are not eligible to declare jihad as they carry no authority. Ordinary men and women, therefore, have every right to exercise jihad, which is an individual obligation on all Muslims. In a bid to clothe his views in a scholarly robe and consequently claim relative legitimacy, Faraj quotes extensively from the interpretations of Ibn Kathīr and al-Suyūṭī.[46] Again, he depends on classic authorities, but this time on the exegetes, another sign that he is selective and biased in formulating his argument.

In Faraj's quotations, he endorses the same narrative of offensive jihad: military jihad is the underlying principle governing Muslim external relations and the "verse of the sword" has abrogated all the verses which indicate that peace with non-Muslims is the norm. The issue of the "verse of the sword" is vividly presented with all its classical and classically-orchestrated debates, while stressing the notion that it abrogates all the verses that advocate peace and forgiveness. According to al-Ḥifnī, the adoption of such an interpretation, in which Muslims may declare war against all non-Muslims, is sheer insanity.[47]

More importantly, Faraj sets a demarcation line between two types of enemy: "the near enemy" (*al-ʿaduww al-qarīb*) and "the far enemy" (*al-ʿaduww al-baʿīd*). The near enemies are the apostate rulers and the far enemies are those who occupy Muslim lands such as Jerusalem (al-Quds). Although defending and freeing occupied Muslim territories is a legal obligation, Faraj wants first to prioritize these options, and he gives fighting "apostate" rulers priority over fighting occupying forces. Critiquing this view, ʿImārah adds that in Faraj's understanding achieving victory over the far enemy entails a tacit approval of Muslim regimes he regards as un-Islamic, as fighting a non-Muslim enemy requires Muslim leadership.[48] It is even more interesting that military jihad comes second, after fighting and eradicating the "apostate rulers" and that this extremist understanding of the medieval legacy and its selectivity in using the textual sources was rejected by scholars who were Faraj's contemporaries. Unlike him, they were well-versed in Islamic scholarship, a sufficient reason why their views regarding this issue are well received.[49]

Having briefly presented and analysed Faraj's thesis of both the internal and external enemy, it is still important to highlight the role played by scholars who were his contemporaries in refuting his extremist views, especially concerning the jihad narrative. Al-Sha'rāwī's response to Faraj and his group mainly took the form of a newspaper reply to an interview on these issues in the Egyptian daily *Al-Ahram* on 8, 16 and 18 November 1981. Unlike 'Imārah's book-length critique of the *Farīḍah*, al-Sha'rāwī's criticism is simply that he is "against them (*ḍiddahum*) ... [and] the murderer and his accomplices are not 'the Helpers of Islam' (*anṣār al-Islām*)".[50] Given the nature of newspaper interviews, al-Sha'rāwī's response may seem somewhat off-the-cuff and reactionary. Unsurprisingly, it is hard to find any reference to Faraj's pamphlet in al-Sha'rāwī's interpretation, although he did propose an initiative to have dialogue with Faraj and his group at the Egyptian Ministry of Interior at the time, which was, however, doomed to failure because of the refusal of the Egyptian Islamic Group to take part.[51] Al-Sha'rāwī may have preferred the matter to be handled officially, particularly by official Azhari officeholders, especially Jād al-Ḥaqq 'Alī Jād al-Ḥaqq, the then Grand Sheikh of the Azhar and 'Atiyyah Saqr (1914–2006), the then head of the Azhar Fatwa Committee.

Both Jād al-Ḥaqq and Saqr provide a scholarly analysis and criticism of the *Farīḍah*. They state in their co-authored book, published as an attachment to the Azhar magazine in 1993, that they prepared their refutation (*naqd*) of the *Farīḍah* after being given a photocopy of the original fifty-four-page pamphlet.[52]

While Kelsay's reference to the *Farīḍah* puts much emphasis on the Sheikh of the Azhar, by virtue of the latter being considered the most authoritative Islamic figure in Egypt and, supposedly, the world of Sunni Islam, the efforts of other scholars, such as ʿImārah and al-Shaʿrāwī, cannot be ignored.[53] Thus, the refutations of Jād al-Ḥaqq, Saqr and ʿImārah and al-Shaʿrāwī's abortive attempt at dialogue constitute the main efforts to refute the extremist ideology of Faraj and his colleagues. While it is impracticable to present these scholarly refutations fully here, it is interesting to highlight the efforts of Faraj's former colleagues, who ultimately renounced their old extremist interpretations. The people who once refused even to meet scholars such as al-Shaʿrāwī have recently started publishing their courageous initiative known as "ideological revisions" (*al-murājaʿāt*) in which the leaders of the Group revoked their original violent stance by publishing self-critical reviews. This started on 5 July 1997 from their cells inside Egyptian prisons.[54]

Ideological Revisions by the Leaders of the Islamic Group

While the refutations of the Egyptian scholars received wide coverage in Western academic discourse, especially by academics such as Jansen, it is hard to find in-depth coverage of the recent literature published by the leaders of the Islamic Group in Egypt in current Western scholarship.[55] Various justifications can be found for this. Firstly, the Group's literature in which they published most of their "ideological revisions" is still in Arabic and, as far as I have been able to determine, not a single book has been published so far in any other language.[56] This gives an indication that the Group members are seemingly talking to themselves, or, let us say, to the wider Egyptian community. Although the English version of their website gives the outside reader some idea of their "ideological revisions", this is limited to translating articles originally published in Arabic on the group's bilingual website.[57] Secondly, from the mid-1990s, the activities of the Group have taken place under strict surveillance by Egyptian state security. The members of the Group can hardly air their new tolerant views in public, and are treated as social outcasts among their local communities.[58] It is thus extremely difficult for them to remove the perceptions created by years of accumulated violence locally, let alone internationally. Thirdly, some Western scholars are unaware of the availability of some of the Group's published "ideological revisions", and others lack objectivity and put all modern extremist groups, including the Group, in one basket, paying little or no attention to these "ideological revisions" as a historical turning point, which constitutes an obstacle in formulating an objective and updated analysis of the Group. For these three reasons, these "ideological revisions" remain almost unheard of in modern Western writings, which usually link Quṭb to Bin Laden and al-Qaeda while ignoring this revisionism from the leaders of the Islamic Group.[59]

While the *murāja'āt* literature started to see the light of day in the late 1990s and early 2000s, it is poorly distributed and difficult to obtain. This literature reveals that most – if not all – of the offensive jihad thesis championed by Faraj has been irrevocably discarded by the current leaders of the Group. They emphasize the Qur'anic verses that incline to peace and forgiveness rather than war and fighting, and assert that Ibn Taymiyyah's opinion regarding the people of Mardin and the Yasa, once suitable for a certain time and place, cannot necessarily be applied to the Egyptian case. Deduction by analogy (*qiyās*) is not acceptable between the two cases. Peaceful co-existence (*musālamah*), coalition (*taḥāluf*), co-operation (*ta'āwun*) and reconciliation (*muṣālaḥah*) are all terms that occur widely in the Group's literature. The Group now argues that "Islam does not consider military confrontation the only available option that has to be followed", and that "the purpose of fighting in Islam is to remove persecution [*fitnah*] ... not just to exercise fighting for the sake of it." The 11 September 2001 attacks, the Bali attacks in Indonesia, and the Riyadh attacks are all rejected as abominable acts that represent a total distortion of jihad.[60]

In addition, clear messages have been presented in other books published by prominent leaders of the Group, messages that call for carefully studying the realities of contemporary times before issuing any legal judgment, giving priority to the voice of reason over that of enthusiasm, and preferring pluralism to dichotomous division. Citations from Ibn Taymiyyah, in addition to being seen as unsuitable, are replaced by statements from modern scholars such as al-Qaraḍāwī.[61]

An Analysis of the Egyptian Islamic Group's Ideological Revisions

Despite the Group's courageous rejection of its earlier views in the late 1990s, its extremist and selective interpretations of the Qur'an in the 1970s and 1980s have nevertheless made favourable public reception difficult. Another reason is the lack of effort by the Azhar's scholars in critiquing these "ideological revisions". Many contemporary Azhar scholars, especially those affiliated to the official institution, have given little or no attention to them, unlike their predecessors who refuted the *Farīḍah*. However, independent Azhar-trained scholars have made concerted efforts, such as al-Qaraḍāwī who hailed the *murāja'āt* initiative,[62] although his analysis is far from the deeper methodological approach applied earlier by those who critiqued the *Farīḍah*.

It is said that 'Umar 'Abd al-Raḥmān (b. 1938), another Azhar-trained scholar who acted as the spiritual guide of the Group from the 1970s onwards, has disowned his radical views.[63] However, this claim is uncertain because he is under strict imprisonment in the US, and has neither published any refutation of his earlier bloodthirsty fatwas nor relinquished his hard-line views.[64] All in all, these "ideological revisions" remain a courageous step in the right direction and should be considered a landmark in the history of an extremist group that first condoned terrorism but later repudiated it.

Nevertheless, not all members of the Group have rejected violence. Some, notably Ayman al-Ẓawāhirī, continue to call for "military jihad", but this time with a special focus on "the far enemy". Omar Ashour remarks that the "process [*al-murāja'āt*] has been only partially successful, however, as three factions within al-Jihad still refuse to uphold it. These factions also refuse to leave the Organization and one of them is in alliance with al-Qa'ida. The process is thus still ongoing at the present time."[65] Moreover, Kepel argues that it is because the terrorists' battle against "the near enemy" has failed, that they must once again consider "the far enemy" as the primary target. With such extremist views, al-Ẓawāhirī and other key leaders of al-Qaeda consider the US as the main representative of this "far enemy".[66] Al-Qaeda's leaders consider anyone who does not embrace their ideology, including hundreds of millions of Muslims, as legitimate military targets.[67] Due to the seriousness of this assertion, it is necessary to examine the ideological basis that al-Qaeda members have adopted when launching their military jihad. This naturally leads one to a consideration of whether or not the 11 September 2001 attacks were justifiable in terms of the Qur'an.

The Qur'an in al-Qaeda's Discourse

Al-Qaeda claims to present its ideology from an Islamic perspective, although this remains limited to Sunni Salafī literalism. To support their claim, its leaders appeal to various Qur'anic verses in a bid to lend authority and legitimacy to their attacks.[68] While some Western authors, such as Shah and Gwynne, have tried to highlight this aspect of al-Qaeda's discourse, noting their declarations of 1996 and 1998 as primarily representative of their justification of jihad, a thorough investigation of all Bin Laden's statements between 1994 and 2004, for example, shows to what extent Qur'anic citations are deeply embedded in almost all of them.[69] Direct reference to classical exegetes such as al-Qurṭubī, and others like Ibn Taymiyyah and ʿAbdullāh ʿAzzām (1941–1989), as well as the indirect influence of Quṭb, show how Bin Laden, al-Ẓawāhirī and their followers give themselves the authority to interpret the Qur'an in service of their ideology.[70] Following the method of Egypt's Islamic Group prior to their ideological revisionism, al-Qaeda's leaders link Qur'anic verses to serve the reality they experience around them.[71] Four main features make al-Qaeda's understanding of military jihad in the Qur'an distinctive.

The first of these distinctive features is that al-Qaeda prioritizes to "the far enemy". Unlike other extremist groups, which saw the deposing of despotic rulers (or "the near enemies") as a necessary step in their ultimate goal of establishing an Islamic caliphate, al-Qaeda considers the far enemy as its top priority. This was the reason behind Bin Laden's claiming responsibility for the devastating attacks of 11 September 2001. In contrast to the classical narrative of offensive jihad explained in Chapter 3, the second feature is that the leaders of al-Qaeda consider their "jihad" as purely "defensive". Bin Laden states that "The United States and their allies are killing us in Palestine, Chechnya, Kashmir, Afghanistan, and Iraq. That's why Muslims have the right to carry out revenge attacks on the US."[72] Yet at the time Bin Laden issued this statement, on 12 November 2001, neither Afghanistan nor Iraq was occupied by the US-led coalition, nor when he issued his declarations in 1996 and 1998. This means that al-Qaeda is practising a form of terrorism in which "Killing the Americans and their allies - civilians and military - is an individual duty for every Muslim who can carry it out in any country where it proves possible."[73]

The third feature is the fact that as a non-state actor al-Qaeda launches its "jihad" with total disregard for Islamic norms, which dictate that only the Muslim ruler or his deputy has the legitimate authority to declare it. The leaders of al-Qaeda and groups of the same ideological ilk consider the rulers to be despots who possess no legal authority and are therefore not entitled to declare a jihad. However, this argument can be easily refuted. The rulers whom al-Qaeda claims are not eligible to launch jihad because they have sided with the enemies of Muslims are the same rulers who declare that Islam is the official religion of their countries. Even when Muslim rulers side with the enemies of Muslims, Muslim leaders can only declare jihad by consensus, not simply as individuals.[74]

The fourth feature of al-Qaeda's fighting is that, while the proponents of the classical jihad narrative depend heavily on the theory of abrogation, Bin Laden and his group do not accept this theory, so al-Qaeda is "far removed" from being faithful to the classical jihad narrative.[75] Indeed, both abrogating (*nāsikhah*) and abrogated (*mansūkhah*) verses are quoted in Bin Laden's statements without distinction.[76] Furthermore, when quoting Qur'anic verses

Bin Laden truncates some verses, including both abrogating and abrogated, removing phrases that qualify how these verses should be understood. In Bin Laden's declaration "The World Islamic Front" issued on 23 February 1998, he applies this methodology when quoting the following verse: *Fight them until there is no more persecution and until worship is devoted to God* but does not cite the remainder of the verse: *If they cease hostilities, there can be no [further] hostility, except towards aggressors* (2: 193).[77] After this selective quoting, Bin Laden declares that "With God's permission we call on everyone who believes in God and wants reward to comply with His will to kill the Americans and seize their money wherever and whenever they find them."[78] To give a separate example of his misuse of abrogated verses, in an interview entitled "Terror for Terror" on 21 October 2001, he cites this verse: *And if you punish [your enemy, O you believers in the Oneness of God], then punish them with the like of that with which you were afflicted* but again *not* the qualifying part *but it is best to show patience* (16: 126).[79] Having presented the main ideological foundations of al-Qaeda, it is now necessary to critique them by highlighting modern scholarly efforts in this regard.

Al-Qaeda's Arguments Refuted

From al-Qaeda's point of view, the attacks of 11 September 2001 as well as other preceding and subsequent attacks are justified Islamically and in terms of the Qur'an, but in my view they are unjustified for the following reasons.[80] Firstly, al-Qaeda's unilateral declaration of war against Muslims and non-Muslims completely disregards the Qur'anic conception of diversity, human brotherhood, and peaceful relations between Muslims and non-Muslims, referred to, for example, in 2: 148; 5: 48; and 49: 13. Anyone who rejects al-Qaeda's ideology is unjustifiably a legitimate target who may be killed; a thing which stands in total contrast to the clear Qur'anic message in which, *if anyone kills a person – unless in retribution for murder or spreading corruption in the land – it is as if he kills all mankind, while if anyone saves a life it is as if he saves the lives of all mankind* (5: 32).[81] Secondly, al-Qaeda's claim that it is exercizing "defensive jihad" against the US and its allies to defend usurpation of Muslim lands is nothing more than a lame excuse because Bin Laden and his followers constitute a very tiny minority representing none but themselves, so they cannot declare "defensive jihad" on behalf of the whole *ummah*.[82] Simply put, the declaration of jihad is the prerogative of the ruler of the Muslim state or his deputy and al-Qaeda members, as non-state actors, are not allowed to declare it.[83] In addition, the "defensive jihad" launched by al-Qaeda against the US and its allies is unjustified because the expansionist American policy against some Muslim countries, such as Iraq and Afghanistan, does not justify shifting the war zone to American soil by attacking its innocent citizens under the pretext that they are "the far enemies".[84] In al-Qaraḍāwī's view, the US and other countries are classed as a territory of covenant (*dār al-ʿahd*) because the international community is bound by the United Nations' Charter.[85] However, according to Shah, the persistent occupation of these two Muslim countries may encourage Muslim rulers – and not al-Qaeda – to declare jihad by consensus. If there were such a consensus, Shah argues, both the Qur'an and international law would support it.[86]

Thirdly, Bin Laden's appeal to a range of classical exegetes, especially al-Qurṭubī, seeks to demonstrate that he is qualified to extract legal rulings from the Qur'an with the aim of attracting more followers to his ideology and gain a presumed authority. However, Gwynne's claim that al-Qurṭubī's exegesis is presumably Bin Laden's "main exegetical source" is questionable, as he refers to other exegetes, including Ibn Kathīr.[87] Bin Laden's attempts to adduce support for his views, regardless of whether the authors he refers to are exegetes or not, are interesting. His citation strategy is both highly selective and decontextualizing: he picks and chooses from the views of classical scholars and exegetes without consideration for the historical contexts in which their views were formulated, and with superficial application to a modern reality that is completely different.[88] As Bin Laden wilfully omits the qualifying parts of Qur'anic verses he quotes, it is unsurprising that he does the same with exegetes such as al-Qurṭubī and Ibn Kathīr.

Fourthly, Bin Laden's belief that the 11 September attackers were martyrs compounds the misunderstanding of jihad, already widely mistaken for a form of terrorism.[89] Faysal Mawlawī (1941–2011) states that those responsible for 11 September cannot be regarded as martyrs, even if they considered their act to be a form of jihad, had sincere intentions and were acting out of ignorance. Good intentions, Mawlawī argues, do not justify illegal acts and 11 September is an action that is prohibited from an Islamic perspective.[90] Mawlawī's balanced fatwa overturns Bin Laden's assertions. It clearly sets a line of demarcation between jihad and terrorism and proposes a clear explanation to Western readers of how the two concepts should be clearly distinguished. Marked by profound juristic understanding of the 11 September attacks, Mawlawī sheds light on the efforts made by the "silent majority" of moderate Muslim scholars, who have allowed the stage to be dominated by "vocal extremists and terrorists".[91] The scholars who condemned the attacks of 11 September, as well as other terrorist attacks throughout the world, are neither a silent majority nor are they less vocal than they should be. The mass media and parts of academia bear responsibility here, as the leaders of al-Qaeda have all too often been projected as spokesmen for Islam, drowning out the contributions of Islamic scholars that remain unknown or unacknowledged. As surveyed earlier in this chapter, concerted collective and individual efforts have been made since 11 September to explain the correct Islamic attitude towards these attacks, e.g. the fourteenth conference of the Supreme Council for Islamic Affairs in Cairo, in addition to the many condemnatory fatwas issued by Muslim scholars in the West and the Muslim world.[92]

These fatwas were generally reactive, as if the muftis were waiting for something to happen before they could explain the Islamic attitude towards it. I have personally lived this experience when I was given the Arabic transcript written by al-Qaraḍāwī to be translated on the day of the 11 September attacks. The general tenor of these fatwas is on the whole apologetic and tepid. The refutations of the extremist views of Bin Laden and his followers were not very vivid. They are short statements of condemnation rather than well-developed scholarly responses. Perhaps, this is another reason why scholars with moderate voices are heard less than the extremists and terrorists who advocate violent interpretations.[93]

While people like Bin Laden and his followers interpret verses from the Qur'an selectively to suit their agendas and add an "authoritative" dressing to their views, modern scholars cite from the Qur'an and the Sunnah to back their arguments while hardly referring to well-versed classical scholars in the field.[94] Perhaps the new genre of online fatwas militates against detailed referencing of classical sources. However, al-Qaraḍāwī's recent monograph *Fiqh al-Jihād* confirms the lack of classical references among contemporary scholars. Al-Qaraḍāwī was one of the first Muslim scholars to condemn the 11 September attacks in an online fatwa, but he hardly gave any space in his two-volume work to refuting the false claims of al-Qaeda's interpretations of the Qur'an and other religious source-texts. Moreover, it is extremely difficult to find the Azhar's scholars exposing the false allegations of Bin Laden and al-Qaeda, as they did with Faraj. The claim that the two are the same can be easily rebutted, as seen from al-Qaeda's main ideological features outlined above, so it is necessary that contemporary Muslim scholars should formulate a modern, comprehensive argument to challenge the ideological legacy of modern terrorists.[95] Having said that, the efforts of individual scholars such as al-Qaraḍāwī and others constitute a laudable endeavour that has the potential to discredit terrorist propaganda, if some of the weaknesses in these efforts are remedied. For example, there is an absence of in-depth academic studies exposing extremist ideas justifying violence taken from the Qur'an, which were evident in the scholarly response to Egypt's Islamic Group. If moderate Muslim scholars do not rise to the challenge, the ferocity of the unfounded "arguments" of al-Qaeda and their impact upon Western opinion will allow the terrorists to continue to monopolize the religious conversation.

Conclusion

The classical jihad narrative is still invoked by today's extremists, such as Bin Laden and al-Ẓawāhirī, who insist on practising terrorism in the name of Islamic jihad. This interpretation of the Qur'an applied by some of the classical exegetes and their modern extremist followers has had its impact on the formulation of the modern Western understanding of jihad in Islam. While the classical exegetes applied the theory of abrogation to justify military jihad as the underlying principle that shapes Muslim external relations with non-Muslims, the extremists distance themselves from this traditional approach, claiming to have a new vision in which they refer to their terrorist actions as a form of jihad, although they stand in total contradiction to what the Qur'an teaches.

Part of the reclaiming of jihad that this chapter and the previous one have presented is to demonstrate that it is a term intrinsic to the Qur'an despite the current misunderstanding and misappropriation that surrounds it. Aspects of such misunderstanding include the failure to: (1) comprehend even the phonological meanings of jihad by mistranslating it as "holy war"; (2) give fair consideration to the Qur'anic verses that emphasize peace and forgiveness while overemphasizing those that speak of war and revenge; (3) recognize a small group of terrorists as utterly marginal and far from being the sole and true representatives of Muslims and Islam; and (4) put the bloody history of some extremist groups into their proper context by considering ideational corrective measures or internal ideological revisionism.

However, this misunderstanding is not limited to Western academia. Rather, there are Muslim scholars who have misconceptions about the Qur'anic concept of war and speak as if it were a completely pacifist book, and there are those who read the Qur'an selectively and portray it as a book that calls for the killing of others for their beliefs. Even when these extremists and terrorists declare their "defensive jihad" against those who invade Muslim lands, they open up the prospect of global warfare without limitation on the basis of a selective reading of the Qur'an, even though it qualifies all the verses that call for fighting non-Muslims.

Between these extremist and the pacifist readings of the Qur'an, I have attempted to bridge a yawning gap by highlighting the role of modern exegetes and scholars who present a lenient yet authoritative view of what relations between Muslims and non-Muslims should be like. This relationship has peace as its underlying principle, except when Muslims are attacked, in which case, they are allowed to retaliate in self-defence. While this peaceful interpretation is widely acknowledged and endorsed by the overwhelming majority of modern scholars in official and unofficial circles, it does not, unfortunately, receive the same degree of attention in Western academic circles as the disproportionately loud voice of terrorist groups such as al-Qaeda and their followers do.

The bipolar division of the world might have succeeded in serving the cause of Islam "at a certain point in history" but its application today will lead to "disastrous consequences".[96] That is why the bipolar view endorsed by classical and modern exegetes cannot be adopted as the final Islamic verdict determining the relationship between Muslims and non-Muslims. In addition, part of the solution to this dilemma lies in understanding all the Qur'anic verses – thought by extremists to promote "aggression" against non-Muslims – in the context of the hostility faced by "the first generation of Muslims from the pagan Arabs" and *not* as a general attitude towards non-Muslims.[97]

As I have attempted to explain, the US is not an enemy of Islam or Muslims, according to Muslim scholars. Therefore, targeting the US and its allies through "defensive jihad", as applied by the late Bin Laden and his current followers, is a faulty interpretation of the Qur'an. The 11 September attacks and those that followed them on American soil were not legitimate, no matter what the motives in the minds of the perpetrators and those who motivated them. In the Qur'anic understanding, these attacks where the blood of human beings is unjustifiably shed are terrorist crimes, for which I will argue the Qur'an prescribes deterrent punishments as will be explained in Chapter 5. In other words, these acts have nothing to do with jihad. Rather, they are acts of terrorism that are poles apart from Islamic jihad.[98]

5

TERRORISM AND ITS QUR'ANIC PUNISHMENT

AT TIMES WE might sympathize with or even support the political cause of a terrorist being tried in a court of law, but should we even momentarily forget the tragic deaths of poor, innocent civilians or what are sometimes the "mass casualties" murdered as a result of such barbaric acts? We might empathize with the anguish of his family, but the grief of one or maybe hundreds of families are weightier. This chapter attempts to anchor in Islamic terms the concept of terrorism as a crime with specific punishments that are capable of deterring the perpetrators in any age or clime.

While little attention has been paid to studying the Qur'anic attitude towards terrorism as a punishable crime, and specifically on the subject of punishment for terrorism; both have received very limited coverage in Western academic literature. In this chapter, I attempt to fill the void. I aim to set out and analyse the Qur'anic penalty for banditry (*ḥirābah*) within the context of the Qur'an's overall concept of crime and punishment, and the views of proponents and opponents of the contention that *ḥirābah* and terrorism can be linked. While I will analyse the discussion of *ḥirābah* by the exegetes whose works I have consulted throughout this study, as *ḥirābah* is a juristic term too, I will also discuss its definitions and various rulings in the four Sunni schools of jurisprudence. Thereafter, I attempt to answer the question of whether or not terrorism should be subject to the same punishment as that set by the Qur'an for *ḥirābah* by reviewing the Sunni exegetical and jurisprudential literatures.

The Qur'anic Concept of Crime and Punishment

The Arabic word *jarīmah* (crime) does not occur in the Qur'an, but related lexemes that convey the sense of committing a crime (e.g. *ijrām*) do occur: *ijrām* once in 11: 35 and *mujrim* (criminal) twice.[1] In 20: 74, al-Shaʿrāwī maintains that *mujrim* refers to a person who commits a criminal act, usually characterized by violation of Allah's divine ordinances.[2] The second occurrence is 70: 11 and al-Alūsī states that it refers to guilty person(s).[3] Other lexemes of *ijrām* such as *mujrimūn* and *mujrimīn* occur fifty times.[4] The last related lexeme is *jarama* (to commit a crime), which occurs five times.[5] Al-Aṣfahāni states that *jarama* originally referred to picking fruit from trees, and it was later used rhetorically to mean committing bad acts.[6] In all of its five Qur'anic occurrences, *jarama* is preceded by the negative particle *lā* forming the phrase *lā jarama* (e.g. 16: 23), which may mean "surely" or "no doubt".[7] However, some modern lexicographers state that the verb *jarama* without the particle *lā* means "to commit a crime or an offence".[8]

The juridical literature related to the concept of crime in Qur'anic discourse shows that, unlike the exegetes, Muslim jurists focus on the definition of crime, and on its types and categories.[9] Explaining such details about the nature of the Islamic rulings on crime is a primary task of the jurist, while the exegete's is to communicate the meaning of the Qur'anic text to a wider audience. However, the two roles may complement each other: the exegete depends on the juristic analysis and the rulings developed by the jurist, and the jurist makes use of the tools employed by the exegete to reach his rulings.

Terrorism is a crime from the Qur'anic perspective, as those who commit it violate Allah's ordinances, and thus become criminals (*mujrimūn*) according to the exegetical explanation of al-Shaʿrāwī and al-Alūsī cited above. Some modern researchers within the field of Islamic criminal law consider that there are differences between a criminal (*mujrim*) and a terrorist (*irhābī*), arguing that criminals usually commit their crimes out of personal interest whereas terrorists commit their actions primarily for political reasons, with the aim of subduing a more powerful authority. Moreover, criminals usually know their victims, while terrorists do not. These differences, however, are not clear-cut because terrorists may clearly have many religious, economic, social, and even personal aims and may not be completely ignorant about their targets, but know full well that helpless civilians will be present at the scenes of their attacks. On the other hand, these researchers state that disseminating fear and alarm among people is a feature common to both crime and terrorism, and that they are therefore similar in effect, although different in nature.[10] The main conditions necessary for the punishment of crime, according to ʿAbd al-Qādir ʿUdah (1906–1954), are a textual source authorizing the punishment, deliberate intent on the part of the criminal, and the criminal's having attained legal maturity (*tamyīz*).[11] ʿUdah is probably generally referring here to crimes that have *ḥudūd* punishments, since *taʿzīr* punishments, for example, do not require textual evidence. The conditions referred to by ʿUdah are applicable to terrorism although it has its own additional criteria as a crime, which will be explained later on in this chapter. From the Qur'anic perspective, according to many modern researchers, terrorism should be considered a crime. Terrorists therefore deserve punishment just as criminals do – which leads us to discuss how the Qur'an generally views punishment for crime to determine the punishment it sets for terrorism in particular.

According to the Qur'an, there are two types of punishments: punishment in this world, which is carried out by the ruler of the Muslim state or those authorized by him to execute it, and the punishment that is postponed until the Day of Judgment. The worldly punishment is usually for a crime related to violating the rights of the community or those of the individual, whereas the "postponed" punishment is for committing a sinful act.[12] Both punishments are referred to in 5: 33, which speaks of *ḥirābah*.[13]

There are two main approaches to the *ḥirābah*-terrorism

relationship. Both propose that the Qur'an sets a punishment for terrorists, but they differ in assigning a category within the Islamic criminal law system under which the punishment for terrorism should fall. One view is that modern terrorism corresponds in its most salient features to *ḥirābah*.[14] If one takes this standpoint, then the punishment for terrorism is referred to in the text of the Qur'an. The other view is that there is little or no relationship between modern terrorism and *ḥirābah*.[15] A preliminary treatment of the thematic handling of the textual Qur'anic discourse on *ḥirābah* itself should be made before presenting both sides of this argument.

The Textual Source of Ḥirābah in the Qur'an

There is a consensus among classical and modern exegetes that the following Qur'anic verses are the textual source of *ḥirābah*:

> *Those who wage war against God and His Messenger and strive to spread corruption in the land should be punished by death, crucifixion, the amputation of an alternate hand and foot, or banishment from the land: a disgrace for them in this world, and then a terrible punishment in the Hereafter, unless they repent before you overpower them – in that case bear in mind that God is forgiving and merciful* (5: 33–34).[16]

'Abd al-Rahīm Ṣidqī claims that 2: 27 is also textual evidence for *ḥirābah*, but his claim is neither supported either by the text of the verse itself nor by its context of revelation.[17] Above all, his claim is not evidence-based. The verse, according to al-Ṭabarī was revealed with reference to the fate of those who break Allah's covenant from among the People of the Book and hypocrites in general, as well as some rabbis who showed animosity towards the Prophetic mission, particularly after his migration to Madinah.[18] Neither al-Ṭabarī nor any of the other classical or modern exegetes refer to this particular verse as textual evidence for *ḥirābah* – which is sufficient to reject Ṣidqī's claim both in theory and practice. Muḥammad Sa'īd al-'Ashmāwī does not consider 5: 33–34 to be textual evidence of *ḥirābah*, but rather as a reference to fighting only against Allah and the person of the Prophet. He does not apply 5: 33–34 to the rightly-guided caliphs or to the jurists after them because, in his view, their morals were marred by sinful acts.[19] Such claims constitute sufficient incentive to examine the exegetical treatment of *ḥirābah* to determine whether or not the context of 5: 33–34 is applicable to *ḥirābah* and other similar crimes.

Although exegetes consider 5: 33–34 to be a textual reference to *ḥirābah*, all of them – especially the classical ones – cite contradictory contexts for the revelation of these two verses: Ibn al-ʿArabī mentions five contradictory contexts for 5: 33–34, al-Qurṭubī, four; al-Ṭabarī, three; and others, such as al-Jaṣṣāṣ, cite only one.[20] Looking at those classical interpretations as a whole shows that there are up to seven sets of reports regarding 5: 33–34 – leaving the reader confused as to which context is the most authoritative.

The first set of reports state that the verses were revealed because a group of the People of the Book broke their covenant with the Prophet and caused corruption on earth.[21] The second set of reports relate that the tribesmen of Abū Barzah al-Aslamī, who had entered into a reciprocal treaty of mutual protection with the Prophet, blocked the way of a group of people who wanted to meet the Prophet in order to embrace Islam.[22] According to a third set of reports, the verses were revealed because of some polytheists who attacked Muslims and fled to a non-Muslim territory before being captured.[23] The fourth set, in which Ibn al-ʿArabī draws upon various reports said to have been related by al-Ṭabarī, contends that the verses were revealed regarding some Jews.[24] Although Ibn al-ʿArabī tries to refute al-Ṭabarī's view by arguing that the Jews did not engage in *ḥirābah* and were not subjected to its punishment when 5: 33–34 was revealed, double-checking the various reports cited by al-Ṭabarī reveals that they contain no reference to the Jews. This throws doubt on Ibn al-ʿArabī's refutation and deepens the contradictory exegetical attitudes concerning the contexts of revelation of 5: 33–34.

The final set of reports revolves around a narration that, according to Abou El Fadl, arouses the most controversy.[25] Although many classical and modern exegetes have referred to this narration, it is important to trace its original hadith source. The Prophet's Companion Anas narrates that:

> A group of men from the tribe of ʿUkl and ʿUraynah came to Madinah and adopted Islam. They then said, "O Prophet of Allah! We were people of the desert and are therefore unable to live in Madinah." The Prophet sent a shepherd and camels with them and ordered them to drink the camels' milk and urine [to regain health]. The men travelled until they reached [a place called] al-Ḥarrah. They then apostatized, killed the shepherd, stole the camels and fled. When the Prophet found out about this he sent a group of Muslims to seize them. When they were brought to him, he ordered that they be blinded, have their hands and feet severed [from opposite sides], and be left to die in a secluded spot at al-Ḥarrah.[26]

This is just one of fourteen narrations cited by al-Bukhārī alone under various headings that range from "the permissibility of drinking camels' urine for medical purposes" to "narrating the stories of ʿUkl and ʿUraynah within the context of the Prophet's raids [*maghāzī*]". The versions narrated by al-Bukhārī are diverse, even in their descriptions of the punishments. Abou El Fadl argues that the debates around the above narration "focused on whether the revelation of the verses meant to chide the Prophet for what he did to the men". He further argues that some reports assert that the prohibition against mutilation (*muthlah*) came after rather than before this incident and that no reproof was applicable because the Prophet blinded the men in retaliation for blinding the shepherd.[27] However, al-Ḥifnī maintains that the Prophet did not order the men to be blinded, arguing that this incident comes in a tradition promulgated by weak narrators.[28]

Even a careful examination of the above set of reports reveals that the whole issue is very complex and it cannot be ascertained which narration or context of revelation is authentic. Moreover, given these various and irreconcilable contexts of revelation, some classical and modern exegetes argue that 5: 33–34 is general textual evidence against those "who wage war against God and His Messenger and strive to spread corruption in the land". Both al-Ṭabarī and Riḍā arrive at this conclusion, although they cite the different contexts of revelation like other exegetes.[29] This leads me to conclude that 5: 33–34 is considered the main Qur'anic textual evidence concerning *ḥirābah*, no matter how diverse or contradictory the contexts of revelation of these two verses may be. Al-Sammān (1917–2007) affirms this view, stating that 5: 33–34 provides a general ruling applicable to all those who spread any kind or form of corruption in the land.[30]

Having reviewed the contexts of revelation of 5: 33–34, the first issue to be tackled in any thematic treatment is the definition of *ḥirābah*. Although the verses are mainly about the punishment, it is necessary to define *ḥirābah* in order to discover the similarities or dissimilarities between *ḥirābah* and terrorism, in order to determine whether the punishment for terrorism is the same for *ḥirābah* or not. It is noteworthy that the phrase "wage war against" (*yuḥāribūna*) is the first use of the term in 5: 33. Thus, a comprehensive definition of *ḥirābah* necessitates defining its lexical and technical aspects.

Definitions of Ḥirābah and Their Evaluation

Lexically, the word *ḥirābah* is derived from the root word *ḥaraba*, the original meaning of which is to despoil someone's wealth or property.[31] *Ḥirābah* is also said to be derived from the word *ḥarb* (war, as the opposite of peace). It thus refers either to fighting or to committing a sinful act. The Qur'an refers to both meanings in 2: 279 and 5: 33. In 2: 279, *ḥarb* refers to fighting those who deal in usury (*ribā*) and keep its outstanding dues. Al-Alūsī states that the war declared by Allah and His Prophet in 2: 279 may denote waging war similar to that declared against the apostates. It may also refer to threatening those who commit such acts with the grave consequences awaiting them in the Hereafter.[32] The second occurrence in 5: 33 refers to people's disobedience when they rebel against the ordinances of Allah and His Prophet.[33]

Thus, the lexical meanings of *ḥirābah* refer to conflict, disobedience and fighting. It also refers to disbelief, banditry, striking terror among the passers-by, and spreading corruption in the land.[34] However, neither the word *ḥirābah* nor the root verb *ḥaraba* occurs in the Qur'an, although the verbal noun form (i.e. *ḥirābah*) is frequently used in classical and modern books of Islamic jurisprudence. In the Arabic lexicons, the lexical definition of the word *ḥirābah* is interchangeable with *muḥārabah*, and this may explain why *ḥirābah* – and not other derivatives – is repeatedly used in various classical and modern works of Islamic jurisprudence.[35] The fact that the Qur'an does not contain the term itself does not necessarily mean that it is silent on identifying its punishment. Rather, the Qur'an refers to *ḥarb* four times, only two of which have been mentioned because of their relevance to this discussion.[36] Riḍā states that three out of the four occurrences of *ḥarb* in the Qur'an refer to war as an antonym to peace, while the fourth refers to those who challenge Allah and His Prophet by insisting on the wrongful consumption of people's possessions, as stated above.[37] Like *ḥirābah*, the word *irhāb* does not occur in the Qur'an either. The Qur'anic discourse shows that there is no link between the term *irhāb* and its lexical origin (i.e. *rahaba*), as was shown in Chapter 1; yet, this is the case with *ḥirābah*, as *ḥarb* and *ḥirābah* have almost the same meaning. Having looked at the lexical definition of *ḥirābah*, it is also essential to this discussion to examine legal definitions of *ḥirābah*.

In the literature of Islamic jurisprudence, *ḥirābah* is classified under the category of crimes with fixed penalties (*ḥudūd*) within the Islamic criminal law system *stricto sensu*.[38] There is an extensive discussion within the four Sunni schools of Islamic jurisprudence about defining *ḥirābah* and distinguishing it from similar legal terms. Within Sunni legal theory, there are three terms that are widely used for *ḥirābah*: (1) *ḥirābah* itself, (2) highway robbery (*qaṭ' al-ṭarīq*), (3) grand theft or larceny (*sariqah kubrā*).[39] For the purposes of this discussion, preference is given to *ḥirābah* because of its strong relevance and similarity to terrorism and the fact in meaning it covers the two other terms.

A comparison between the exegeses of 5: 33–34 and legal definitions of *ḥirābah* reveals that all classical and modern exegetes cite the various juristic definitions of *ḥirābah* without presenting new or adapted definitions of their own. There are many reasons why exegetes largely follow the legal definition of *ḥirābah*. They appear to consider *ḥirābah* a purely juristic term, and prefer those juristic definitions that best suit their exegetical approach or follow, as is often the case, the legal school of thought to which they belong. The exegetes also appear to consider the definition of *ḥirābah* as a legal term to be of secondary importance to the primary goal of the exegetical endeavour, which is to convey the overall meaning of the Qur'anic text rather than focus on some of the terminological aspects that it may include. As both classical and modern exegetes mostly cite from the four Sunni schools of jurisprudence in their discussions of the technical definition of *ḥirābah*, it is necessary to examine them further given the reliance of the exegetes upon them.

The prominent Ḥanafī jurist al-Kāsānī (d. 587/1191) defines *ḥirābah* as:

> Setting out for the purpose of forcibly stealing travellers' property in a way in which travel on the road is obstructed. This is irrespective of whether the act is committed by an individual or a group as long as the one(s) who carries it out uses force by means of offensive weapons (*asliḥah*) or other means such as sticks and rocks.[40]

The Ḥanafī jurist Abū Bakr al-Sarakhsī (d. 483/1090) adds that it makes no difference whether either those who obstruct the road or the targeted personnel are Muslims or protected non-Muslim minorities in Muslim lands (*ahl al-dhimmah*).[41] It is clear that the Ḥanafī school restricts the concept of *ḥirābah* to what they call "the great theft" (*al-sariqah al-kubrā*). In his *Ḥāshiyah*, Ibn 'Ābidīn (1198–1252) treats *ḥirābah* as equivalent to *al-sariqah al-kubrā*.[42] However, this restriction cannot be accepted at face value within the context of discussing the link between *ḥirābah* and terrorism because, in the Ḥanafī view, there is no apparent link between the two crimes.

The second definition is that of Imām al-Shāfi'ī (d. 204/819–20), who defines the *muḥāribūn* as follows, "They are a group of people who use offensive weapons to rob another group, either in the desert, on the highway, in a Bedouin camp or in a village."[43] In *Al-Aḥkām al-Sulṭāniyyah*, the Shāfiʿī jurist al-Māwardī (d. 450/1058), defines the *muḥāribūn* as, "A group of corrupt people who use weapons and obstruct the way (or the highway) for the purpose of seizing travellers' property, killing them or obstructing their way."[44] The emphasis on the communal sense understood from the word "group" in these two Shāfiʿī definitions indicates that if an individual person commits *ḥirābah* he or she cannot be punished because the punishment for *ḥirābah* requires the act to be carried out by a group of individuals. Compared with the definition of terrorism arrived at in Chapter 1, the Shāfiʿī definition of *ḥirābah* is apparently dissimilar, giving special weight to the "communal act" rather than treating terrorist acts by an individual, a group or a state with complete equality.[45] However, al-Shāfiʿī's view that the seriousness of *ḥirābah* remains the same whether committed in a city, village or a desert, and al-Māwardī's reference to the *muḥāribūn* as "corrupt people" whose heinous acts go beyond stealing or killing, provide grounds to argue that in this respect the Shāfiʿī school recognizes a similarity between *ḥirābah* and terrorism.[46] This seemingly see-saw relationship between *ḥirābah* and terrorism is typically presented by two modern scholars who hold opposing views on this issue. The first, al-ʿUmayrī, states that the Shāfiʿī definition of *ḥirābah* is very restrictive, whereas al-Majālī adopts a more nuanced view, stating correctly that one opinion of the Shāfiʿī school restricts the concept of *ḥirābah* to robbing others, whereas the other opinion broadens it to include any act that can be described as corruption.[47]

A third definition is that of the Ḥanbalī jurist Ibn Qudāmah (d. 620/1223–4), who defines the *muḥāribūn* as "people armed with offensive weapons who rob others in the desert, where the victims find it very hard to expect help from others."[48] Ibn Qudāmah restricts the site where the crime of *ḥirābah* can be committed to the desert and rules out the possibility that it can be committed in the city on the premise that a person attacked there is readily aided. Like al-Shāfiʿī, Ibn Qudāmah restricts the tools used in *ḥirābah* to offensive weapons. Unlike Ibn Qudāmah, another Ḥanbalī jurist, al-Buhūtī (d. 1051/1651) stresses that it does not matter whether the act of *ḥirābah* is committed in a desert or city or at sea.[49] A close examination of the Ḥanbalī definitions of *ḥirābah* reveals that they bear no similarity to the modern definition of terrorism. Restricting the "site" of the commission of *ḥirābah* to the desert, and the "act" to mere robbery makes the Ḥanbalī definition appear distant from the definition of terrorism.

The fourth definition is that of Imam Mālik, who defines *ḥirābah* as "the act of terrorizing people whether to rob them or for any other purposes."[50] Additionally, the Mālikī jurist Ibn ʿAbd al-Barr (d. 463/1071), defines the *muḥārib* as "the one who blocks the way of the passers-by, terrifies them, spreads corruption in the land by robbing the possessions of others, shedding their blood, and violating the sanctity of what Allah makes unlawful."[51] According to Ibn ʿAbd al-Barr, the person who commits such acts is considered a *muḥārib*, whether he is "Muslim or non-Muslim, free or enslaved, or whether or not his acts end in robbing and killing or not".[52] Unlike the other Sunni definitions, the Mālikī definition of *ḥirābah* broadens the concept to include all acts that lead to terrorizing people. Wajis asserts that the Mālikī definition excludes the instruments (i.e. the weapons) as well as the site of the commission from the criteria used to define *ḥirābah*.[53] In fact, there is evidence of "semi-consensus" among many contemporary scholars, who see the Mālikī definition as the most comprehensive.[54]

Limitation of the concept of *ḥirābah* is an important aspect of the discussion that can be easily identified in these Sunni definitions. Al-Shāfiʿī, for example, clearly limits the site of the commission to the land rather than sea or air. Although some of the juristic definitions of *ḥirābah* mention the sea, none mention the air. Al-Ghunaymī states the obvious in remarking that this is because airpower was unknown at the time the classical jurists lived and they did not speculate on it. As some classical jurists considered the sea as a site for *ḥirābah*, this also makes hijacking an aeroplane an act of *ḥirābah* if analogical deduction (*qiyās*) is applied.[55] Al-Ghunaymī's view reflects a distinctive contribution in which modern scholarly efforts link modern forms of *ḥirābah* with the classical Sunni theory by using the principles of jurisprudence – namely analogical deduction – as a tool. His view refers to the necessity of widening the concept of *ḥirābah* beyond the limitations of classical Sunni theory.

Another important aspect about the above four definitions is that they are similar in many aspects, although their focus differs in certain respects. This becomes clear when they are examined through a unifying concept, something which is now sought after by many modern researchers, who attempt to link *ḥirābah* as a Qur'anic crime dealt with extensively in the classical juristic literature with current reality. However, Wajis, while attempting to reach a seemingly comprehensive definition of *ḥirābah*, pays special attention to what he calls "the most important element", which is causing corruption. Wajis argues that the overriding importance of this element has been seemingly ignored by jurists and that the addition of causing corruption to the Mālikī definition would render it comprehensive.[56] His arrival at this conclusion may be attributed to the fact that Imam Mālik's definition is the only one used in his thesis. After analysing it, he suggests adding a missing element to make it comprehensive. He does this without referring to or quoting other definitions of *ḥirābah* by authoritative jurists in the Mālikī school such as Ibn ʿAbd al-Barr, whose definition is quoted above. It would have been better if Wajis had included this definition in his thesis, because it specifically refers to "spreading corruption", which he erroneously asserts is missing from the Mālikī legal school. Wajis also treats the definition from Imam Mālik's *Mudawwanah* as the sole one representing the Mālikī school, despite citing two Shāfiʿī definitions of *ḥirābah* in his discussion. In addition to Wajis, the efforts of ʿAbd al-Fattāḥ Qā'id, al-ʿUmayrī and al-Majālī make substantial contributions towards a unified definition of *ḥirābah*. For Qā'id, the terrorizing of innocents is a common element in all the Sunni definitions of *ḥirābah*,[57] whereas al-Majālī stresses that some followers of the Shāfiʿī and many followers of the Mālikī schools focus on corruption as a common denominator in *ḥirābah*.[58] Al-ʿUmayrī tries to reach a collective definition based on all the definitions of the classical Sunni jurists, while taking modern reality into account.[59]

A critical review of the definitions formulated by these modern researchers reveals that they omit the "tools" used in *ḥirābah*, even though most of the Sunni jurists include this as a criterion that ought to be taken into account when attempting to define *ḥirābah*.[60] However, this is excusable, given that what matters is the act itself and not the "tools" used. These definitions also refer more to individual than to collective action in *ḥirābah*, which might make it appear as though collective *ḥirābah* is deemed to be not as serious as an individual act, albeit that the consequences of both are serious. In addition, the targets of the *ḥirābah* are either Muslims, protected non-Muslim minorities (*mu'āhadīn*) or "scriptuaries" (*ahl al-kitāb*).[61] In my view, it would have been better if those researchers had specified innocent civilians as the target rather than referring to Muslims and scriptuaries. Having said that, I will conclude by formulating a definition of *ḥirābah* that may be deemed comprehensive and more applicable to the present day, as follows:

> *Ḥirābah* is the premeditated act of a sane and mature individual (or group of individuals) aimed at frightening, robbing, killing or transgressing against non-combatants' dignity, carried out from a position of power (*shawkah*). The targets in *ḥirābah* may be Muslims or non-Muslims, in any setting, be it a village, a city, at sea or in the air.

As referred to previously, the exegetes did not give their own definitions of *ḥirābah* but rather referred to their "school's definitions". Sherman A. Jackson stresses that modern exegetes, such as Riḍā, 'Abduh, and Quṭb, would for the most part follow the contours laid down by their classical predecessors, providing definitions that are essentially the same, and do not provide any additional guidance to the extent that nothing of note can be said to have been added or taken away from the classical definitions.[62]

As the classical exegetes cite their school's views, they did not come to agreement on common elements in *ḥirābah*, as each apparently discusses either his own or his school's view. However, many common elements can be extracted: (1) the use of weapons, (2) the site of the action, (3) the act of robbery, (4) the act of terrorizing people, and (5) causing corruption in the land. All of these elements of *ḥirābah* are found in the Sunni jurisprudential literature.

The four schools of Sunni jurisprudence hold different views as to whether the use of weapons may be an element in the definition of *ḥirābah*. The Ḥanafī, Shāfiʿī and Ḥanbalī jurists generally emphasize the use of weapons as a necessary element of *ḥirābah*, whether or not they are used offensively. However, the Mālikī school does not refer to weapons in its various definitions, implying that weapons need not be used. The Mālikīs would even consider someone who uses no weapons but only frightens others to be a *muḥārib*.[63] This Mālikī view is more akin to modern reality, in which sophisticated means are used to spread terror without the use of weapons. Modern terrorist operations certainly use weaponless tactics to carry out their deadly attacks. Excluding the Mālikī view would prevent people and governments from challenging such terrorist tactics and they would continue to suffer serious consequences as a result.

The site of commission of *ḥirābah* is an important element according to the Ḥanafī and the majority of the Ḥanbalī jurists.[64] Al-Sarakhsī and Ibn Qudāmah consider one of the main criteria for classifying an act as *ḥirābah* is that it should be committed in an uninhabited place or a desert.[65] It may be understood from this view that a crime committed in a town or a village, where the victims can receive help, is not considered *ḥirābah*.[66] On the other hand, the Shāfiʿī and Mālikī definitions of *ḥirābah* clearly indicate that the *muḥārib* is to be punished wherever his criminal act is committed. This view is apparently favoured by El-Awa who much prefers the Shāfiʿī opinion on this issue to those of the other Sunni schools.[67] In addition, Wajis prefers the Shāfiʿī and Mālikī opinions as he argues that the verse about *ḥirābah* is general in its application, as it specifies neither a city nor a desert for an act to be considered *ḥirābah*. As al-Ghunaymī maintains, it should be considered irrelevant whether *ḥirābah* or any other similar criminal act is committed in a city, village or uninhabited place, or on earth, in the air or at sea. In modern times, there is no compelling rationale to restrict the definition of an act of *ḥirābah* either topographically or geographically, as most would say a crime is a crime regardless of where it is committed.

The Ḥanafī, Shāfiʿī, and Ḥanbalī jurists consider the act of robbery a significant and essential element of *ḥirābah*. All the juristic definitions mentioned above, including the Mālikī definition, refer to the act of robbery. However, the Mālikī definition seemingly considers the act of robbery as one of the objectives of *ḥirābah* rather than one of its main elements. Whether robbery is involved or not, Wajis argues that the crime of *ḥirābah* has been committed, as long as the remaining criteria are met.[68] Wajis is apparently affected by the Mālikīs, whose view he favours here over the other Sunni legal schools. Although *ḥirābah* is generally linked to armed robbery in the juristic discourse, it may be said that robbery is only a limited demonstration of what constitutes *ḥirābah*. The adoption of this view widens the overlap between *ḥirābah* and terrorism, and paves the way for discussing the two most important elements of *ḥirābah*: (1) the act of terrorizing people and (2) causing corruption.

Terrorizing people is one of the two most important elements of *ḥirābah*. It plays a major role in determining whether or not the act is considered *ḥirābah*. Of all the four juristic definitions mentioned above, only the Mālikī definition specifies the act of terrorizing people as an element of *ḥirābah*. The Mālikīs consider any action intended to terrorize people to be an act of *ḥirābah*, irrespective of whether a weapon is used or not. Wajis understands this to include all the other elements mentioned by other jurists.[69] This element can be considered the greatest common denominator between *ḥirābah* and terrorism because it is a distinctive characteristic of both crimes.

Causing corruption is the second most important element in the definition of *ḥirābah*. Of all the previous elements, it can be argued that this is the most comprehensive because of the general nature of corruption. Wajis argues that, with the exception of the site where *ḥirābah* is committed, all the other elements can be included under this comprehensive heading.[70] Abou El Fadl states that almost without exception the classical jurists argued that those who attack residents and wayfarers in order to terrorize them are corrupters of the earth.[71]

Having examined the elements of *ḥirābah*, it can be said that terrorizing people and causing corruption are the most important so far as the link between *ḥirābah* and terrorism is concerned. This is because any crime that meets either of these two criteria can be considered to be both *ḥirābah* and terrorism. It is therefore necessary to present the exegetical explanations of these two elements, with special reference to corruption. The Qur'anic attitude towards *fasād* (corruption) as a central element in terrorism has already been dealt with in Chapter 1, although 5: 33, which also refers to *fasād* was not discussed there. It has been left for discussion here as a textual and contextual link with *ḥirābah* needed to be established first of all. Frederick Mathewson Denny considers that 5: 33 refers to committing destructive deeds as one of two general aspects of corruption as referred to in the Qur'an.[72]

Exegetes, both classical and modern, take much interest in discussing the various meanings and aspects of *fasād* in 5: 33, and some link this verse to the immediately preceding one that also refers to *fasād*. Al-Sha'rāwī noticeably focuses on *fasād* when discussing 5: 32, stating that "corruption on earth" (*al-fasād fī al-arḍ*) has human beings as its targets, as well as fauna and flora.[73] He adds that causing corruption to those inanimate objects negatively affects human beings, and then cites the violation of people's possessions as an example of *fasād*.[74] Al-Sha'rāwī's discussion of this verse shows that he relies heavily on *al-arḍ* as the scene for corruption in which human beings can be held legally accountable. However, in modern times, settings such as the sea and space are also considered the site of modern forms of corruption in a time when the international community struggles to confront piracy and global warming. In addition, Mawdūdī states that *al-arḍ* in this verse refers to "either country or territory" that is ruled by an Islamic state.[75] It can be said that al-Sha'rāwī, Mawdūdī and other exegetes such as al-Ṭabarī, al-Jaṣṣāṣ, and Riḍā apparently limit the scene of corruption to *al-arḍ* because it is this word that is used in 5: 32–33. Yet while the literal Qur'anic reference to *al-arḍ* points to it as the main setting where corruption can be committed, this does not rule out the occurrence of corruption in the sea, the air or elsewhere.

Moreover, according to the exegetes, the aspects of corruption in 5: 33 take many forms. Al-Ṭabarī states that corruption refers to several different sinful acts, such as terrifying Muslim passers-by, obstructing their path, seizing their possessions, and infringing their rights. Al-Ṭabarī apparently favours these explanations of *fasād*, although he cites other exegetical views held by Mujāhid (d. 104/722), who states that *fasād* refers to killing, adultery and theft.[76] He does not attempt to refute Mujāhid's views, but rather cites them among others and then concludes by giving his own opinion. Riḍā, on the other hand, goes to great lengths to refute Mujāhid's explanation of *fasād*, asserting that Muslim jurists, whom he did not name, are of the opinion that these sinful acts are crimes for which there are specified punishments, whereas the punishments mentioned in 5: 33 are for people who combine *muḥārabah* and *fasād* as two textually linked actions.[77] Riḍā adds that these actions are not only textually linked, but are also related to each other.[78] Riḍā's view here is precise and evidence-based, and it may therefore be given priority over other explanations.

However, in a view which is apparently similar to al-Ṭabarī's, Frank E. Vogel argues that 5: 33 refers to two different crimes: the first is *ḥirābah*, understood from the phrase "wage war", while the second is the crime of "corruption in the land", understood from the clause "strive to spread corruption in the land".[79] Vogel ascribes this interpretation of this "vague text" to classical scholars, but his claim cannot be accepted.[80] He does not say who are those scholars or how they formulated this view and he does not refer to any of their works. A survey of all the available exegetical interpretations of this part of the verse finds not one exegete who has singled out *ḥirābah* as one crime and corruption in the land as another. On the contrary, most (if not all) exegetes refer to the two clauses as inextricably united elements in the crime of *ḥirābah*, and not as two separate crimes.[81]

According to al-Shaʿrāwī, the targeted audience of *fasād* in 5: 32–33 is inextricably linked to the perpetrator. He argues that *fasād* is of two types. In the first type, the perpetrator attempts to take personal revenge for a previous aggression against him initiated by the other party. For al-Shaʿrāwī, this personal revenge is prohibited because of violating the principle in Islamic law that people should not take the law into their own hands, and not because it is reciprocating aggression. They would be applying their own laws in disregard of the authoritative bodies appointed to settle personal grudges primarily through legal channels.[82] This type of *fasād* bears no similarity to *ḥirābah*, but is more akin to repelling aggression, although in a prohibited way. The second type, according to al-Shaʿrāwī, is the terrorization of people with whom there is no cause for dispute. This is the most apt example of *ḥirābah*, as it relates perfectly to the essence of the two verses under discussion.[83] Indeed, this description of *ḥirābah* generally corresponds to terrorism as with the latter there is also no dispute between the terrorist and his innocent victims. The targets are taken hostage not because of their own status but to subdue those in authority, such as rulers or governments, so that they succumb to terrorist demands. I will now explore further the similarities and differences between *ḥirābah* and terrorism.

Ḥirābah and Terrorism: Similarities and Differences

Having defined *ḥirābah* and discussed its elements, I want to examine the arguments of those who consider that there is close or complete similarity between *ḥirābah* and terrorism. An in-depth look at the definition of terrorism in Chapter 1 and the definition of *ḥirābah* above shows that there are many common characteristics between the two.

The first characteristic is that terrorism and *ḥirābah* lead to very similar results: the spreading of corruption in the land through threatening national and international security by killing innocents unjustly, sometimes robbing them of their possessions, and spreading fear among them, which result in destabilizing the whole society.[84] The second characteristic is the elements of intimidation and spreading fear, which are central to the definitions of terrorism and *ḥirābah*.[85] These two elements are clear in most of the juristic definitions of *ḥirābah* reviewed here, especially in the Mālikī definitions. They also represent the main features in the definition of terrorism arrived at earlier in this book. The third characteristic is that some researchers such as Abū Zahrah, Sayyid Sābiq and Muḥammad Kheir Haykal have literally equated terrorism with *ḥirābah*, and even state that they are synonymous within the context of Islamic law.[86] Abou El Fadl maintains that researchers who follow this view argue that the word terrorism is an honest translation of the term *ḥirābah*, although he believes that this is anachronistic because terrorism, according to him, is a modern action that is related to the notions of political crime and national liberation. He stresses that while terrorism and *ḥirābah* have many similarities, they are not literally or conceptually the same. However, a stark contradiction of this view is to be found in another work by Abou El Fadl, where he says that "*ḥirābah* and terrorism are fundamentally the same thing" and this is "nothing short of remarkable".[87] This clear contradiction makes it difficult to determine Abou El Fadl's position on this issue. Directly questioned on this difference, Abou El Fadl answered that the punishment for terrorism is dealt with in Islamic jurisprudence within a legally complex discourse, and referred to his *Rebellion and Violence in Islamic Law*, which indicates that he is apparently of the view that there is a strong similarity rather than complete equivalence between *ḥirābah* and terrorism.[88]

Salwā al-ʿAwwā is another researcher who agrees that the closest equivalent to the Western notion of "terrorism" in Islamic jurisprudence is *ḥirābah*, arguing that *ḥirābah* includes, among other things, declaring war against a society as a whole.[89] This view, which is also held by some others, summarizes the optimal norm of the relation between terrorism and *ḥirābah* - that it is an exaggeration then to claim that the terms are synonymous, but safe to maintain that they have far more similarities than dissimilarities.[90] However, this view has its staunch opponents who see terrorism as completely divorced from *ḥirābah*.

Opponents of the majority view see very little similarity or none at all between terrorism and *ḥirābah*.[91] Ḥārib considers that terrorism bears little resemblance to *ḥirābah* as it is usually associated with political or ideological aims without the destruction of property being a central objective, as it is in the case of *ḥirābah*. Although terrorism may involve destruction, its foremost intention is to achieve political aims.[92] Ḥārib thus admits that there may be some overlap between the two but considers that *ḥirābah* is the more general term. Yet, as shown above, there is no consensus among the four Sunni legal schools that "robbery" is the main objective of *ḥirābah*, as Ḥārib maintains. Al-'Umayrī considers that disseminating fear is the main intention in *ḥirābah*, arguing that the four Sunni legal schools support his view. He also believes that the main objective of many terrorism-related crimes (such as hijacking aeroplanes and assassination) is to threaten the security of society, which means they are all acts of *ḥirābah*.[93] His view is shared by Sherman A. Jackson, who argues that spreading terror and fear are foundational aspects of both *ḥirābah* and terrorism.[94]

Ḥārib's view is only as one opinion among many others. He overemphasizes political objectives as if they were the only factor to be considered when assessing the relationship between *ḥirābah* and terrorism. Al-Rubaysh states that adopting a more general attitude concerning the objectives of terrorism, taking the political aim as one among others, which brings some acts of terrorism within the definition of *ḥirābah*.[95] Moreover, Ḥārib also considers that the lack of similarity between *ḥirābah* and terrorism is because of the difference in the type of force used: *ḥirābah* is limited to traditional weapons whereas terrorism may extend to environmental, biological and economic attacks, which may take various sophisticated forms.[96] However, the Mālikī definition of *ḥirābah* points to the conclusion that terrorism is close to *ḥirābah* by virtue of the fact that both include a very strong element of intimidation. Thus, I would conclude that the similarities between terrorism and *ḥirābah* exceed their dissimilarities, despite the case made by some that there is no similarity at all.

The first of these is Ṣalāḥ al-Ṣāwī who says there is no similarity between *ḥirābah* and terrorism as far as punishment is concerned. This opinion came in al-Ṣāwī's refutation of a fatwa originally written by Mohamed S. El-Awa and ratified by al-Qaraḍāwī and others on 27 September 2001.[97] Al-Qaraḍāwī's fatwa is a response to a question submitted to him about whether or not it is permissible for American Muslim soldiers to participate in their country's military operations against Afghanistan and other Muslim countries.[98] It is beyond the scope of this chapter to discuss the content of this fatwa or the circumstances surrounding it, but what is relevant to our discussion is the punishment El-Awa and al-Qaraḍāwī set for those who perpetrated the attacks of 11 September 2001.[99] They argue that, according to the texts of the Sharīʿah and the rulings of Islamic jurisprudence, the punishment for the perpetrators of those attacks is the same as that set by 5: 33–34 for the crime of *ḥirābah*.

Al-Ṣāwī cites various justifications for rejecting any link between *ḥirābah* and terrorism, arguing that the punishment for the perpetrators of the 11 September attacks cannot be the same as the punishment for *ḥirābah*.[100] He argues that *ḥirābah* is equivalent to armed robbery with the intention of injuring and terrifying the victim (i.e. *al-sariqah al-kubrā*). He further claims that there is no link between *ḥirābah* and terrorism and cites one of the contexts of revelation as an example of the difference between the two.[101] Al-Ṣāwī adds that, on basis of the supposition that al-Qaeda and its leader Osama Bin Laden were the perpetrators of the 11 September attacks, as the American media claim, the devastating terrorist act has nothing to do with *ḥirābah*, as al-Qaraḍāwī's fatwa attempts to show. Al-Ṣāwī gives some reasons for his assertion. Firstly, al-Qaeda and its leader Osama Bin Laden, according to him, are not regarded by Muslims as plunderers or in any way linked to immorality. Secondly, he says that those who carried out the attacks were among the casualties and this goes against any possibility that their actions were motivated by "worldly gain".[102]

Al-Ṣāwī's refutation of al-Qaraḍāwī's fatwa has its weak points that cast doubt on whether it is well-structured or evidence-based. Firstly, he considers *ḥirābah* as essentially equivalent to *al-sariqah al-kubrā* by apparently adopting the clearly limited Ḥanafī concept of *ḥirābah* while turning a blind eye to the other three main juristic Sunni views. In particular, he disregards the Mālikī view, which broadens the concept of *ḥirābah* as discussed previously. Secondly, al-Ṣāwī states that "going back to the books of jurisprudence and exegesis will help make clear this issue",[103] but fails to provide a single exegetical reference that is considered within the Sunni tradition to be a main reference concerning punishment.[104] Thirdly, he singles out one narration about the contexts of revelation of 5: 33–34 without referring to the other six contradictory narrations (that I set out above) in order to clarify the difference between *ḥirābah* and terrorism, and does not explain that there are different narrations. He then leaves the text of al-Qaraḍāwī's fatwa - which he has tried in vain to refute - and focuses on information that is related to the topic of the fatwa in general but irrelevant to the punishment for *ḥirābah* and terrorism or the relationship between them. Fourthly, al-Ṣāwī tries to portray *ḥirābah* as a crime inextricably linked to plunder while considering the perpetrators of the 11 September attacks as being far above worldly gain, thus attempting to destroy the link between *ḥirābah* and terrorism. In fact, this weakens his refutation, as *ḥirābah* goes beyond plundering to encompass other forms of corruption and terrorizing innocents. It is also impossible to ascertain the true intentions of the 11 September attackers, who, as al-Ṣāwī remarks, "died, and their secrets have died with them".[105] Fifthly, although al-Ṣāwī rejects applying the punishment for *ḥirābah* to terrorists, he presents no alternative punishment. Basheer M. Nafi argues that al-Ṣāwī considers the 11 September attacks as rebellion (*baghy*) rather than *ḥirābah*, but in doing so ignores the fact that *baghy* in its original meaning is a crime of rebellion against a Muslim ruler that also has its set punishment.[106] Neither the Arabic nor English versions of al-Ṣāwī's refutation to al-Qaraḍāwī'a fatwa make reference to the punishment for *baghy* as applicable to the perpetrators of the 11 September attacks.[107]

The second staunch opponent to the majority view is Haytham Muḥammad, who adopts a stance very similar to al-Ṣāwī's. He argues that the absence of an Islamic concept of terrorism is a reason why it is confused with *ḥirābah*. He backs the view that *ḥirābah* refers essentially to an assault and that, although terrorism may be similar, terrorists exclusively target an enemy whose blood and property are violable in the first place, and *ḥirābah* is different from terrorism because its perpetrators are primarily seeking illicit financial gain, while terrorists are politically motivated. He argues that while terrorizing others is common to both *ḥirābah* and terrorism, it is a subsidiary element in *ḥirābah*, which usually targets a small group of people. This is unlike terrorism in which terror is the main element and is intended to affect all members of society.[108]

Haytham ignores the efforts of the various Islamic institutions to define terrorism, and his depiction of the confusion between *ḥirābah* and terrorism belittles them. [109] As he does not refer to these definitional efforts, it is no wonder that he can then go on to argue that their supposed absence is a cause of the problem. Like al-Ṣāwī, Haytham is keen to narrow *ḥirābah* down to pillage and plunder while giving little attention to its broader scope as the Mālikīs do. Moreover, to say that terrorism targets an enemy whose blood and property are violable is a risky judgment that throws doubt upon whether this view is religiously acceptable. It is also imprecise to claim that terrorism targets society at large while *ḥirābah* targets a very small group. The reality shows otherwise and the catastrophic 11 September attacks are just a single example. The targets of terrorism need not be the whole society, as claimed by Haytham, in order for such an act to be distinguished from one of *ḥirābah*.

The discussion shows that the view that there is a relationship between *ḥirābah* and terrorism constitutes the mainstream attitude. Its arguments are evidence-based, have withstood the arguments and refutations against it, and provide a strong basis for saying that terrorism has some equivalence to *ḥirābah*, at least in its effects, nature and aims.[110] Compared to the main trend, the proponents of the opposing view are fewer in number and clearly lacking in influence. Their views do not carry weight because they contain so many weaknesses and contradictions. This brings us to an important point, which is that, although it cannot be claimed that *ḥirābah* and terrorism are synonymous, the majority view at least is that the punishment for terrorism should be the same as that for *ḥirābah*. This view has strong justifications in contrast to the opponents' view.[111]

As has been argued, it is appropriate to apply the Mālikī definition of *ḥirābah* to terrorism. Wajis gives several justifications in support of this view. Firstly, he says that 5: 33 does not refer specifically to property as the main objective in *ḥirābah*.[112] It is therefore safest to interpret the meaning of the verse in a general sense, which includes all the elements of *ḥirābah*. Secondly, 5: 33 indicates that an act of *ḥirābah* takes place when corruption is spread in the land, and certainly terrorizing and killing innocents, and causing destruction to fauna and flora fulfils this criterion.[113] Thirdly, armed robbery is much less harmful in its destructive effects than terrorism, whose main aim is to cause death and destruction of the fabric of society.

Moreover, Wajis argues that one who sets out with the intention to rob, with or without being involved in homicide, is treated as a *muḥārib*. Consequently, terrorists who set out with the sole intention of causing death and destruction should also be treated as *muḥāribūn*. Thus, terrorist acts are considered *ḥirābah* and terrorists are considered *muḥāribūn*.[114] It cannot be claimed that robbery is a main objective of *ḥirābah*; Muslim scholars, according to Vogel, "frequently omit the requirement of the motive of taking property", considering that "spreading terror" deserves the same punishment as that set for *ḥirābah*.[115] Wajis's arguments and the view cited by Vogel provide enough support for the proposition that terrorists should receive the same punishment as that set by the Qur'an for *muḥāribūn*,[116] especially when they are supported by other proponents of the mainstream approach referred to above.

As an exegete, Darwazah provides a unique contribution to the argument for applying the punishment for *ḥirābah* to terrorism. He argues that "those who forcibly transgress against peoples' properties and honour by instilling fear are committing acts of terrorism, and hence they should receive the punishment set by the Qur'an for *ḥirābah*." Darwazah maintains that terrorist acts can justifiably be named *ḥirābah* acts. He rules out but does not categorically deny that Muslims could commit such terrorist acts.[117] Al-Maṭrūdī adds that the similarity between *ḥirābah* and terrorism necessitates similarity in the way terrorists should be punished once the prerequisites necessary for applying the punishment are met.[118] Having reached this important conclusion, it is then necessary to discuss the forms of punishment for terrorism in 5: 33 discussed in the exegetical literature.

The Punishment for Terrorism in the Qur'an

As a preliminary to discussing the forms of punishment set for terrorists, it is essential to look at how the punishment in general is presented in the Qur'an. As stated earlier, the Qur'an prescribes two punishments for *muḥāribūn*: one in this world and one in the Hereafter. A worldly punishment applies to terrorists (or other criminals) because they have violated human rights; their punishment in the Hereafter applies because they have violated the Divine ordinances of Allah.[119] Each punishment has its own setting. The worldly punishment is executed by those who apply the criminal law of a given country. Contrary to what devout Muslims would wish for, Sharīʿah law is not applied in most Muslim-majority countries. Punishment in the Hereafter is decreed by Allah. Kamali opposes reading a distinction into the Qur'an between violating the rights of man and violating the ordinances of Allah, because he regards it as being primarily the result of intellectual reasoning in understanding laws (*ijtihād*). There is no need for such "hard and fast" divisions between the rights of Allah and the rights of man.[120] Sherwani, who clearly favours Kamali's view, states that sins and crimes affect the rights of individuals and those of society.[121] Moreover, classical and modern exegetes consider *ḥirābah* a punishable crime without distinguishing between the rights of man and the rights of Allah. More importantly, they take the view that two punishments await the *muḥāribūn*: one in this world and another in the Hereafter.

Indeed, the two phrases used in the Qur'an to describe the punishments of the *muḥāribūn*: "disgrace in this world" (*khizy fī al-dunyā*) and "punishment in the Hereafter" (*fī al-ākhirati ʿadhāb*) are interpreted by the exegetes as referring to these two punishments. Both al-Ṭabarī and Ibn Kathīr interpret *khizy* to mean "punishment"; this is in addition to other ignominies, such as disgrace, humiliation, and being made an example of.[122] The punishment that awaits the *muḥāribūn* in the Hereafter is Hellfire.[123] Quṭb and al-Shaʿrāwī refer to this double punishment for *ḥirābah*, however, each of them focuses on a specific aspect of each punishment.[124] Al-Shaʿrāwī emphasizes the worldly punishment for *muḥāribūn*, stressing that they should receive their just deserts as they obstruct and attack helpless passers-by, who should enjoy security.[125] He extracts two linguistically different, yet complementary meanings for the word *khizy* stating that it denotes disgrace and humiliation for the criminal.[126] For him, the disgraceful exposure of the criminal is in itself a humiliation.[127] However, Quṭb and Darwazah assert that *khizy* indicates that worldly punishment does not waive the punishment in the Hereafter, so the two punishments must be considered in detail.[128]

The Worldly Punishment for Terrorists

In 5: 33, four severe worldly punishments for the *muḥāribūn* are outlined. Quṭb states that these severe punishments are essential for the security of both the Muslim community and individuals.[129] However, Quṭb's emphasis on securing the "Muslims", whether as communities or as individuals, may be used loosely here. Although he does not refer to non-Muslims in his interpretation, it can be easily understood from his explanation of 60: 8, for example, that Islam is keen to promote peace among all people.[130]

Moreover, al-Qurṭubī favours the prescription of severe worldly punishment for the *muḥāribūn* if it prevents "people", irrespective of whether they are Muslims or not, from earning their living.[131] His reasoning, although limited the protection of livelihoods, is general as it makes no creedal distinctions with regard to victims of this crime. The worldly punishment for the *muḥāribūn* is the most severe in Islam, as al-Sayyid Sābiq (d. 2000) confirms.[132] This may explain the unanimity of exegetes and jurists, both past and present, on the punishment itself, which may be – according to 5: 33 – (1) execution, (2) crucifixion, (3) the amputation of a hand and a foot on opposite sides, or (4) banishment from the land. Exegetes and jurists alike take two main approaches to these four alternative punishments.[133] The first approach seeks to establish proportionality between the crime and the punishment (*tartīb*) whereas the second approach authorizes the Muslim ruler to use his discretion in applying the punishment (*takhyīr*).[134]

The emergence of these two approaches can be traced back to the different linguistic meanings of the conjunction *aw*, which generally means "or" in English and occurs three times in 5: 33. The *tartīb* and *takhyīr* meanings of *aw* are the two alternative meanings that underpin the two different approaches. These two meanings of *aw* decisively influence the views of exegetes and jurists with respect to punishing the *muḥāribūn*, splitting them into a majority who adopt the *tartīb* approach and a minority who take the *takhyīr* approach. It is worth noting here that *aw* occurs 280 times in the Qur'an conveying numerous meanings, which include in addition to *tartīb* and *takhyīr*, other specific meanings such as vagueness and division.[135]

The majority of exegetes adopt the *tartīb* approach as a determining factor in establishing the punishment for *muḥāribūn*, and almost all of them follow their school's views when they attempt to interpret the meanings of the conjunction *aw*. However, an analysis of the classical interpretations reveals that there are exegetes who limited their discussion to noting the two approaches without stating a preference for one or the other. As a result, one is left unable to determine where exactly an exegete stands and it can then fairly be assumed that the exegete in question may be grouped with the first or the second approach, depending on his interpretation.

Al-Ṭabarī is a leading exegete who adopts the *tartīb* approach, stating that the punishments for the *muḥāribūn* are dependent upon the offences committed by them. He cites a narration discussed earlier in this chapter in which the Prophet was guided by the Angel Gabriel to follow the *tartīb* approach in the punishment of the people of ʿUraynah in the context of 5: 33. He argues further that as the conjunction *aw* has various meanings, it is illogical to restrict its meaning to *takhyīr* in this particular verse. However, he limits its meaning to *tartīb* without strong justification, apart from giving a linguistic example. The only narration cited by al-Ṭabarī to support his view cannot be found in the authentic collections of Hadith: he does not mention the source of this narration and admits it is questionable.[136] Although the use of *aw* in the verse may imply *takhyīr*, for al-Alūsī the context shows that the *tartīb* approach is the most correct. This is because the crime of *ḥirābah* carries different punishments that should be attached proportionately to its different categories.[137] Al-Ṭabarī and al-Alūsī both adduce different arguments to support their claims. Al-Ṭabarī applies what may be regarded as a textual evidence whereas al-Alūsī depends on reason. Interestingly, both arguments are open to refutation if they are thoroughly investigated by the proponents of *takhyīr*.

In attempting to explain why the majority prefer the *tartīb* approach, ʿAbd al-Fattāḥ Qā'id notes that the *takhyīr* approach authorizes the Muslim ruler to exercise discretion with regard to the punishment. However, this leaves room for error, with the possible execution of a person who did not commit homicide. Qā'id argues further for its prohibition on the basis of a Prophetic hadith, which states that "No Muslim person who bears witness that there is no deity other than God and that Muhammad is God's Messenger may be killed except for one of three reasons: a life for life, a married adulterer and a rebel who renounces his faith and abandons his community."[138] According to this Prophetic hadith, it is not permitted for the Muslim ruler to execute the *muḥāribūn* if they have not committed homicide. However, Abū Zahrah and al-Maghrabī take the view that this hadith cannot be used as evidence in support of the *tartīb* approach because it is applicable to personal rather than community cases. They consider that *ḥirābah* is equivalent to declaring internal war within a country and so requires exceptional punishment that transcends the literal application of this hadith.[139] In addition, although al-Ṭabarī, al-Alūsī and Qā'id are clearly staunch proponents of the *tartīb* approach, they do not rule out the *takhyīr* approach either, which is an indication that *takhyīr* may have tacit support among its opponents.[140]

Furthermore, some exegetes are strong supporters of the *takhyīr* approach. Al-Qurṭubī and Ibn al-ʿArabī provide very clear examples of this, with both sticking to the Mālikī view. Whilst referring to the *tartīb* approach, al-Qurṭubī declares that he follows Imam Mālik's view because the latter applies equity (*istiḥsān*) as legal support for the adoption of the *takhyīr* approach.[141] However, Sābiq argues that the ruler resorts to *takhyīr* out of consideration for the public interest (*maṣlaḥah*).[142] The claim that adopting *takhyīr* is a misapplication of the public interest principle as it will lead to injustice being committed by the ruler can be easily dismissed. This is because checking political absolutism cannot be achieved by deeming the public interest test to be inapplicable in this case. Instead, as Zidān argues, subjects correct rulers by addressing an injustice or by deposing them from the authority with which they are entrusted.[143] Whichever legal principle may be applied here, i.e. equity or public interest, al-Qurṭubī's view is unswervingly loyal to the Mālikī school, which has a diverse discourse on both principles within the context of Islamic law.[144] Ibn al-ʿArabī is the second main supporter of the *takhyīr* approach. He establishes his position by refuting al-Ṭabarī's argument that the conjunction *aw* originally means *takhyīr* in 5: 33. He also rejects the use of the hadith about the tribe of ʿUkl and ʿUraynah as evidence, indicating that it is cited in the context of punishing renegades (*murtaddūn*) and not *muḥāribūn*.[145] Quṭb is the third main supporter of *takhyīr*, although he admits that this goes against the opinion of the majority. He states that he follows the Mālikī view because it provides the Muslim community with the necessary peace and security it requires.[146]

Having discussed the two main approaches to punishment, it is worth mentioning that there are some modern exegetes, such as al-Shaʿrāwī and Riḍā, whose views are difficult to categorize because they seem to support neither *takhyīr* nor *tartīb* and are in a grey area between the two.[147] Although neither has a clear preference, Riḍā shows the basis for his argument. By weighing both views and summarizing the key elements in the debate, Riḍā puts forward a stronger argument than al-Shaʿrāwī. Interestingly, there are classical exegetes whose interpretations are submerged in this grey area even if they are normally considered as *takhyīr* or *tartīb* supporters.[148]

After analysing these different exegetical approaches to the punishment of the *muḥāribūn*, I propose that *takhyīr* is the most applicable approach for the punishment of terrorism. Aside from the exegetes, modern researchers suggest various other reasons for following the *takhyīr* approach; in most of their arguments, consideration of the public interest principle (*maṣlaḥah*) is a common element.[149] Haytham states that, although the *takhyīr* approach is seemingly harsh, it is the most suitable option that is capable of stopping terrorism. He argues that *maṣlaḥah* provides the ruler with the flexibility required to secure the best interests for Muslims, and in fact also serves the general aim of ensuring safety for the whole community regardless of creedal affiliation.[150] Abū Zahrah adopts the *takhyīr* opinion on the basis of its being an effective deterrent applied by the ruler within the options laid down by 5: 33, although it may be indirectly inferred that he applies *maṣlaḥah* in so arguing.[151]

On the basis of the foregoing discussion, *takhyīr* appears to me to be the safer approach. This is because modern terrorism has generated and will continue to generate different situations that require flexible handling by the ruler or his deputies, who are responsible for finding suitable punishments in an ever-challenging reality. Thus, the flexibility provided by the public interest principle is the approach that should be adopted because it helps the ruler to take effective pre-emptive measures to stop any attempt at jeopardizing the security of his subjects.[152]

Execution is the first type of punishment mentioned in 5: 33, however, little attention has been paid to it by classical or modern exegetes.[153] Al-Alūsī states that the *muḥāribūn* are only to be executed if they commit homicide. He also raises two important issues that are hardly discussed by other exegetes: (1) whether a pardon by the murder victim's relatives waives the execution, and (2) the method of execution to be used. In his view, the *muḥāribūn* are executed because they have committed a crime with fixed legal penalties (*ḥadd*), but it makes no difference whether they are executed with an offensive weapon or not. He maintains that forgiveness by the murder victim's relatives does not waive the execution because the crime of *ḥirābah* is a violation of the rights of the Lawgiver.[154]

Moreover, the four Sunni schools of Islamic law concur with al-Alūsī's position, especially concerning these two issues. Qā'id argues that the majority of jurists maintain that *muḥāribūn* are executed because they have committed a *ḥadd*-related crime. Thus, the forgiveness of the victim's relatives does not waive the execution.[155] As for the method of execution, the use of the sword was the commonest in early times, to the extent that Wajis argues that there is a consensus among jurists on this issue.[156] However, today's circumstances dictate that the lives of terrorists be taken by other methods that minimize their suffering. This is in harmony with the general rulings of the Qur'an and the Prophetic hadiths.[157]

Ṣalb or "crucifixion" is the second form of punishment referred to in 5: 33, and is used both in the Qur'an and in Islamic law.[158] The Arabic lexeme *ṣ-l-b* occurs eight times in five different forms in the Qur'an.[159] *Ṣalb*, according to al-Aṣfahānī, generally refers to hanging someone until death.[160] Riḍā adds that the criminal is tied to a wooden prop or a similar object with his arms stretched out until death.[161] The *muḥāribūn* are "crucified" when they combine homicide with usurping others' properties. The reason for this, according to Darwazah, is to deter others who may contemplate committing this crime. He claims that *ṣalb* may refer to death by hanging, arguing that this was practised in earlier times, but this lacks credence because it is divorced from the linguistic origin of the word *ṣalb* (from *ṣalīb* or cross) and has no circumstantial evidence to support it.[162] The fact that death by hanging was an ancient practice is not a pretext for saying that it replaces *ṣalb* with no conclusive evidence.

Al-Jaṣṣāṣ cites conflicting views as to whether *ṣalb* is to be carried out before or after execution, but argues that *ṣalb* is prohibited once the criminal is executed because it is forbidden to crucify the dead. This argument is in harmony with the general spirit of Islam, which is against mutilation. Thus, for *ṣalb* to be carried out, it should be prior to execution. With reluctance, al-Jaṣṣāṣ cites two views about the duration of *ṣalb*, saying that it can be either three days or one.[163] However, it is meaningless to dishonour the sanctity of the corpse by leaving it for one or three days as this is against the ordinances of the Sunnah, which dictates that burial should be performed quickly after death occurs.[164] Thus, although *ṣalb* is meant to shame the criminal, according to the Qur'an (17: 70), there should be no violation of the deceased person's dignity after death.

Finally, it is suggested that *ṣalb* is the punishment of last resort for the Muslim ruler. This is supported by the precedent of the Prophet, who did not impose this punishment upon the people of 'Ukl and 'Uraynah, according to the various sets of reports cited earlier. Moreover, the historical record shows that this punishment has rarely been applied by Muslim rulers. When asked about *ṣalb*, Imam Mālik answered that he had "never heard of anyone who applied *ṣalb* except 'Abd al-Malik bin Marwān who crucified a man named al-Ḥārith because he claimed to be a prophet."[165]

The third form of punishment is amputation. It refers to cutting off an alternate hand and foot, i.e. a hand and a foot on opposite sides of the body. Classical and modern exegetes have paid little attention to explaining this punishment. It may simply be that it is self-explanatory: the right hand and left foot are to be cut off if the *muḥārib* robs but does not kill, and, if he is convicted for the second time, then his left hand and right foot are to be cut off. Al-Alūsī considers that the hands are cut off as a punishment for robbery and the feet are amputated for terrorizing the public.[166] Whatever justification is given, the most important issue is to carry out the punishment in a swift manner, inflicting the least amount of pain.[167] This reflects the common concern of all exegetes not to cause humiliation to the bodies of criminals, but secure them an honourable death right until the last minute of their lives.

The last form of punishment specified in 5: 33 is banishment (*nafy*). Linguistically, banishment means exile.[168] Two interpretations dominate the exegetical discussion. The first interpretation argues that it refers to banishing the criminal from his homeland to another land. This is in order to end his criminal acts by placing him in a new environment where he will find it difficult to adapt thus preventing him from committing criminal acts.[169] Ibn al-'Arabī gives a second interpretation arguing that *nafy* here means imprisonment. For him, the criminal can easily spread corruption in exile, but it is difficult to do that in prison.[170] However, al-Shaʿrāwī vehemently opposes this view by arguing that modern prisons may provide too comfortable a haven for criminals, so they are no longer a suitable form of punishment for this particular crime.[171] Al-Ṭabarī combines both interpretations by claiming that *nafy* refers to banishing to another country and then having the criminal incarcerated there until he repents.[172]

In my view, the best choice is to enable the ruler to apply the punishment as he sees fit, taking into consideration the nature of each terrorist act, its repercussions, the best way to deter the perpetrators, and the benefits and harms to the whole of society. This is simply because many terrorists would nowadays consider asylum or living in luxurious exile compared with facing oppression in their home countries, due to the lack of basic human rights there. This scenario would apply if asylum or exile to foreign countries with good human rights records were available. This would entice terrorists to adopt a strategy of mobility to perpetrate more terrorist acts in a more fertile environment. On the other hand, imprisonment in one's own country might not fulfil the basic meaning of banishment. This is why it is clearly correct for the ruler to exercise his discretion.

The Repentance of the Muḥāribūn

After discussing the four punishments for the *muḥāribūn*, the Qur'an keeps open the way for the sincere declaration of repentance, which is stated unequivocally in 5: 34. It is worth noting that out of the eighty-seven occurrences of derivatives of the word repentance (*tawbah*) in the Qur'an, only one refers specifically to repentance by the *muḥāribūn*.[173] In this context, repentance has one of two meanings: (1) the *muḥāribūn* willingly surrender themselves to the ruler before being apprehended, or (2) they relinquish all their criminal acts in the presence or absence of the ruler.[174] A thorough analysis of the exegetical literature on 5: 34 shows that two issues dominate this discussion. The first refers to the prerequisites for repentance and the second deals with whether waiving the punishment for the *muḥāribūn* exempts them from civil liability (*ḥaqq al-'ibād*).

In order for repentance to be counted as sincere, certain conditions must be fulfilled. Al-Nawawī (d. 676/1277) refers to three conditions for the validity of repentance. Firstly, the criminal must completely desist from committing crime. Secondly, he must show remorse for what he has done. Thirdly, he must firmly commit himself not to repeat his sinful action. This is required if the act committed infringes the right of Allah. If it infringes the rights of human beings, al-Nawawī adds a fourth condition, which is to discharge all personal obligations owed to the offended party, whether financial or otherwise.[175] Riḍā addresses the necessity of sincere repentance in interpreting 5: 34. His explanation is in total harmony with the four conditions referred to by al-Nawawī. He further stresses the importance of the *muḥāribūn* making a sincere declaration of repentance while they still have their strength.[176] This is apparently the reason for waiving the punishment as it gives the criminals the chance to reintegrate themselves into their respective societies and become good citizens again.

However, the fourth condition for repentance leads to extensive controversy as to whether the *muḥāribūn* will be exempted from civil liability. Riḍā is in favour of the view that repentance exempts the criminal from all the punishments due to Allah whether in this world or in the Hereafter. However, the rights of wronged human beings are waived only with their approval.[177] Riḍā's view is perfectly harmonious with the main conditions for repentance. However, modern terrorist acts perpetrated against societies that cause collective damage are to be assessed by the ruler, who should champion the rights of the victims or their heirs by executing the perpetrator or requiring compensation for damage. Although the claimant or his heirs can either claim their rights from the offender or forgive him, it is not proper for them to take the matter into their own hands because this role should be played by the imam or judge.[178]

Conclusion

By explaining the Qur'anic concept of crime and punishment in this chapter, I have argued that terrorism is a heinous crime against humanity, through an examination of its definition and punishment under Islamic law. Like terrorism, *ḥirābah* is a term that triggers much controversy among classical and modern exegetes and jurists, as seen in the discussion surrounding 5: 33–34. Despite the diverse and contradictory nature of the occasions of revelations regarding these verses, it is significant that the exegetes are unanimous that 5: 33–34 constitutes textual evidence for the punishment of the *muḥāribūn*.

Although not explicitly referred to by classical or modern exegetes (with the exception of Darwazah), the punishment for terrorism is an issue on which modern Muslim scholars have made remarkable contributions. They have done this by applying analogical deduction (*qiyās*), exploring the common elements between *ḥirābah* as a crime that is textually-supported, and terrorism, which poses a real danger in today's world but has no clearly-defined Qur'anic punishment.

The Qur'an does not condone terrorism in any way; in fact, it prescribes the most severe of punishments for acts of terror. The four alternative punishments, ranging from execution to exile, are set as deterrents for this heinous crime. Although it is outside the scope of this discussion, while these punishments may seem barbaric at first glance, when the interests of the whole of society are taken into consideration, a case for their deterrent value in preventing suffering and carnage may be made. The four worldly punishments for terrorism put forward by the Qur'an provide workable mechanisms for those in authority if they want to develop a moral and practical basis to deter terrorism in terms of formal legal measures.[179] Finally, this discussion has served as a response to those who claim that the punishments referred to in 5: 33 target "those who fight against Allah and Muhammad"[180] with no regard to the contextual or even linguistic interpretations given by classical and modern exegetes.

CONCLUSION: TERRORISM AND THE PATH OF PERSUASION

THROUGHOUT THIS STUDY, I have attempted a systematic analysis of terrorism in the light of the Qur'an exegetical tradition. My focus was to highlight the views of selected classical and modern exegetes, as well as some modern scholars, in order to understand some of the main constituents of terrorism in modern times. The selected exegetes draw attention to the importance of *tafsīr* in general, and particularly *al-tafsīr al-mawḍūʿī*, the exegetical genre that has most informed my own approach in analysing terrorism.

One of the main aspects of terrorism is its definition. The attempts by some leading Muslim and non-Muslim organizations to define terrorism have shown definitional challenges, prominent among which are "relativism" and "dynamism". These problems emerge from specific convictions, agendas and understandings about terrorism internationally. While in Chapter 1 I have proposed a "semi-collective" definition of terrorism taking a Qur'anic perspective into consideration, further investigation by terrorism researchers remains necessary in this field.

Both the Arabic term *irhāb* and the English term "terrorism" are alien to classical Arabic and English literatures. Lexically, both terms have been adopted and loaded with violent connotations in the last few decades. Long before, the Western usage of the term dating back to the time of the French Revolution, shows how "terrorism" was used to indicate positive meanings. Similarly, *irhāb* has only been used in Arabic to denote a modern sense of terrorism since the 1980s.

As far as the Qur'an is concerned, this study has shown that neither its verses nor the selected commentaries on them refer directly to terrorism in its modern sense. It is very clear from the selected exegeses, however, that the Qur'an and its interpreters have contributed to and anticipated some aspects of the international debate in combating various forms of terrorism, unjustified killing, destruction of property, and other forms of aggression against animals and the natural environment. This is in addition to the prohibition of other physical or non-physical measures capable of harming others through aggression in terms of their properties, intellect, honour and religion.

The lexical root *r-h-b* and its lexemes in the Qur'an such as, *istarhaba*, *al-rahab*, *irhabūnī* refer to fearing Allah out of fear of His punishment and hope in His reward. The only word around which much controversy arises as a result of being ab(used) by some extremist Muslims and non-Muslims to call for or justify terrorism is *turhibūna* in 8: 60. Extremist interpretations of this particular verse have gone as far as to name it "the verse of terrorism". Therefore, this study has paid special attention to this verse and given an analysis of its main themes to provide better understanding of it. The erroneous naming of it as "the verse of terrorism" has also been rebutted. Instead, the verse is a universal call for Muslims to possess various intellectual, educational, economic and military worldly powers. It was originally revealed in reference to the imminent outbreak of war between Muslims and non-Muslims and ordered Muslims to prepare for unavoidable battle; its modern application, according to most classical and modern exegetes, is to help Muslims attain dominance in various fields for the purpose of strategic defence. However, Sayyid Quṭb misinterprets *quwwah* in this verse as the force that is intended to subdue non-Muslims to Islam. It is on the basis of his extreme interpretations of *quwwah* that some Muslim terrorist groups and some ill-informed circles in the West have taken the verse as a pretext to justify acts of terrorism perpetrated by some Muslims, in an attempt to establish this as a "fact" based on the text of the Qur'an. Yet, as I have shown, Quṭb's extreme interpretation stands in sharp contrast to that of the classical exegetes, especially al-Ṭabarī and al-Rāzī, as well as other modern ones who, while they have broadened the domain of military force, have limited its use to self-defence.

Moreover, it should always be borne in mind that exegetes are human beings whose surrounding circumstances have an impact on their interpretations. In other words, their exegeses do not exist in a vacuum. This is quite noticeable in the wide range of disagreements among classical and modern exegetes concerning the issue of jihad. A clear example of this, as clarified in Chapter 3, is whether peace or war is the underlying principle of relations between Muslims and non-Muslims. Classical exegetes including al-Ṭabarī, al-Qurṭubī, Ibn al-ʿArabī, al-Suyūṭī, al-Jaṣṣāṣ, al-Rāzī and al-Alūsī maintain that war is the underlying principle that governs external relations between Muslims and non-Muslims. Consequently, they adopted the dichotomous division of the world into *dār al-Islam* and *dār al-ḥarb*. They used the theory of abrogation in the so-called the "verse of the sword" as evidence through which all other verses in the Qur'an calling for peace with non-Muslims are abrogated. On the one hand, this view of classical exegetes has been critiqued by explaining that there is no uniform view concerning the theory of abrogation, according to which the proponents of all opposing views have to agree about. On the other hand, differences between classical exegetes concerning the "verse of the sword" itself further weaken their argument.

With regard to the objectives of this work as well as the foregoing discussion, it can be further concluded that, insofar as the Qur'anic verses related to military jihad are concerned, the classical exegetes employed an exclusivist rather than inclusivist attitude towards non-Muslims. As I argued in Chapter 3, the binary division of the world they arrived at has proved to be without foundation in the Qur'an itself, and they therefore failed to communicate the meanings of the Qur'an regarding this particular point to a wider audience. In addition, their interpretation remained hostile in its attitude and they were affected by their historical circumstances and geographical horizons, which had a great impact on their exegeses, as can be seen from the biographies I provided in the introduction to this study.

It is no wonder then to see the leaders of modern terrorist groups, such as the late Bin Laden, selecting from these classical exegeses what suits their own terrorist agendas. As mentioned, some classical exegetes, especially al-Qurṭubī, are mentioned by name in Bin Laden's speeches and letters. On the basis of this classical hard-line attitude in the understanding of jihad in the Qur'an, it is sometimes understood as being equivalent to terrorism in modern times, a claim that this study has set out to refute.

As for the modern exegetes, I have shown that most of them, with the exception of Quṭb, maintain that peace is the underlying principle governing external relations between Muslims and non-Muslims. Riḍā opposed the interpretations of the classical exegetes, and especially their interpretation of the "verse of the sword". Al-Shaʿrāwī shared Riḍā's view and stated that the historical circumstances in which most of the classical exegetes lived excuses their intolerant interpretation. Darwazah's view stands in total opposition to the classical interpretative theory because it contradicts *al-aḥkām al-muḥkamah*, which enjoins Muslims to refrain from fighting non-hostile entities.

Sayyid Quṭb is the only modern exegete whose view contrasts sharply with those of modern exegetes and scholars; he is also quite distinctive from the views of the classical exegetes too. Although he was influenced by authors of the classical period, such as Ibn Taymiyyah, Quṭb introduced his unique interpretation of transitional texts (*al-nuṣūṣ al-marḥaliyyah*) and final texts (*al-nuṣūṣ al-nihā'iyyah*) arguing that what is applicable nowadays are the latter, whose rulings are definitive. Quṭb severely criticized many of the exegetes of his time, Riḍā and Darwazah in particular, calling them "the defeatists" because they adopted peace as the governing principle upon which Muslim and non-Muslim relations are based. The historical circumstances in Egypt in the 1950s and 1960s, the harsh conditions Quṭb experienced when he was incarcerated, and the fact that he wrote most of his revolutionary ideas in his *Ẓilāl* are evidence of how an exegete is influenced by his surroundings and further confirms that exegetes do not exist in a vacuum.

Of all the modern commentaries referred to in this book, it is clear that Quṭb's is the most influential, as the number of academic studies by modern Muslim and Western authors about Quṭb's exegesis and his other revolutionary works shows. Quṭb's writings, especially the *Ẓilāl* and *Milestones*, have actually inspired a generation of extremists and terrorists since his death until the present time. In an attempt to highlight this influence, I examined critically the original violent ideas of the Islamic Group of Egypt. The advocacy of extremist interpretations can lead to disastrous consequences that have no geographical limitations in today's world. The violent Egyptian experience led by the Islamic Group inspired members in other countries. When some of the imprisoned members of the Islamic group began a process of ideological revision, it was welcomed by the local authorities and emulated by some members outside Egypt. Others who, by that time, had joined al-Qaeda were adamant about refusing to reconsider their extremist stance towards their fellow Muslims and fellow human beings.

As explained in Chapter 4, the Islamic Group's leaders unilaterally initiated violence and approved the killing of innocents, and initially acted in total defiance of trained Muslim scholars from reputable seminaries such as the Azhar, whom they described as agents and state-salaried employees. However, after inaugurating the process of ideological revision, they also sought conciliation with the Egyptian authorities, which still employs salaried religious scholars.

One of the laudable contributions that did not yield immediate fruit was al-Shaʿrāwī's initiative with the Islamic Group, discussed in Chapter 4, which was in the tradition of using persuasion, in the tradition of "wisdom and fair exhortation", to refute extremism. He did not record this personal initiative in his exegesis and his initiative also reveals that talking to terrorists was not a systematic approach adopted by governments in Muslim-majority societies in his day. While his personal initiative was generally unsuccessful at the time, it sowed seeds that bore fruit long afterwards, when the leaders of the Islamic Group re-examined their historical attitudes and initiated their process of moderating ideological revision.

State authorities should prioritize the use of persuasion in combating extremists for the religious justification they give for violence. As a start, this approach can at least be applied to those subjected to brainwashing by terrorist organizations. A sizeable number of terrorists or would-be terrorists could thus be persuaded to mend their ways. I would suggest that dedicated teams of Muslim scholars who enjoy independence from state influence, are well-versed in Islamic knowledge, and adopt moderation (*wasaṭiyyah*) could enjoy a degree of success in the path of persuasion. This approach could make an enormous contribution to international peace and security and be an effective means of combating terrorism that relies upon religious justification.

Another method of combating terrorism, discussed in Chapter 5, is the punishment for terrorists set out in the Qur'an. From a comparison of *ḥirābah* and terrorism, it would appear that they are alike because their similarities far exceed their dissimilarities. Given that the exegetes surveyed in this book are unanimous about the Qur'anic textual evidence (i.e. 5: 33–34) for the punishment for *ḥirābah*, I inferred that this same punishment should be applied to terrorism. To recapitulate the argument briefly, four alternate earthly punishments are prescribed by the Qur'an for terrorists. They are execution, crucifixion, amputation of the alternate hand and foot, and banishment. Another very severe but unspecified punishment awaits terrorists in the Hereafter. The Qur'an opens the door for terrorists who sincerely repent of what they have perpetrated. This approach, in which the sincere repentance of terrorists is encouraged, complements the suggestion I make for the path of persuasion, i.e. the importance of talking to terrorists or those strongly inclined to commit terrorist acts. The severity of the punishments for terrorists shows the extent to which the Qur'an respects the human soul regardless of its faith, race or geography.

Of all the modern exegetes, only Darwazah specifically refers to the punishment for terrorism as set out in the Qur'an. He points out too that it is the same as that prescribed for *ḥirābah*. The fact that other modern exegetes, such as Riḍā, Quṭb, and al-Sha'rāwī do not consider this important point, even indirectly, shows that some modern exegetes lack the ability to respond to world events. While none should be criticized for a lack of foresight, given that modern terrorism is a relatively new phenomenon in the Muslim world (as discussed in Chapter 1), the approach of modern exegetes in interpreting the *ḥirābah* verses takes a traditional line with few new interpretations.

It is also noticeable that the attitude of modern scholars concerning the punishment for terrorism in Islam is still at an immature stage. Even with the high number of international conferences about terrorism that take place in the Muslim world, which have been convened as reactionary procedures to major terrorist acts, it is hard to find a single one dedicated to specifying the punishment for terrorism in Islam, let alone in the Qur'an. This is a serious gap which this research has attempted to fill by discussing the permissibility or otherwise of the 11 September attacks in light of the Qur'an.

Besides the corrective measures set by the Qur'an for combating terrorism, there is also its approach of peace and tolerance with people of other faiths. The study of these and many other topics related to modern Qur'anic political ethics in light of the rich thematic interpretations of the Qur'an is needed more today than ever before.

This study argues that in Islamic ethico-legal terms the 11 September attacks were terrorist acts whose perpetrators should be tried and sentenced according to the scale of punishments for terrorism in the Qur'an. These atrocious crimes were sheer acts of terrorism perpetrated by al-Qaeda on the basis of highly selective interpretations of the Qur'an, which they use to serve their own agendas. They were committed in total defiance of the clear, moderate and inclusive message of the Qur'an as it is understood by almost all modern Muslim scholars. The extreme interpretations of those who justified the 11 September attacks have been highlighted, critiqued, and refuted by Muslim scholars, and it has been proven that the Qur'anic texts referred to by Bin Laden and other terrorists have been quoted out of their original contexts. The same is true of their erroneous attempts to quote from classical exegetical sources to cloak their bloody, irresponsible and prohibited terrorist acts in a false, unbloodied, morally justified, permitted and even laudable guise.

Nowadays, there are still al-Qaeda-like organizations operating in different countries that launch perverted attacks based on the same misguided, ill-informed misinterpretations of the Islamic core sources and their established commentary literatures. I would contend that there is still much to be done to provide an adequate ideological challenge to these organizations and groups through primary recourse to the Qur'an, as I have attempted to do in this book. Of course, combating terrorism cannot be done overnight. Rather, it needs dedicated work and clear mechanisms, not just militarily on the battlefield but ideologically in society as well. This path of persuasion also needs to be supported by the further study of terrorism and many other topics related to modern Qur'anic political ethics in light of the rich thematic interpretations of the Qur'an, and it is needed more today than ever before.

ENDNOTES

(Full references are given at their first citation.)

Introduction: Why Does The Qur'an Matter In Confronting Terrorism?

1. Nadia Mahmoud Mostafa, "The Missing Logic in Discourses of Violence and Peace in Islam: The Necessities of a Middle View after the 11th of September 2001", in Abdul Aziz Said, Mohammed Abu-Nimer and Meena Sharify-Funk, eds., *Contemporary Islam: Dynamic, Not Static* (London: Routledge, 2006), p. 174. See also John L. Esposito, "The Future of Islam and U.S.-Muslim Relations", *Political Science Quarterly*, vol. 126, no. 3, 2011, pp. 365–401, citation at p. 367.
2. T.P. Schwartz-Barcott, *War, Terror and Peace in the Qur'an and in Islam: Insights for Military and Government Leaders* (Carlisle, PA: Army War College Foundation Press, 2004), pp. 2–4.
3. Amritha Venkatraman, "Religious Basis for Islamic Terrorism: The Quran and Its Interpretations", *Studies in Conflict and Terrorism*, vol. 30, no. 3, 2007, pp. 229–248, citation at p. 231.
4. Hussein Abdul-Raof, *Schools of Qur'anic Exegesis: Genesis and Development* (London: Routledge, 2010), p. 14.
5. According to M.A.S. Abdel Haleem, "The Qur'an was the starting point for all the Islamic sciences: Arabic grammar was developed to serve the Qur'an, the study of Arabic phonetics was pursued in order to determine the exact pronunciation of Qur'anic words, the science of Arabic rhetoric was developed in order to describe the features of the inimitable style of the Qur'an, the art of Arabic calligraphy was cultivated through writing down the Qur'an, the Qur'an is the basis of Islamic law and theology." M.A.S. Abdel Haleem, *The Qur'an: A New Translation* (Oxford: Oxford University Press, 2005), p. 9.

6. See example, Abdel Haleem, *Qur'an*, p. 14; Richard Bonney, *Jihād: From the Qur'ān to bin Laden* (Basingstoke: Palgrave Macmillan, 2004), pp. 21 f.; Tamara Sonn, "Introducing", in Andrew Rippin, ed., *The Blackwell Companion to the Qur'ān* (Oxford: Wiley-Blackwell, 2009), p. 3; J.M.S. Baljon, *Modern Muslim Koran Interpretation (1880–1960)* (Leiden: Brill, 1968), p. 1.
7. David Cook, *Martyrdom in Islam* (Cambridge, New York: Cambridge University Press, 2007), p. 36. For the significant role of the Sunnah as the second main source of Islamic legislation after the Qur'an, see for example, Mawil Izzi Dien, *Islamic Law: From Historical Foundations to Contemporary Practice* (Edinburgh: Edinburgh University Press, 2004), pp. 38–40.
8. Literally, the Arabic word *tafsīr* refers to interpretation, exegesis and explanation. While it refers mostly to the interpretation of the Qur'anic text, it also refers to commentaries on Greek scientific and philosophical works, being equivalent in this last meaning to the Arabic word *sharḥ* (explanation). Technically, it refers to exerting the utmost human effort to communicate the meanings of the Qur'an. See for example, Muṣṭafā ibn 'Abdullāh al-Qusṭanṭīnī, *Kashf al-Ẓunūn 'an Asāmī al-Kutub wa al-Funūn* (Beirut: Dār al-Kutub al-'Ilmiyyah, 1413/1992), vol. 1, p. 427; Muḥammad Ḥusayn al-Dhahabī, *'Ilm al-Tafsīr* (Cairo: Dār al-Ma'ārif, n.d.), pp. 5 f. According to one expert view, "Reading the Qur'ān without commentary (*tafsīr*) is almost impossible. The text is too general to be understood without additional explanation or detail, and these are generally supplied in the *tafsīr*.", see Leah Kinberg, "Contemporary Ethical Issues", in Rippin, ed., *Blackwell Companion to the Qur'ān*, p. 465.
9. Abdul-Raof, *Schools of Qur'anic Exegesis*, p. 2; see also Kate Zebiri, *Maḥmūd Shaltūt and Islamic Modernism* (Oxford: Clarendon Press, 1993), p. 128.
10. Muḥammad Ḥusayn al-Dhahabī, *Al-Tafsīr wa al-Mufassirūn: Baḥth Tafṣīlī 'an Nash'at al-Tafsīr wa Taṭawwuruh wa Alwānuh wa Madhāhibuh ma'a 'Arḍ Shāmil li Ashhar al-Mufassirīn wa Taḥlīl Kāmil li Ahamm Kutub al-Tafsīr min 'Aṣr al-Nabiyy Ṣallā Allāhu 'alayhi wa Sallam ilā 'Aṣrinā al-Ḥāḍir* (Cairo: Dār al-Ḥadīth, 1426/2005), vol. 1, p. 43.
11. According to one expert, this is because they "understood the Qur'ān and witnessed its circumstances of revelation at first hand", Abdul-Raof, *Schools of Qur'anic Exegesis*, p. 3; see also Jane Dammen McAuliffe, *Qur'ānic Christians: An Analysis of Classical and Modern Exegesis* (Cambridge: Cambridge University Press, 1991), p. 13.
12. The view of considering some of the Companions of Muḥammad as exegetes follows the traditional Muslim perspective. The Orientalist

view, however, questions the reliability of exegesis in this period. According to Claude Gilliot, "additional research is needed, including work on manuscripts, to elucidate more fully the problems of the beginnings and early development of qur'ānic exegesis." See Claude Gilliot, "Exegesis of the Qur'ān: Classical and Medieval", in Jane Dammen McAuliffe, ed., *The Encyclopaedia of the Qur'ān* (Leiden: Brill, 2002), vol. 2, pp. 99–124, citation at pp. 102 f.

13. Jane Dammen McAuliffe, "Preface", in idem, ed., *Encyclopaedia of the Qur'ān*, vol. 1, p. 4; Abdul-Raof, *Schools of Qur'anic Exegesis*, p. 7.

14. Fred Leemhuis, "Origins and Early Development of the Tafsīr Tradition", in Andrew Rippin, ed., *Approaches to the History of the Interpretation of the Qur'ān* (Oxford: Oxford University Press, 1988), pp. 13–30, citation at p. 30; Abdul-Raof, *Schools of Qur'anic Exegesis*, p. 7; al-Dhahabī, *'Ilm al-Tafsīr*, p. 36.

15. Abdul-Raof, *Schools of Qur'anic Exegesis*, p. 11.

16. Andrew Rippin, "Tafsīr", *Encyclopaedia of Islam*, vol. 10, pp. 83–88 (Leiden: Brill, 1954–2007), citation at p. 87.

17. According to Andrew Rippin, "In tracing the historical developments of the genre, it is possible to separate out four periods of expression: formative, classical, mature, and contemporary. The separation is artificial, particularly fuzzy at the edges and certainly in need of refinement." Rippin, "Tafsīr", p. 85. See also Abdullah Saeed, *Interpreting the Qur'ān: Towards a Contemporary Approach* (London: Routledge, 2006), pp. 8–12; Abdul-Raof, *Schools of Qur'anic Exegesis*, p. 11. See also Shuruq Abdul Qader Naguib, "The Meaning of Purity in Classical Exegesis of the Qur'ān" (PhD Thesis, Department of Middle Eastern Studies, University of Manchester, 2003), p. 41; Rotraud Wielandt, "Exegesis of the Qur'ān: Early Modern and Contemporary", in McAuliffe, ed., *Encyclopaedia of the Qur'ān*, vol. 2, pp. 124–142.

18. Two other fundamental genres can also be identified on the basis of the source of exegesis: First, *al-tafsīr bi al-ma'thūr* (traditional exegesis), in which the exegete depends on the Prophetic Tradition, the sayings of the Prophet's Companions, and other early authorities. Second, *al-tafsīr bi al-ra'y* (rational/hypothetical exegesis), in which the exegete employs his personal opinion. See Jane Dammen McAuliffe, "The Tasks and Traditions of Interpretation", in idem, ed., *The Cambridge Companion to the Qur'ān* (Cambridge: Cambridge University Press, 2006), pp. 189 f.; 'Abd al-Mun'im al-Nimr, *'Ilm al-Tafsīr: Kayfa Nasha' wa Taṭawwara ḥattā Intahā ilā 'Aṣrinā al-Ḥāḍir* (Cairo: Dār al-Kitāb al-Miṣrī, 1405/1985), pp. 99–105; Mannā' al-Qaṭṭān, *Mabāḥith fī 'Ulūm al-Qur'ān* (Cairo: Maktabat Wahbah, eleventh edn., 2000), pp. 337–356.

19. Al-Dhahabī, *'Ilm al-Tafsīr*, p. 39–52; Abdul-Raof, *Schools of Qur'anic Exegesis*, pp. 92–98.

20. For the significance of thematic exegesis of the Qur'an, see Aḥmad As-Sayyid al-Kūmī and Muḥammad Aḥmad Yūsuf al-Qāsim, *Al-Tafsīr al-Mawḍūʿī li al-Qur'ān al-Karīm* (Cairo: N.p., 1402/1982), pp. 17–20. See also ʿAbd al-Sattār Fatḥallah Saʿīd, *Al-Madkhal Ilā al-Tafsīr al-Mawḍūʿī* (Cairo: Dār al-Ṭibāʿah wa al-Nashr al-Islāmiyyah, 1986), p. 21; ʿAbd al-Ḥayy al-Faramāwī, *Al-Bidāyah fī al-Tafsīr al-Mawḍūʿī: Dirāsah Manhajiyyah* (Cairo: N.p, second edn., 1397/1977), p. 52.

21. According to Ziyād al-Daghāmīn, while it is believed that interest in thematic exegesis started during the second/eighth century at the hands of Qatādah ibn Diʿāmah al-Sadūsī (d. 118/736), author of *Al-Nāsikh wa al-Mansūkh*, Abū ʿUbaydah al-Qāsim ibn Sallām (d. 224/838) and Abū Bakr al-Sijistānī (d. 330/942), these efforts cannot be considered a contribution in thematic exegesis. Rather, they are best described as studies in Qur'anic scholarship. See Ziyād Khalīl Muḥammad al-Daghāmīn, *Manhajiyyat al-Baḥth fī al-Tafsīr al-Mawḍūʿī li al-Qur'ān al-Karīm* (Amman: Dār al-Bashīr, 1416/1995), pp. 18 f.

22. Al-Kūmī and al-Qāsim, *Al-Tafsīr al-Mawḍūʿī li al-Qur'ān al-Karīm*, pp. 6–35; Mohamed El-Tahir El-Mesawi, "The Methodology of al-Tafsīr al-Mawḍūʿī: A Comparative Analysis", *Intellectual Discourse*, vol. 13, no. 1, 2005, p. 2. For more on the significance of this important conference, see http://www.sharjah.ac.ae/Arabic/Conferences/tehq/Pages/default.aspx; Internet; accessed 25 May 2010. To download the research papers, see http://www.4shared.com/dir/37950284/e8816d3b/_____.html; Internet; accessed 25 May 2010. For a useful survey of some modern studies on thematic exegesis, see Al-Daghāmīn, *Manhajiyyat al-Baḥth fī al-Tafsīr al-Mawḍūʿī*, pp. 21–27.

23. Al-Faramāwī, *Al-Bidāyah fī al-Tafsīr al-Mawḍūʿī*, p. 51; Riyāḍ al-Akhra, *Al-Mujrayāt al-Ijtimāʿiyyah wa al-Tawajjuh Naḥwā al-Tafsīr al-Mawḍūʿī* (Beirut: Dār al-Hādī li al-Ṭibāʿah wa al-Nashr wa al-Tawzīʿ, 1427/2006), p. 98.

24. See Muḥammad ʿAbdullāh Dirāz, *Al-Nabā' al-ʿAẓīm* (Kuwait: Dār al-Qalam, second edn., 1970); idem, *The Qur'ān: An Eternal Challenge, Al-Nabā' al-ʿAẓīm*, trans. and ed. Adil Salahi (Leicester: Islamic Foundation, 2001/1421); Muḥammad al-Ghazālī, *Naḥwā Tafsīr Mawḍūʿī li Suwar al-Qur'ān al-Karīm* (Cairo: Dār al-Shurūq, third edn., 1997); idem, *Thematic Commentary on the Qur'ān*, trans. Ashur A. Shamis, rev. Zaynab Alawiye (Herndon, VA: International Institute of Islamic Thought, 1421/2000).

25. Al-Faramāwī, *Al-Bidāyah fī al-Tafsīr al-Mawḍūʿī*, p. 52; Abdul-Raof, *Schools of Qur'anic Exegesis*, p. 97. See also Mohamed El-Arabawy

Hashem, "The Concept of Human Being in the Qur'ān with Special Reference to the Interpretations of 'Abduh (1226/1849–1323/1905), Quṭb (1323/1906–1385/1966), al-Sha'rāwī (1329/1911–1419/1998) and al-Azhar Magazine (*Majallat al-Azhar*) (1384/1965-)" (PhD Thesis, Department of Theology and Religion, School of Philosophy, Theology and Religion, College of Arts and Law, University of Birmingham, March 2009), p. 7.

26. Hassan Hanafi, "Method of Thematic Interpretation of the Qur'an", in Stefan Wild, ed., *The Qur'an as Text* (Leiden: Brill, 1996), p. 204.

27. Kāmil Salāmah al-Daqs, *Āyāt al-Jihād fī al-Qur'ān al-Karīm: Dirāsah Mawḍū'iyyah wa Tārīkhiyyah wa Bayāniyyah* (Kuwait: Dār al-Bayān, 1392/1972), pp. 5–181.

28. Another very famous figure in mysticism if not in the field of exegesis is Ibn 'Arabī (d. 638/1240). See Farid Esack, *The Qur'an: A User's Guide* (Oxford: Oneworld, 2007), p. 135.

29. According to Fudge, "Almost all of Islamic history's great exegetes were known primarily as some other type of scholar: for example, al-Ṭabarī (d. 311/923) was a Sunnī traditionist and legal scholar...." Bruce Fudge, "Qur'ānic Exegesis in Medieval Islam and Modern Orientalism", *Die Welt des Islams*, vol. 46, no. 2, 2006, pp. 115-147, citation at p. 117.

30. McAuliffe, "The Tasks and Traditions of Interpretation", p. 192.

31. For more on the biography of al-Ṭabarī and his exegesis, see for example, 'Abd al-Ḥayy al-Faramāwī, "Al-Ṭabarī" in Maḥmūd Ḥamdī Zaqzūq, ed., *Mawsū'at A'lām al-Fikr al-Islāmī* (Cairo: al-Majlis al-A'lā li al-Shu'ūn al-Islāmiyyah, 1428/2007), pp. 551–553; Aḥmad Muḥammad al-Ḥūfī, *Al-Ṭabarī* (Cairo: al-Mu'assasah al-Miṣriyyah al-'Āmmah li al-Ta'līf wa al-Tarjamah wa al-Ṭibā'ah wa al-Nashr, 1382/1963), pp. 31–179; Ibrāhīm 'Awaḍ, *Min al-Ṭabarī ilā Sayyid Quṭb: Dirāsāt fī Manāhij al-Tafsīr wa Madhāhibuh* (Cairo: Dār al-Fikr al-'Arabī, 1421/2000), pp. 9–69; Helmut Gätje, *The Qur'ān and Its Exegesis: Selected Texts with Classical and Modern Muslim Interpretations* (Oxford: Oneworld, 1996), pp. 34 f.; 'Abdullāh Shiḥātah, *'Ulūm al-Tafsīr* (Cairo: Dār al-Shurūq, 2001/1421), pp. 176–183. See also Naguib, "The Meaning of Purity in Classical Exegesis", pp. 48–53; al-Dhahabī, *Al-Tafsīr wa al-Mufassirūn*, vol. 1, pp. 180–195; McAuliffe, *Qur'ānic Christians*, pp. 38–45; Muḥammad al-Shabīb and Muḥammad al-Shamlāwī, *Al-Madāris al-Tafsīriyyah: 'Arḍ Mūjaz li Ashhar al-Mufassirīn wa Manāhijihim fī al-Tafsīr, Mu'jam Yaḍumm Akthar min 100 Tafsīr wa Mufassir* (Beirut: Mu'assasat al-'Ārif li al-Maṭbū'āt, 1427/2006), pp. 29 f.

32. Shalahudin Kafrawi, "Fakhr al-Dīn al-Rāzī's Methodology in Interpreting the Qur'ān" (MA diss., Faculty of Graduate Studies and Research, Institute of Islamic Studies, McGill University, Montreal, Canada, 1998), p. 22.

33. According to al-Faramāwī, al-Rāzī's focus on thematic exegesis at that time was an interest that did not reach the level of a clear methodology, but was rather a brief theme noticeable in his exegesis, see al-Faramāwī, *Al-Bidāyah fi al-Tafsīr al-Mawḍū'ī*, p. 55. However, al-Daghāmīn states that al-Rāzī's exegesis bears strong relevance to thematic exegesis, See his *Manhajiyyat al-Baḥth fi al-Tafsīr al-Mawḍū'ī*, pp. 98 f.

34. Al-Nimr, *'Ilm al-Tafsīr*, p. 128.

35. For further biographical information on the life of al-Rāzī and his exegesis, see for example 'Abd al-'Azīz al-Majdūb, *Al-Imām al-Ḥakīm Fakhr al-Dīn al-Rāzī min Khilāl Tafsīrih* (Tunisia: al-Dār al-'Arabiyyah li al-Kutub, second edn., 1400/1980), pp. 12–62; Fatḥallah Khalīf, *Fakhr al-Dīn al-Rāzī* (Alexandria, Egypt: Dār al-Jāmi'āt al-Miṣriyyah, 1976), pp. 4–49; Kafrawi, "Fakhr al-Dīn al-Rāzī's Methodology", pp. 8–114; 'Abd al-Ḥayy al-Faramāwī, "Al-Fakhr al-Rāzī" in Zaqzūq, ed., *Mawsū'at A'lām al-Fikr al-Islāmī*, pp. 793–795. See also Naguib, "The Meaning of Purity in Classical Exegesis", pp. 57–60; al-Nimr, *'Ilm al-Tafsīr*, pp. 123–129; al-Dhahabī, *Al-Tafsīr wa al-Mufassirūn*, vol. 1, pp. 248–253; McAuliffe, *Qur'ānic Christians*, pp. 63–71; al-Shabīb and al-Shamlāwī, *Al-Madāris al-Tafsīriyyah*, pp. 117–122.

36. Mashhūr Ḥasan Maḥmūd Sulaymān, *Al-Imām al-Qurṭubī: Shaykh A'immat al-Tafsīr* (Damascus: Dār al-Qalam, 1413/1993), pp. 22 f.

37. For more biographical information on the life and exegesis of al-Qurṭubī, see for example, Sulaymān, *Al-Imām al-Qurṭubī*, pp. 11–179; 'Abd al-Ḥayy al-Faramāwī, "Al-Qurṭubī", in Zaqzūq, ed., *Mawsū'at A'lām al-Fikr al-Islāmī*, pp.831 f.; Shiḥātah, *'Ulūm al-Tafsīr*, pp. 192–194. See also al-Qaṭṭān, *Mabāḥith*, pp. 368 f.; Naguib, "The Meaning of Purity in Classical Exegesis", pp. 61–64; al-Nimr, *'Ilm al-Tafsīr*, p. 110; al-Faramāwī, *Al-Bidāyah fi al-Tafsīr al-Mawḍū'ī*, p. 55; al-Dhahabī, *Al-Tafsīr wa al-Mufassirūn*, vol. 2, pp. 401–407; al-Shabīb and al-Shamlāwī, *Al-Madāris al-Tafsīriyyah*, pp. 123 f.

38. Al-Daghāmīn, *Manhajiyyat al-Baḥth fi al-Tafsīr al-Mawḍū'ī*, p. 37. For more on the biography of al-Alūsī and his exegesis, see Muḥammad Rajab al-Bayyūmī, "Al-Alūsī al-Mufassir", in Zaqzūq, ed., *Mawsū'at A'lām al-Fikr al-Islāmī*, pp. 13–18; al-Nimr, *'Ilm al-Tafsīr*, p. 103; al-Dhahabī, *Al-Tafsīr wa al-Mufassirūn*, vol. 1, pp. 300–308; al-Shabīb and al-Shamlāwī, *Al-Madāris al-Tafsīriyyah*, pp. 133–135.

39. One of the faculties of Cairo University at that time. It is now called Dār al-ʿUlūm.

40. For more on the biography of ʿAbduh, see for example, Kenneth Cragg, "ʿAbduh, Muḥammad", in John L. Esposito, ed., *The Oxford Encyclopedia of the Modern Islamic World* (New York: Oxford University Press, 1995), vol. 1, pp. 11 f.; Muḥammad ʿImārah, "Muḥammad ʿAbduh (al-Imām)", in Zaqzūq, ed., *Mawsūʿat Aʿlām al-Fikr al-Islāmī*, pp. 969–971; ʿAbdullāh Maḥmūd Shiḥātah, "Manhaj al-Imām Muḥammad ʿAbduh fī Tafsīr al-Qur'ān al-Karīm" (MA diss., Faculty of Dār al-ʿUlūm, Cairo University, Egypt, 1380/1960), pp. 3–30; al-Dhahabī, *Al-Tafsīr wa al-Mufassirūn*, vol. 2, pp. 483–504. See also Zebiri, *Maḥmūd Shaltūt*, pp. 132–140; Baljon, *Modern Muslim Koran Interpretation*, pp. 4 f.; Johannes J. G. Jansen, *The Dual Nature of Islamic Fundamentalism* (London: Hurst & Company, 1997), pp. 26–33; idem, *The Interpretation of the Koran in Modern Egypt* (Leiden: Brill, 1974), pp. 18–34.

41. Umar Ryad, "Islamic Reformism and Christianity: A Critical Reading of the Works of Muḥammad Rashīd Riḍā and His Associates (1898–1935)" (PhD Thesis, Faculty of Humanities, Institute for Religious Studies, Leiden University, The Netherlands, 2008), p. 3.

42. For more on the biography of Riḍā, see for example Emad Eldin Shahin, "Rashīd Riḍā, Muḥammad", in Esposito, ed., *Oxford Encyclopedia of the Modern Islamic World*, vol. 3, pp. 410–412; idem, "Muḥammad Rashīd Riḍā's Perspectives on the West as Reflected in *Al-Manar*", *The Muslim World*, vol. 79, no. 2, April 1989, pp. 113–132; Muḥammad ʿImārah, "Muḥammad Rashīd Riḍā", in Zaqzūq, ed., *Mawsūʿat Aʿlām al-Fikr al-Islāmī*, pp. 946 f.; Aḥmad al-Sharabāṣī, *Rashīd Riḍā: Al-Ṣaḥafī, al-Mufassir, al-Shāʿir, al-Lughawī* (Cairo: al-Majlis al-Aʿlā li al-Shu'ūn al-Islāmiyyah, 1977), pp. 10–90; Ibrāhim Aḥmad al-ʿAdawī, *Rashīd Riḍā: Al-Imām al-Mujāhid* (Cairo: al-Mu'assasah al-Miṣriyyah al-ʿĀmmah li al-Ta'līf wa al-Anbā' wa al-Nashr, n.d.), pp. 208–214; Ana Belén Soage, "Rashīd Rida's Legacy", *The Muslim World*, vol. 98, no. 1, January 2008, pp. 1–23; al-Dhahabī, *Al-Tafsīr wa al-Mufassirūn*, vol. 2, pp. 505–517; McAuliffe, *Qur'ānic Christians*, pp. 78–85.

43. Shahin, "Rashīd Riḍā, Muḥammad", in Esposito, ed., *Oxford Encyclopedia of the Modern Islamic World*, vol. 3, p. 410.

44. According to Rotraud Wielandt, "ʿAbduh's actual share in it [i.e. of *Tafsīr al-Manār*] consists of the record of a series of lectures that he gave at al-Azhar University around the year 1900 which covered the text of the Qur'ān from the beginning to Q 4: 124. His pupil Muḥammad Rashīd Riḍā took notes of these lectures which he afterwards elaborated and showed to his teachers for approval or correction." Wielandt, "Exegesis of the Qur'ān", p. 128.

45. Al-Dhahabī, *Al-Tafsīr wa al-Mufassirūn*, vol. 2, p. 507.

46. Muḥammad Rashīd Riḍā, *Tafsīr al-Qur'ān al-Ḥakīm: al-Mushtahir bi ism Tafsīr al-Manār* (Cairo: Dār al-Manār, second edn., 1366/1947), vol. 7, pp. 499 f. See also al-Daghāmīn, *Manhajiyyat al-Baḥth fī al-Tafsīr al-Mawḍū'ī*, p. 20.

47. Ismail K. Poonawala, "Muḥammad 'Izzat Darwaza's Principles of Modern Exegesis: A Contribution towards Quranic Hermeneutics", in G.R. Hawting and Abdul-Kader A. Shareef, eds., *Approaches to the Qur'ān* (London: Routledge, 1993), p. 238.

48. For further information on the life of Darwazah and his exegesis, see Poonawala, "Muḥammad 'Izzat Darwaza's Principles of Modern Exegesis" in Hawting and Shareef, eds., *Approaches to the Qur'an*, pp. 225–246; Muḥammad 'Azzah Darwazah, *Al-Tafsīr al-Ḥadīth: Tartīb al-Suwar Ḥasab al-Nuzūl* (Beirut: Dār al-Gharb al-Islāmī, second edn., 2000), vol. 1, pp. 276–278; Zebiri, *Maḥmūd Shaltūt*, pp. 145 f.

49. Barbara H.E. Zollner, *The Muslim Brotherhood: Hasan al-Hudaybi and Ideology* (London: Routledge, 2009), p. 3.

50. Ibid., p. 2.

51. Mhd. Syahnan, "A Study of Sayyid Quṭb's Qur'ān Exegesis in Earlier and Later Editions of His *Fī Ẓilāl al-Qur'ān* with Special Reference to Selected Themes" (MA diss., Faculty of Graduate Studies and Research, Institute of Islamic Studies, McGill University, Montreal, Canada, 1997), p. 39.

52. The translated volumes of the *Ẓilāl* appear under the title *In the Shade of the Qur'ān*, trans. and ed. Adil Salahi (Markfield and Leicester, Islamic Foundation, 1999–2009), 18 vols. This research refers to the relevant translated volumes, although the main Arabic edition remains the basic reference. For more on the biography of Quṭb and his works, see for example Shahrough Akhavi, "Quṭb, Sayyid", in Esposito, ed., *Oxford Encyclopedia of the Modern Islamic World*, vol. 3, pp. 400–404; Aref Ali Nayed, "The Radical Qur'ānic Hermeneutics of Sayyid Quṭb", *Islamic Studies*, vol. 31, no. 3, Autumn 1413/1992, pp. 355–363; Ronald L. Nettler, "Guidelines for the Islamic Community: Sayyid Qutb's Political Interpretation of the Qur'ān", *Journal of Political Ideologies*, vol. 1, no. 2, 1996, pp. 183–196; John C. Zimmerman, "Sayyid Qutb's Influence on the 11 September Attacks", *Terrorism and Political Violence*, vol. 16, no. 2, Summer 2004, pp. 222–252; Ibrahim M. Abu-Rabi', *Intellectual Origins of Islamic Resurgence in the Modern Arab World* (Albany: State University of New York Press, 1996), pp. 166–195; Mohammed Shah Bin Jani, "Sayyid Qutb's View of Jihād: An Analytical Study of His Major Works" (PhD Thesis,

Department of Theology, Islamic Studies, Faculty of Arts, University of Birmingham, United Kingdom, 1998), pp. 30–82; Syahnan, "A Study of Sayyid Quṭb's Qur'ān Exegesis", pp. 1–74; Ibrāhim Munīr and Tawfīq al-Wā'ī, *Sayyid Quṭb: Ṣāḥib al-Ẓilāl* (Kuwait: Maktabat al-Manār al-Islāmiyyah, 1426/2005), pp. 11–82.

53. Johannes J.G. Jansen, *The Neglected Duty: The Creed of Sadat's Assassins and Islamic Resurgence in the Middle East* (New York: Macmillan, 1986), p. 121.

54. See http://www.elsharawy.com/, accessed 26 June 2009. For more on the biography of al-Sha'rāwī and his exegesis, see for example Muḥammad Rajab al-Bayyūmī, "Muḥammad Mutawallī al-Sha'rāwī", in Zaqzūq, ed., *Mawsū'at A'lām al-Fikr al-Islāmī*, pp. 1,003–1,006; Jansen, *The Neglected Duty*, pp. 121–150; Maḥmūd Mahdī, *Al-Sha'rāwī Mufakkiran* (Cairo: Dār al-Bayān li al-Ṭab' wa al-Nashr wa al-Tawzī', 2003), pp. 12–15; al-Shabīb and al-Shamlāwī, *Al-Madāris al-Tafsīriyyah*, pp. 157 f.

55. Mark Easterby-Smith, Richard Thorpe and Andy Lowe, *Management Research: An Introduction* (London: Sage, second edn., 2002), p. 118.

56. Bilal Sambur, "The Insider/Outsider Problem in the Study of Islam", *Islamic Quarterly*, vol. 46, no. 1, 2002, pp. 95–106; see also Ahmed Mohsen Al-Dawoody, "War in Islamic Law: Justifications and Regulations" (PhD Thesis, University of Birmingham, Department of Theology and Religion, School of Philosophy, Theology and Religion, College of Arts and Law, August 2009), p. 17.

57. Jabal Muḥammad Buaben, *Image of the Prophet Muḥammad in the West: A Study of Muir, Margoliouth and Watt* (Leicester: Islamic Foundation, 1417/1996), pp. 328 f; and idem, "The Life of Muḥammad (S.A.W.) in British Scholarship: A Critique of Three Key Modern Biographies of the Prophet Muḥammad (S.A.W.)" (PhD Thesis, Department of Theology and Religion, University of Birmingham, May 1995), pp. 374, 377. See also David Marshall, *God, Muhammad and the Unbelievers: A Qur'ānic Study* (Richmond: Curzon, 1999), p. 6.

58. This is because "the same term can mean different things to different people", Radwan A. Masmoudi, "Struggles Behind Words: Shariah, Sunnism, and Jihad", *SAIS Review*, vol. 21, no. 2, Summer-Fall 2001, p. 19. Yusuf Işicik also adds that "one can understand an oral or written statement only when one is aware of the distinction between the literal and terminological senses of words and of differences in meaning over time." See Yusuf Işicik, "Two Fundamental Concepts in the Qur'ān: Ta'wīl and Mutashābih", *Islamic Quarterly*, vol. 53, no. 1, 1430/2009, p. 82; and also Adam L. Silverman, "Just War, Jihad, and Terrorism: A Comparison of Western and Islamic Norms for the Use

of Political Violence", *Journal of Church and State*, vol. 44, no. 1, 2002, pp. 73–92, citation at p. 90.

59. Specifically, I have relied on the al-Shamirlī edition authorized by al-Azhar in Egypt and published and distributed by al-Shamirlī, no. 62, 21/10/1999.

1. Defining Terrorism: Secular and Islamic Perspectives

1. According to one expert, "Analysis of international terrorism cannot easily proceed without first defining 'terrorism'.", see David Aaron Schwartz, "International Terrorism and Islamic Law", *Columbia Journal of Transnational Law*, vol. 29, 1991, pp. 629–652, citation at p. 631.
2. Karima Bennoune, "Terror/Torture", *Berkeley Journal of International Law*, vol. 26, no. 1, 2008, pp. 19–27; Alex Schmid, "Terrorism - The Definitional Problem", *Case Western Reserve Journal of International Law*, vol. 36, nos. 2 and 3, 2004, pp. 375–419, citation at p. 395.
3. Brian Kingshott, "Terrorism: The 'New' Religious War", *Criminal Justice Studies*, vol. 16, no. 1, 2003, pp. 15–27, citation at p. 15.
4. Amir Taheri, *Holy Terror: The Inside Story of Islamic Terrorism* (London: Sphere, 1987), p. 4.
5. According to one account, "Walter Laqueur simply threw up his hands, arguing that terrorism had appeared in so many different forms and under so many different circumstances that a comprehensive definition was impossible." Leonard Weinberg, Ami Pedahzur, and Sivan Hirsch-Hoefler, "The Challenges of Conceptualizing Terrorism", *Terrorism and Political Violence*, vol. 16, no. 4, Winter 2004, pp. 777–794, citation at p. 777.
6. According to Zdzislaw Galicki, "the question of defining international terrorism remains the most difficult and unsatisfactorily solved for all engaged in the process of elaboration of antiterrorist treaties, either universal or regional." See his "International Law and Terrorism", *The American Behavioral Scientist*, vol. 48, no. 6, February 2005, pp. 743–757, citation at p. 745.
7. Aref M. Al-Khattar, *Religion and Terrorism: An Interfaith Perspective* (Westport, Conn.: Praeger, 2003), p. 36.
8. 'Abd al-Raḥmān Sulaymān al-Maṭrūdī, "Naẓrah fī Mafhūm al-Irhāb wa al-Mawqif minhu fī al-Islām", [article online]; available from http://

alminbar.al-islam.com/images/books/367.pdf; accessed 31 December 2007, p. 85.

9. Dawn Perlmutter, *Investigating Religious Terrorism and Ritualistic Crime* (New York: CRC Press LLC, 2004), p. 1; Haytham ʿAbd al-Salām Muḥammad, *Mafhūm al-Irhāb fī al-Sharīʿah al-Islāmiyyah*, (Beirut: Dār al-Kutub al-ʿIlmiyyah, 2005), pp. 19–21.

10. Philip Cryan, "Defining Terrorism", in Aftab Ahmad Malik, ed., *With God on Our Side: Politics & Theology of the War on Terrorism* (Bristol: Amal Press, 2005), p. 98.

11. Walter Gary Sharp, "The Use of Force against Terrorism: American Hegemony or Impotence?", *Chicago Journal of International Law*, vol. 1, no. 1, 2000, pp. 37–47, citation at p. 39; Ben Saul, "Attempts to Define 'Terrorism' in International Law", *Netherlands International Law Review*, vol. 52, no. 1, 2005, pp. 57–83, citation at p. 58.

12. Muhammad ʿAwaḍ al-Tartūrī and Aghādīr ʿArafāt Guwayḥān, *ʿIlm al-Irhāb: Al-Usus al-Fikriyyah wa al-Nafsiyyah wa al-Ijtimāʿiyyah wa al-Tarbawiyyah li Dirāsat al-Irhāb* (Amman: Dār al-Ḥāmid li al-Nashr wa al-Tawzīʿ, 2006), p. 19.

13. ʿAbd al-Rahmān Sulaymān al-Maṭrūdī, "Al-Irhāb wa Ra'y al-Qur'ān Fīh," *Journal of Qur'anic Studies*, vol. 6, no. 1, 2004, pp. 159-199, citation at pp. 196 f.

14. Perlmutter, *Investigating Religious Terrorism*, p. 1; Colin Wight, "Theorising Terrorism: The State, Structure and History", *International Relations*, vol. 23, no. 1, 2009, pp. 99–106, citation at p. 102.

15. Colin Turner, *Islam: The Basics* (New York: Routledge, 2006), p. 190.

16. Javaid Rehman, *Islamic State Practices, International Law and the Threat from Terrorism: A Critique of the "Clash of Civilizations" in the New World Order* (Oxford: Hart Publishing, 2005), p. 73 f.

17. Jenny Teichman, "How to Define Terrorism", *Philosophy*, vol. 64, no. 250, October 1989, pp. 505–517, citation at p. 514.

18. Asma Barlas, "Jihad, Holy War, and Terrorism: The Politics of Conflation and Denial," *American Journal of Islamic Social Sciences*, vol. 20, no. 1, Winter 2003, pp. 46–62, citation at p. 53.

19. Richard Goldstone and Janine Simpson, "Evaluating the Role of the International Criminal Court as a Legal Response to Terrorism", *Harvard Human Rights Journal*, vol. 16, 2003, pp. 12–26, citation at p. 13.

20. Haytham, *Mafhūm al-Irhāb*, p. 20.

21. Although the phrase "combating terrorism" is here translated from the Arabic, researchers such as Bruce Hoffman would argue that it is "a global war on terrorism", as declared by former US President Bush after 11 September, and currently dubbed the "strategy against violent extremism". See Bruce Hoffman, *Inside Terrorism* (New York: Columbia University Press, second edn., 2006), p. 129.
22. Haytham, *Mafhūm al-Irhāb*, pp. 20 f.
23. Jörg Friedrichs, "Defining the International Public Enemy: The Political Struggle behind the Legal Debate on International Terrorism", *Leiden Journal of International Law*, vol. 19, 2006, pp. 69–91.
24. Augustus Richard Norton, "Terrorism" in Esposito, ed., *Oxford Encyclopedia of the Modern Islamic World*, vol. 4, p. 206.
25. Ben Saul, *Defining Terrorism in International Law* (Oxford: Oxford University Press, 2006), p. 4.
26. Chapters Two and Three of this monograph critique the proponents of such extremist views.
27. Robert W. Taylor and Harry E. Vanden, "Defining Terrorism in El Salvador: 'La Matanza'", *Annals of the American Academy of Political and Social Science*, vol. 463, September 1982, pp. 106-118, citation at p. 107.
28. Saul, *Defining Terrorism*, p. 5.
29. Susan Tiefenbrun, "A Semiotic Approach to a Legal Definition of Terrorism", *ILSA Journal of International and Comparative Law*, vol. 9, 2002–2003, pp. 357–402, citation at p. 358.
30. Roberta Senechal de la Roche, "Toward a Scientific Theory of Terrorism", *Sociological Theory*, Theories of Terrorism: A Symposium, vol. 22, no. 1, March 2004, pp. 1–4, citation at p. 1.
31. Abdel Haleem, *Qur'an*, p. 71.
32. For a detailed discussion of this point, please refer to Chapter 5 of this monograph.
33. Indeed, it is beyond the scope of this chapter to discuss the differences between jihad and terrorism. Chapters 3 and 4 of this book deal with this issue in detail.
34. E.g. Mark A. Gabriel, *Islam and Terrorism: What the Quran Really Teaches about Christianity, Violence and the Goals of the Islamic Jihad* (Lake Mary, Florida: FrontLine, 2002), pp. 34–37.
35. Geoffrey Levitt, "Is 'Terrorism' Worth Defining?", *Ohio Northern University Law Review*, vol. 13, 1986, pp. 97–116, citation at p. 97. The 109 definitions of terrorism were provided between 1936 and 1981. See Walter Laqueur, "Reflections on Terrorism", *Foreign Affairs*,

vol. 65, no. 1, Fall 1986, pp. 86–100, citation at p. 88, with the quote coming from Alex P. Schmid and Albert J. Jongman, *Political Terrorism: A New Guide to Actors, Authors, Concepts, Data Bases, Theories, and Literature* (Amsterdam: SWIDOC, rev. and enl. edn., 1988); Saul, *Defining Terrorism*, p. 57.

36. Leonard Weinberg and William L. Eubank, *What Is Terrorism?* (New York: Chelsea House, 2006), p. 10.

37. Seyyed Hossein Nasr, “Islam & the Question of Violence”, in Malik, ed., *With God on Our Side*, p. 273.

38. See for example Terrence K. Kelly, “The Just Conduct of War against Radical Islamic Terror and Insurgencies”, in Charles Reed and David Ryall eds., *The Price of Peace: Just War in the Twenty-First Century* (Cambridge: Cambridge University Press, 2007), pp. 203–205.

39. Mahathir Mohamad, *Terrorism and the Real Issues: Selected Speeches of Dr Mahathir Mohamad*, ed. Hashim Makaruddin (Subang Jaya: Pelanduk Publications, 2003), pp. 12–14.

40. See for example Muḥammad ʿAbd al-Raḥīm Sulṭān al-ʿUlamāʾ, “Mawqif al-Islām min al-Irhāb”, in *Tolerance in the Islamic Civilization*, Researches and Facts. The Sixteenth General Conference of the Supreme Council for Islamic Affairs (Cairo: Maṭābiʿ al-Ahrām al-Tujāriyyah, 2004), p. 1,167; Niaz A. Shah, *Self-defence in Islamic and International Law: Assessing al-Qaeda and the Invasion of Iraq* (Basingstoke: Palgrave Macmillan, 2008), p. 66.

41. Muḥammad ʿAbd al-Raḥīm, “Mawqif al-Islām min al-Irhāb”, p. 1,158.

42. Kuṭb Muṣṭafā Sano, “Fī Muṣṭalaḥ al-Irhāb wa Ḥukmuh: Qirāʾah Naqdiyyah fī al-Mafhūm wa al-Ḥukm min Manẓūr Sharʿī”, [article online]; available from http://alminbar.al-islam.com/Mehwar_erhabM.aspx?View=Page&PageID=6&PageNo=1&BookID=207&word=images/books/220.doc&pdf=images/books/220.pdf; Internet; accessed 1 January 2008, p. 6.

43. This phrase is inspired by a statement made by Colin Turner referred to earlier in this chapter.

44. Haytham, *Mafhūm al-Irhāb*, p. 39.

45. *Oxford Advanced Learner's Dictionary of Current English*, ed. Jonathan Crowther (Oxford: Oxford University Press, fifth edn., 1995), p. 1,233.

46. Shawqī Ḍayf, et al., *Al-Muʿjam al-Wasīṭ* (Cairo: Maktabat al-Shurūq al-Dawliyyah, fourth edn., 2004), p. 376.

47. Majmaʿ al-Lughah al-ʿArabiyyah, *Al-Muʿjam al-Wajīz* (Cairo: Egyptian Ministry of Education, 1415/1994), p. 279.

48. Aḥmad Jalāl 'Izziddīn, *Al-Irhāb wa al-'Unf al-Siyāsī* (Cairo: Dār al-Ḥurriyyah li al-Ṣaḥāfah wa al-Ṭibā'ah wa al-Nashr, 1986), p. 21 quoted in Abdulhafiz ibn Abdullah Al-Malki, "Naḥwā Binā' Istirātījiyyah Waṭaniyyah", [article online]; available from http://www.nauss.edu.sa/NAUSS/Arabic/Menu/ELibrary/ScLetterResearch/Doctorate/year1/part1/dps12006.htm; Internet; accessed 2 March 2008, p. 96.

49. *Fear of you [believers] is more intense in their hearts than fear of God because they are people devoid of understanding*, Abdel Haleem, *Qur'an*, p. 366; Scott C. Alexander, "Fear", in McAuliffe, ed., *Encyclopaedia of the Qur'ān*, vol. 2, p. 197.

50. Grant Wardlaw, *Political Terrorism: Theory, Tactics, and Counter-measures* (Cambridge: Cambridge University Press, 1982), p. 18; Parvez Ahmed, "Terror in the Name of Islam - Unholy War, Not Jihad", *Case Western Reserve Journal of International Law*, vol. 39, no. 3, 2007–2008, pp. 759–788, citation at p. 764; Reuven Young, "Defining Terrorism: The Evolution of Terrorism as a Legal Concept in International Law and Its Influence on Definitions in Domestic Legislation", *Boston College International and Comparative Law Review*, vol. 29, no. 1, 2006, pp. 23–106, citation at p. 27.

51. Charles Tilly, "Terror, Terrorism, Terrorists", *Sociological Theory*, vol. 22, March 2004, pp. 5–13, citation at p. 8.

52. Hoffman, *Terrorism*, p. 3.

53. Ibid., pp. 16 f.

54. David J. Whittaker, ed., *The Terrorism Reader* (New York: Routledge, 2001), p. 13.

55. Ibid.

56. *Oxford Advanced Learner's Dictionary*, p. 1,233.

57. Some researchers, such as al-Maṭrūdī and others, would argue that citing as many individual definitions of terrorism as possible would help make the definition of terrorism more comprehensive by having many definitions supporting one another, see al-Maṭrūdī, "Al-Irhāb", pp. 192 f. However, this would still not lead to a fully comprehensive definition and would perplex readers.

58. Mahmoud Samy, "The League of Arab States", in Giuseppe Nesi, ed., *International Co-operation in Counter-terrorism* (Hampshire: Ashgate, 2006), p. 157; Ali ibn Faiz al-Jahni, *Al-Irhāb: Al-Fahm al-Mafrūḍ li al-Irhāb al-Marfūḍ* (Riyadh: Naif Arab University for Security Sciences, Centre for Studies and Researches, 1421/2001), pp. 18, 363; Aḥmad 'Alī al-Imām, "Ru'yah Ta'ṣīliyyah li mafhūm al-Irhāb", *Scientific Review of the European Council for Fatwa and Research*, no. 6, January 2005, p. 27.

59. Sālim al-Bahnasāwī, *Al-Taṭarruf wa al-Irhāb fī al-Manẓūr al-Islāmī wa al-Dawlī* (Al-Mansūrah: Dār al-Wafā' li al-Ṭibā'ah wa al-Nashr wa al-Tawzī', 2004, p. 64.

60. For a thought-provoking discussion on the definitions of individual, group and state-sponsored terrorism see Majorie Cohn, "Distinguishing Terrorism", *The Guild Practitioner*, vol. 60, no. 1, Winter 2003, pp. 74–79.

61. Bayān Makkah al-Mukarramah Bisha'n al-Irhāb, "Ta'rīf al-Irhāb", *Majallat al-Majma' al-Fiqhī al-Islāmī*, vol. 13, no. 15, 2002, p. 491; Zakī 'Ali al Sayyid Abū Ghaḍḍah, *Al Irhāb fī al-Yahūdiyyah wa al-Masīḥiyyah wa al-Islām wa al-Siyāsāt al-Mu'āṣirah* (Al-Mansūrah: Dār al-Wafā', 2002), p. 37.

62. From the seventeenth session of the International Islamic Fiqh Academy affiliated to the OIC, "Mawqif al-Islām min al-Ghulūww wa al-Taṭarruf wa al-Irhāb" [article online]; available from http://www.fiqhacademy.org.sa/qrarat/17-3.htm; accessed 25 June 2013.

63. Sano, "Fī Muṣṭalaḥ al-Irhāb", p. 8.

64. Ibid., p. 18.

65. For a comprehensive exposition of this point, see ibid., pp. 15–18.

66. Ibid., p. 10.

67. Boaz Ganor, "An International Objective Definition of Terrorism as a Crucial Tool for New International Framework" [article online]; available from http://www.ewi.info/pdf/Attachments171.pdf; accessed 29 February 2008, p. 24.

68. See for example "Jihad Debated", http://www.islamonline.net/servlet/Satellite?c=Article_C&cid=1203515459722&pagename=Zone-English-News/NWELayout; accessed 29 February 2008; Mark Trevelyan, "Security Professionals Gloomy on Terrorism Outlook", [article online]; available from http://www.reuters.com/article/worldNews/idUSL2126797520070223; accessed 25 June 2013.

69. Jørgen S. Nielsen, "The Discourse of 'Terrorism' between Violence, Justice and International Order", in Tahir Abbas, ed., *Islamic Political Radicalism: A European Perspective* (Edinburgh: Edinburgh University Press, 2007), p. 22.

70. Cherif Bassiouni, "Legal Control of International Terrorism: A Policy-Oriented Assessment," *Harvard International Law Journal*, vol. 43, no. 1, Winter 2002, pp. 83–103, citation at p. 84.

71. Ganor, "An International Objective Definition of Terrorism", p. 24. The original source refers to the journal of the MWL (i.e. *Majallat al-Majma' al-Fiqhī al-Islāmī*) referred to earlier in this chapter. The official website of the MWL is http://www.themwl.org/; accessed 2 March 2008.

72. See the English word "aggression" translated as *'udwān* at http://dictionary.reference.com/search?q=aggression&r=66; accessed 28 June 2013.

73. Perlmutter, *Investigating Religious Terrorism*, pp. 4–5; Hoffman, *Terrorism*, pp. 83–85.
74. RAND Terrorism Incident Database quoted in Hoffman, *Terrorism*, p. 88.
75. Hoffman, *Terrorism*, p. 82.
76. Ibid., 33.
77. Al-Khattar, *Religion and Terrorism*, pp. 17, 37.
78. Perlmutter, *Investigating Religious Terrorism*, p. 2; Hoffman, *Terrorism*, p. 33.
79. This definition is available from the FBI website at: http://www.fbi.gov/albuquerque/about-us/what-we-investigate, accessed 26 July 2014; al-Khattar, *Religion and Terrorism*, p. 19.
80. See Department of Defense Dictionary of Military and Associated Terms; available from http://www.dtic.mil/doctrine/jel/doddict/data/t/05482.html; accessed 28 June 2013. See also Robert A. Pape, "The Strategic Logic of Suicide Terrorism", *American Political Science Review*, vol. 97, no. 3, August 2003, pp. 343–361, citation at p. 345.
81. Perlmutter, *Investigating Religious Terrorism*, pp. 4–5.
82. Sano, "Fī Muṣṭalaḥ al-Irhāb", p. 7.
83. Al-Malkī, "Naḥwā Binā' Istirātījiyyah Waṭaniyyah", pp. 100 f.
84. Perlmutter, *Investigating Religious Terrorism*, p. 2.
85. Al-Maṭrūdī, "Al-Irhāb", pp. 189 f.
86. According to Sano, the other Islamic definition is that attributed to the Islamic Research Academy at al-Azhar cited and evaluated earlier in this chapter.
87. Hoffman, *Terrorism*, p. 31; Sano, "Fī Muṣṭalaḥ al-Irhāb", p. 7.
88. Ibid., pp. 9, 33.
89. For a comprehensive discussion of these three main reservations, see Sano, "Fī Muṣṭalaḥ al-Irhāb", pp. 7–11.
90. Hoffman, *Terrorism*, p. 33.
91. Perlmutter, *Investigating Religious Terrorism*, p. 2.
92. Ibid., pp. 83–107.
93. Sherman A. Jackson, "Domestic Terrorism in the Islamic Legal Tradition," *The Muslim World*, vol. 91, nos. 3–4, September 2001, p. 293-310. This article has been recently reprinted in David Cook, ed. *Jihad and Martyrdom*, vol. 4, pp. 166–181.
94. For 'Īsāwī's definition of terrorism see Aḥmad 'Īsāwī, "Mafhūm al-Irhāb fī al-Qur'ān: Muqārabah li Dirāsat Dilālat al-Muṣṭalaḥ al-Qur'ānī", *Al-Wa'y al-Islāmī*, Rabī' I 1426 AH/April–May 2005, p. 48.

95. Chapter 5 of this book discusses this issue in detail.

96. For a comprehensive account of the history of the Assassins, see Bernard Lewis, *The Assassins: A Radical Sect in Islam* (London: Phoenix, Orion Books, 2003); Farhad Daftary, *The Assassin Legends: Myths of the Isma'ilis* (London: I.B. Tauris, 1994).

97. Lewis, *The Assassins*, p. 9; J.P. Larsson, *Understanding Religious Violence: Thinking outside the Box on Terrorism* (Aldershot: Ashgate, 2004), pp. 37–41.

98. Daftary, *The Assassin Legends*, p. 4.

99. Olivier Roy, *Globalised Islam: The Search for a New Ummah* (London: Hurst, rev. & enl. ed., 2004), p. 42.

100. Larsson, *Understanding Religious Violence*, p. 37. Larsson considers that Lewis' *The Assassins* as one of very few authoritative writings about the Assassins.

101. Ibid., pp. 37–40.

102. For comprehensive definitions of all these sects, see Haytham, *Mafhūm al-Irhāb*, pp. 77–79; and al-Tartūrī and Guwayḥān, *'Ilm al-Irhāb*, p. 83. On the non-violent nature of modern descendants of the Assassins, see Larsson, *Understanding Religious Violence*, p. 41.

103. According to Iqbal and Lewis, "In the Qur'an and Sunna, corruption refers to a broad range of behavioral digressions that threaten the social, economic and ecological balance (see 11: 85; 28: 4, 77, 83; 29: 28–30; 30: 41; 89: 12)." Zafar Iqbal and Mervyn K. Lewis, "Governance and Corruption: Can Islamic Societies and the West Learn from Each Other?", *American Journal of Islamic Social Sciences*, vol. 19, no. 2, Spring 2002, p. 8.

104. According to al-Aṣfahānī, the opposite of *fasād* is *ṣalāḥ* (righteousness), see al-Rāghib al-Aṣfahānī, *Mufradāt Alfāẓ al-Qur'ān*, ed. Ṣafwān 'Adnān Dawūdī (Damascus: Dār al-Qalam, second edn., 2002), p. 636. On its occurrence in the Qur'an, see Muḥammad Fu'ād 'Abd al-Bāqī, *Al-Mu'jam al-Mufahras li Alfāẓ al-Qur'ān al-Karīm* (Cairo: Dār al-Ḥadīth, 1988), pp. 518 f; and Elsaid M. Badawi and Muhammad Abdel Haleem, *Arabic-English Dictionary of Qur'anic Usage* (Leiden: Brill, 2008), pp. 709 f.

105. Mustansir Mir, *Dictionary of Qur'ānic Terms and Concepts* (New York: Garland, 1987), p. 42.

106. On declaring disbelief in Allah, e.g. 16: 88, 21: 22; on hypocrisy, e.g. 2: 11–12; on extravagance, e.g. 26: 151–152; on magic, e.g. 10: 80–82. For general uses of *fasād*, see Badawi and Abdel Haleem, *Arabic-English Dictionary of Qur'anic Usage*, pp. 709 f.

107. Khaled Abou El Fadl, *The Great Theft: Wrestling Islam from the Extremists* (New York: HarperCollins, 2005), p. 242.

108. Abdur Rahman Hassan Al Nafisah, "Al-I'tidā' 'alā al-Āminīn wamā Yatarattab 'alayh", *Contemporary Jurisprudence Research Journal*, vol. 16, no. 64, Sep-Oct-Nov 2004, pp. 291 f.; Maḥmūd Shaltūt, *Al-Islām: 'Aqīdah wa Sharī'ah* (Cairo: Dār al-Shurūq, fifteen edn., 1408/1988), p. 337.

109. Abdel Haleem, *Qur'an*, p. 177.

110. Fakhr al-Dīn Muḥammad ibn 'Umar al-Tamīmī al-Rāzī, *Al-Tafsīr al-Kabīr aw Mafātīḥ al-Ghayb* (Beirut: Dār al-Kutub al-'Ilmiyyah, 2000), vol. 20, pp.159 f.

111. 'Abd al-Raḥmān ibn al-Kamāl Jalāl al-Dīn al-Suyūṭī, *Al-Durr al-Manthūr fī al-Tafsīr bi al-Ma'thūr* (Beirut: Dār al-Fikr, 1993), vol. 5, p. 282.

112. Muḥammad Mutawallī al-Sha'rāwī, *Tafsīr al-Sha'rāwī* (Cairo: Akhbār al-Yawm, 1991), vol. 14, p. 8,511.

113. Abdel Haleem, *Qur'an*, p. 348.

114. For the five occurrences in the Qur'an, see 6: 164, 17: 15, 35: 18, 39: 7, and 53: 38.

115. Abou El Fadl, *The Great Theft*, pp. 244, 306.

116. Sayyid Quṭb, *Fī Ẓilāl al-Qur'ān* (Cairo: Dār al-Shurūq, twelfth edn., 1406/1986), vol. 4, p. 2, 224; idem: *In the Shade*, vol. 11, p. 157.

117. Al-Bukhārī, *Ṣaḥīḥ al-Bukhārī*, no. 6,878, in *Mawsū'at al-Ḥadīth al-Sharīf: Al-Kutub al-Sittah*, ed. Ṣāliḥ ibn 'Abd al-'Azīz Āl al-Shaykh (Riyadh: Dār al-Salām li al-Nashr wa al-Tawzī', 1999), p. 573.

118. Ismā'īl ibn 'Umar ibn Kathīr, *Tafsīr al-Qur'ān al-'Aẓīm* (Beirut: Dār al-Fikr, 1401/1980–1), vol. 3, p. 39.

119. Muḥammad ibn 'Abdullah ibn al-'Arabī, *Aḥkām al-Qur'ān*, ed. Muḥammad 'Abd al-Qādir 'Aṭā (Beirut: Dār al-Kutub al-'Ilmiyyah, 1996), vol. 3, pp. 194–198.

120. Darwazah, *Al-Tafsīr al-Ḥadīth*, vol. 3, p. 382.

121. Al-Bukhārī, *Ṣaḥīḥ al-Bukhārī*, no. 6,862, in *Mawsū'at al-Ḥadīth*, p. 572.

122. Al-Tirmidhī, *Jāmi'*, no. 1,395, in *Mawsū'at al-Ḥadīth*, p. 1,793.

123. Aḥmad ibn 'Alī al-Rāzī al-Jaṣṣāṣ, *Aḥkām al-Qur'ān,* ed. Muḥammad al-Ṣādiq Qamḥāwī (Beirut: Dār Iḥyā' al-Turāth al-'Arabī, 1405/1984–5), vol. 1, p. 174.

124. 'Abd al-Raḥmān Spīndārī, *Al-Irhāb min Manẓūr Qur'ānī* (Kurdistan: Hawār, 2006), p. 24.

125. Quṭb, *Ẓilāl*, vol. 5, p. 2,678; idem, *In the Shade*, vol. 13, p. 204.

126. Ibid., vol. 13, p. 205.

127. Al-Sha'rāwī, *Tafsīr*, vol. 17, pp. 10,871–10,875; Quṭb, *Ẓilāl*, vol. 5, p. 2,677; idem, *In the Shade*, vol. 13, p. 205; Darwazah, *al-Tafsīr al-Ḥadīth*, vol. 3, p. 311; and Muḥammad ibn Jarīr ibn Yazīd ibn Khālid al-Ṭabarī, *Jāmi' al-Bayān 'an Ta'wīl Āy al-Qur'ān* (Beirut: Dār al-Fikr, 1405/1984–5), vol. 20, pp. 27 f.

128. Spīndārī, *Al-Irhāb*, pp. 24 f.

129. Ibid., p. 26. 130. Al-Maṭrūdī, "Naẓrah fī Mafhūm al-Irhāb", p. 2.

131. Ibid.

132. Al-Ṭabarī, *Jāmi' al-Bayān*, vol. 1, p. 206; Muḥammad ibn Aḥmad al-Anṣārī al-Qurṭubī, *Al-Jāmi' li Aḥkām al-Qur'ān* (Cairo: Dār al-Sha'b, n.d.), vol. 1, p. 275; Ibn Kathīr, *Tafsīr al-Qur'ān*, vol. 1, p. 71.

133. Al-Sha'rāwī, *Tafsīr*, vol. 1, pp. 235–247; Riḍā, *Tafsīr al-Qur'ān al-Ḥakīm*, vol. 1, pp. 258 f; Sayyid Abul A'lā Mawdūdī, *Towards Understanding the Qur'ān*, trans. & ed. Zafar Ishaq Ansari (Leicester: The Islamic Foundation, 1988), vol. 1, pp. 59 f.

134. Abū Ghaḍḍah, *Al-Irhāb*, p. 41. 135. Ibid., p. 40 f.

136. Al-Qurṭubī, *Al-Jāmi'*, vol. 6, p. 133; al-Sha'rāwī, *Tafsīr*, vol. 5, p. 3,072.

137. Badawi and Abdel Haleem, *Arabic-English Dictionary of Qur'anic Usage*, pp. 709 f.

138. It is beyond the scope of this chapter to discuss the Qur'anic punishment for *fasād* and terrorism. Chapters 2 and 5 of this book discuss this issue.

139. Badawi and Abdel Haleem, *Arabic-English Dictionary of Qur'anic Usage*, pp. 709 f.

140. Al-Rāzī, *Al-Tafsīr al-Kabīr*, vol. 2, p. 162.

141. Al-Suyūṭī, *Al-Durr al-Manthūr*, vol. 3 p. 70; al-Sayyid Maḥmūd al-Alūsī, *Rūḥ al-Ma'ānī fī Tafsīr al-Qur'ān al-'Aẓīm wa al-Sab' al-Mathānī* (Beirut: Dār Iḥyā' al-Turāth al-'Arabī, n.d.), vol. 16, p. 39; vol. 21, p. 47 f.

142. Frederick Mathewson Denny, "Corruption", in McAuliffe, ed., *Encyclopaedia of the Qur'ān*, vol. 1, p. 439.

143. The five surahs are 2, 7, 11, 26, 28.

144. 'Abd al-Bāqī, *Al-Mu'jam al-Mufahras*, pp. 518 f; Badawi and Abdel Haleem, *Arabic-English Dictionary of Qur'anic Usage*, p. 599.

145. Al-Alūsī, *Rūḥ al-Ma'ānī*, vol. 12, pp. 116, 118. According to the authors of *Al-Mu'jam al-Wasīṭ*, there are two other verbal noun forms of *'athā*.

They are *'uthuwwan* and *'athayānan*. Shawqī Ḍayf et al., *Al-Mu'jam al-Wasīṭ*, p. 584.

146. Abdel Haleem, *Qur'an*, p. 250.

147. Ibid., p. 103.

148. Ibid., p. 98.

149. Mawdūdī, *Towards Understanding*, vol. 3, p. 35.

150. 'Abd al-Fattāḥ Idrīs, "Manhaj al-Islām fī Muḥārabat al-Fasād", [article online]; available from http://www.islamonline.net/servlet/Satellite?pagename=IslamOnline-Arabic-Ask_Scholar/FatwaA/FatwaA&cid=1122528612952; accessed 29 April 2008.

151. Al-Qurṭubī, *Al-Jāmi'*, vol. 2, p. 226.

152. Al-Alūsī, *Rūḥ al-Ma'ānī*, vol. 8, p. 140.

2: Arming for Deterrence in the Qur'an

1. Abdel Haleem, *Qur'an*, p. 114.
2. I sometimes refer to the Islamic Group as the "Group" in the book. According to Habeck, "Based on one verse in the Qur'an [i.e. 8: 60] as well as few ahadith, the jihadis are convinced that creating fear in the hearts of the unbelievers is not only a sound tactic in their war, but one that is supported by Islamic law." Mary R. Habeck, *Knowing the Enemy: Jihadist Ideology and the War on Terror* (New Haven: Yale University Press, 2006), p. 132.
3. Spīndārī, *Al-Irhāb*, p. 34.
4. Liam Martin and M.L.R. Smith, "Every Kingdom Divided Against Itself Will Be Ruined: A Reflection, a Deflection, and a Qualified Reinterpretation of the Global Jihad", *Studies in Conflict and Terrorism*, vol. 34, no. 9, September 2011, pp. 672–695, citation at pp. 674 f.
5. Wilders published a film on the internet under the title "Quran license to Kill". I watched the film before it was later removed from the website after it sparked huge protest from Muslims. The original link was "Quran: License to Kill"; http://www.liveleak.com/view?i=7d9_1206624103; accessed 27 March 2008.
6. "Response to Wilders' Anti-Koran Film: Saudi Blogger Releases Christian Version of 'Fitna'"; available from http://www.spiegel.de/international/world/0,1518,546534,00.html; accessed 9 June 2013.
7. John Tyler, "The Opportunity Geert Wilders Has Waited for", [article online]; available from http://news.bbc.co.uk/1/hi/world/europe/8549155.stm; accessed 9 June 2013; see also Liz Fekete, "The

Muslim Conspiracy Theory and the Oslo Massacre", *Race & Class*, vol. 53, no. 3, January–March 2012, pp. 30–47, citation at p. 36.

8. Nielsen, "The Discourse of 'Terrorism' between Violence, Justice and International Order", p. 17.
9. 'Abd al-Bāqī, *Al-Mu'jam al-Mufahras*, p. 587 f.
10. Badawi and Abdel Haleem, *Arabic-English Dictionary of Qur'anic Usage*, p. 787.
11. Al-Alūsī, *Rūḥ al-Ma'ānī*, vol. 1, p. 281.
12. Abdel Haleem, *Qur'an*, p. 247.
13. Muḥammad Bassām Rushdī al-Zayn, *Al-Mu'jam al-Mufahras li Ma'ānī al-Qur'ān al-'Aẓīm* (Damascus: Dār al-Fikr, second edn., 1417/1996), vol. 2, p. 969.
14. Al-Qurṭubī, *Al-Jāmi'*, vol. 8, p. 35; al-Suyūṭī, *Al-Durr al-Manthūr*, vol. 4, p. 83; Ibn Kathīr, *Tafsīr al-Qur'ān*, vol. 2, p. 322; al-Jaṣṣāṣ, *Aḥkām al-Qur'ān*, vol. 4, pp. 252 f.
15. Abū Dāwūd, *Sunan Abū Dāwūd*, no. 2514, in *Mawsū'at al-Ḥadīth*, ed. Āl al-Shaykh, p. 1,409.
16. Al-Rāzī, *Al-Tafsīr al-Kabīr*, vol. 15, p. 148.
17. Al-Ṭabarī, *Jāmi' al-Bayān*, vol. 10, p. 32.
18. Al-Suyūṭī, *Al-Durr al-Manthūr*, vol. 4, p. 83; Ibn al-'Arabī, *Aḥkām al-Qur'ān*, vol. 2, p. 424; on the usage of *khayl* see for example Majma' al-Lughah al-'Arabiyyah, *Al-Mu'jam al-Wajīz*, p. 217; Shawqī Ḍayf et al., *Al-Mu'jam al-Wasīṭ*, p. 266.
19. Al-Rāzī, *Al-Tafsīr al-Kabīr*, vol. 15, p. 185; al-Qurṭubī, *Al-Jāmi'*, vol. 10, p. 30.
20. Al-Alūsī, *Rūḥ al-Ma'ānī*, vol. 10, p. 23; Nielsen, "The Discourse of 'Terrorism' between Violence, Justice and International Order", p. 17.
21. Quṭb, *Ẓilāl*, vol. 3, p. 1,543; idem, *In the Shade*, vol. 7, p. 185.
22. Sayed Khatab, "Hakimiyyah and Jahiliyyah in the Thought of Sayyid Qutb," *Middle Eastern Studies*, vol. 38, no. 3, July 2002, p. 151; Nettler, "Guidelines for the Islamic Community", p. 189.
23. Quṭb, *Ẓilāl*, vol. 3, p. 1,544; idem, *In the Shade*, vol. 7, p. 186.
24. Bin Jani "Sayyid Quṭb's View of Jihad", p. 362.
25. Chapter 3 of this book deals with this point in detail.
26. Al-Sha'rāwī, *Tafsīr*, vol. 8, p. 4,776.
27. Ibid., vol. 8, p. 4,778.
28. Riḍā, *Tafsīr al-Qur'ān al-Ḥakīm*, vol. 10, pp. 69–70.

29. Mawdūdī, *Towards Understanding*, vol. 3, p. 146 f.; Darwazah, *Al-Tafsīr al-Ḥadīth*, vol. 7, p. 81.

30. See for example Aḥmad Nār, *Al-Qitāl fī al-Islām* (Ḥumṣ: Al-Maktabah al-Islāmiyyah, second edn., 1968), pp. 23–125; Yūsuf al-Qaraḍāwī, *Fiqh al-Jihād: Dirāsah Muqāranah li Aḥkāmihi wa Falsafatihi fī Ḍaw' al-Qur'ān wa al-Sunnah* (Cairo: Maktabat Wahbah, 1430/2009), vol. 1, p. 533.

31. Nār, *Al-Qitāl*, pp. 23–125; Ẓāfir al-Qāsimī, *Al-Jihād wa al-Ḥuqūq al-Dawliyyah al-'Āmmah fī al-Islām* (Beirut: Dār al-'Ilm li al-Malāyīn, 1982), p. 246.

32. Nār, *Al-Qitāl*, pp. 26, 97.

33. Ibid., p. 126.

34. Indeed, El-Awaisi's article is a very clear example of that, see Abd Al-Fattah El-Awaisi, "The Conceptual Approach of the Egyptian Muslim Brothers towards the Palestine Question, 1928–1949", *Journal of Islamic Studies*, vol. 2, no. 2, 1991, pp. 225–244, citation at p. 239.

35. Al-Qaraḍāwī, *Fiqh al-Jihād*, vol. 1, pp. 536, 590 f.

36. Azhar Institute of Fatwa, "Imtilāk al-Ummah lī al-Asliḥah al-Nawawiyyah", [article online]; available from http://www.islamonline.net/servlet/Satellite?pagename=IslamOnline-Arabic-Ask_Scholar/FatwaA/FatwaA&cid=1122528620106; accessed 29 August, 2007.

37. Anne-Marie Delcambre, *Inside Islam* (Milwaukee, Wisc.: Marquette University Press, 2005), p. 18.

38. Muzammil Siddiqi, "How Islam Views Possession of Nukes", [article online]; available from http://www.onislam.net/english/ask-the-scholar/international-relations-and-jihad/relations-during-peace/175739.html, accessed 26 July 2014.

39. See Wael B. Hallaq, "Was the Gate of Ijtihād Closed?", *International Journal of Middle Eastern Studies*, vol. 16, no. 1, March 1984, pp. 3 f.

40. 'Abd al-Mun'im al-Ḥifnī, *Mawsū'at al-Qur'ān al-'Aẓīm* (Cairo: Maktabat Madbūlī, 2004), vol. 2, p. 1,880.

41. Majma' al-Lughah al-'Arabiyyah, *Al-Mu'jam al-Wajīz*, p. 252; Shawqī Ḍayf et al., *Al-Mu'jam al-Wasīṭ*, p. 323; al-Rāghib al-Aṣfahānī, *Mufradāt Alfāẓ*, p. 338 f.

42. Al-Aṣfahānī, *Mufradāt Alfāẓ*, p. 338 f; Muḥammad al-Raḥmānī, *Al-Dīn wa al-Ayduyulūjyā: Jadaliyyat al-Dīnī wa al-Siyāsī fī al-Islām wa fī al-Markisiyyah* (Beirut: Dār al-Ṭalī'ah li al-Ṭibā'ah wa al-Nashr, 2005), p. 53; Quṭb, *Ẓilāl*, vol. 3, p. 1,543; idem, *In the Shade*, vol. 7, p. 185; and see also Muḥammad Muṣṭafā Muḥammad, *Al-Fihris al-Mawḍū'ī li Āyāt al-Qur'ān al-Karīm* (Beirut: Dār al-Jīl, fourth edn., 1409/1989), p. 335.

43. Al-Qaraḍāwī, *Fiqh al-Jihād*, vol. 1, p. 590; The Islamic Fiqh Council,

"Bayān Makkah al-Mukarramah bi-Sha'n al-Irhāb wa Qarārāt al-Dawrah al-Sābi'ah 'Asharah", *The Islamic Fiqh Council Journal*, no. 17, 1425/2004, p. 272.

44. For more details about the principal Qur'anic concepts that are usually translated by the English word "fear", see Scott C. Alexander, "Fear" in McAuliffe, ed., *Encyclopaedia of the Qur'ān*, vol. 2, pp. 194–198; 'Abd al-Bāqī, *Al-Mu'jam al-Mufahras*, p. 325; Badawi and Abdel Haleem, *Arabic-English Dictionary of Qur'anic Usage*, pp. 384 f.

45. See 2:40, 5: 82, 7: 116, 7: 154, 8: 60, 9: 31, 9: 34, 16: 51, 21: 90, 28: 32, 57: 27, 59: 13. See also al-Zayn, *Al-Mu'jam al-Mufahras li Ma'ānī al-Qur'ān*, vol. 1, p. 515.

46. Al-Ṭabarī, *Jāmi' al-Bayān*, vol. 1, p. 251, on 2: 40; vol. 14, p. 118 on 16: 51; vol. 9, p. 20 on 7: 116; vol. 9, p. 71 on 7: 154; vol. 28, p. 47 on 59: 13; and vol. 27, p. 241 on 57: 154; al-Aṣfahānī, *Mufradāt Alfāẓ*, p. 367; Muḥammad ibn Abī Bakr ibn 'Abd al-Qādir al-Rāzī, *Mukhtār al-Ṣaḥḥāḥ*, ed. Maḥmūd Khāṭir (Beirut: Maktabat Lubnān Nashirūn, 1995), p. 109.

47. Badawi and Abdel Haleem, *Arabic-English Dictionary of Qur'anic Usage*, pp. 384 f.

48. Abū Ghaḍḍah, *Al-Irhāb*, p. 132.

49. Schwartz-Barcott, *War, Terror and Peace in the Qur'an and in Islam*, p. 60; Laurence Andrew Dobrot, "The Global War on Terrorism: A Religious War?", [article online]; available from http://www.strategicstudiesinstitute.army.mil/pdffiles/pub822.pdf; accessed 20 July 2013, p. 8; Joseph Grinstein, "Jihad and the Constitution: The First Amendment Implications of Combating Religiously Motivated Terrorism", *The Yale Law Journal*, vol. 105, no. 5, March 1996, pp. 1,347–1,381, citation at p. 1,353.

50. Al-Maṭrūdī, "Al-Irhāb", p. 176.

51. Ibid.

52. Ibid., p. 175.

53. Al-Ṭabarī, *Jāmi' al-Bayān*, vol. 10, p. 30; Ibn Kathīr, *Tafsīr al-Qur'ān*, vol. 2, p. 323.

54. *Jizyah* is a tax paid by non-Muslims in return for their protection by Muslims against outside aggression. See Quṭb, *In the Shade*, vol. 7, p. 188. Nowadays, with military conscription imposed on the nationals of certain countries regardless of whether they are Muslims or non-Muslims, there is no way to claim money from non-Muslims under the name of *jizyah* or under any other name. See Yūsuf al-Qaraḍāwī, *Al-Dīn wa al-Siyāsah: Ta'ṣīl Warad Shubuhāt* (Cairo: Dār al-Shurūq, 1428/2007), p. 184.

55. Al-Rāzī, *Al-Tafsīr al-Kabīr*, vol. 15, p. 149.

56. Riḍā, *Tafsīr al-Qur'ān al-Ḥakīm*, vol. 10, p. 74; Darwazah, *Al-Tafsīr al-Ḥadīth*, vol. 7, p. 81.

57. Al-Sha'rāwī, *Tafsīr*, vol. 8, p. 4,776.

58. Ibid., vol. 8, p. 4,780.

59. Riḍā, *Tafsīr al-Qur'ān al-Ḥakīm*, vol. 10, p. 75. See also Aḥmad 'Alī al-Imām, "Ru'yah Ta'ṣīliyyah li Mafhūm al-Irhāb", p. 31.

60. Muṣṭafā Zayd, *Sūrat al-Anfāl: 'Arḍ wa Tafsīr* (Cairo: Dār al-Fikr al-'Arabī, third edn., 1377/1957), pp. 147 f. and 147 f., footnote (a).

61. *Bughāh* (sing. *bāghī*) are those who attempt to overthrow a legitimate ruler by violence; see Muḥyī al-Dīn ibn Sharaf al-Nawawī, *Al-Majmū': Sharḥ al-Muhadhdhab*, ed. Maḥmūd Maṭrajī (Beirut: Dār al-Fikr, 2000), vol. 20, p. 337. Zayd, *Sūrat al-Anfāl*, pp. 147 f., footnote (a).

62. Quṭb, *Ẓilāl*, vol. 3, p. 1,544; idem, *In the Shade*, vol. 7, p. 186.

63. For detailed lexical differences between *rahbah* and *ir'āb,* see for example Muhammad ibn Ya'qūb al-Fayrūz Ābādī, *Al-Qamūs al-Muḥīṭ* (Beirut: Mu'assasat al-Risālah, n.d.), pp. 115–118.

64. 'Abdullāh Mabrūk al-Najjār, "Taḥdīd al-Mafāhīm fī Majāl al-Ṣirā' al-Basharī: al-Jihād, al-Qitāl, al-'Unf, al-Irhāb", *The Truth about Islam in a Changing World*, Researches and Proceedings. The Fourteenth General Conference of the Supreme Council for Islamic Affairs (Qalyūb: Al-Ahram Commercial Press, 2003), pp. 820 f.

65. Al-Maṭrūdī, "Al-Irhāb", p. 175.

66. Spīndārī, *Al-Irhāb*, p. 34.

67. Ibid.; Sayyid Imām al-Sharīf, "Al-Irhāb min al-Islām wa Man Ankara Daḥliya Faqad Kafara", [article online]; available from http://archive.muslimuzbekistan.com/arb/arnews/2004/03/marsad31032004.html; accessed 8 March 2010.

68. Salwā Muḥammad al-'Awwā, *Al-Jamā'ah al-Islāmiyyah al-Musallaḥah fī Miṣr 1974–2004* (Cairo: Maktabat al-Shurūq al-Dawliyyah, 2006), p. 146; Usāmah Ibrāhīm Ḥāfiẓ et al, *Mubādarat Waqf al-'Unf: Ru'yah Wāqi'iyyah wa Naẓrah Shar'iyyah* (Cairo: Maktabat al-'Ubaykān, 2004), pp. 52 f.; Ḥamdī 'Abd al-Rahmān 'Abd al-'Aẓīm et al, *Taṣlīṭ al-Aḍwā' 'alā mā Waqa' fī al-Jihād min Akhṭā'* (Cairo: Maktabat al-Turāth al-Islāmī, 2002/1422), p. 78; Sayyid Imām al-Sharīf, "Al-Ḥalaqah al-Tāsi'ah min Wathīqat Tarshīd al-'Amal al-Jihādī: Ḍawābiṭ al-Takfīr", [article online]; available from http://www.islamonline.net/servlet/Satellite?c=ArticleA_C&cid=1195032611220&pagename=Zone-Arabic-Daawa%2FDWALayout; accessed 6 December 2007.

69. Al-Najjār, "Taḥdīd al-Mafāhīm fī Majāl al-Ṣirā' al-Basharī", p. 823.

70. Yūsuf al-Qaraḍāwī, *Al-Islām wa al-'Unf: Naẓarāt Ta'ṣīliyyah* (Cairo: Dār al-Shurūq, 2005), p. 49.

71. Badawi and Abdel Haleem, *Arabic-English Dictionary of Qur'anic Usage*, p. 606; ʿAbd al-Bāqī, *Al-Muʿjam al-Mufahras*, pp. 449 f.

72. Al-Ṭabarī, *Jāmiʿ al-Bayān*, vol. 10, pp. 29, 32.

73. Darwazah, *Al-Tafsīr al-Ḥadīth*, vol. 7, p. 78.

74. Al-Rāzī, *Al-Tafsīr al-Kabīr*, vol. 15, p. 115.

75. Riḍā, *Tafsīr al-Qur'ān al-Ḥakīm*, vol. 10, p. 74.

76. Al-Shaʿrāwī, *Tafsīr*, vol. 8, p. 4,780.

77. Ibn al-ʿArabī, *Aḥkām al-Qur'ān*, vol. 2, p. 426.

78. Al-Ṭabarī, *Jāmiʿ al-Bayān*, vol. 10, p. 33.

79. Al-Shaʿrāwī, *Tafsīr*, vol. 8, p. 4,781; Quṭb, *Ẓilāl*, vol. 3, p. 1,544; idem, *In the Shade*, vol. 7, p. 186; Riḍā, *Tafsīr al-Qur'ān al-Ḥakīm*, vol. 10, pp. 75 f.

80. Al-Shaʿrāwī, *Tafsīr*, vol. 8, p. 4,781.

81. Quṭb, *Ẓilāl*, vol. 3, p. 1,544; idem, *In the Shade*, vol. 7, p. 186.

82. Riḍā, *Tafsīr al-Qur'ān al-Ḥakīm*, vol. 10, p. 76.

3: Jihad versus Terrorism in the Qur'an

1. To understand the importance of jihad in the Qur'an, see ʿĀrif Khalīl Abū ʿĪd, *Al-ʿAlāqāt al-Dawliyyah fī al-Fiqh al-Islāmī* (Amman: Dār al-Nafā'is, 1427/2007), pp. 114–118.

2. Al-Aṣfahānī, *Mufradāt Alfāẓ*, p. 208; Jamāl al-Dīn Muḥammad ibn Makram ibn Manẓūr, *Lisān al-ʿArab* (Beirut: Dār Ṣādir, sixth edn., 1417/1997), vol. 3, p. 133.

3. Badawi and Abdel Haleem, *Arabic-English Dictionary of Qur'anic Usage*, pp. 177 f.; ʿAbd al-Bāqī, *Al-Muʿjam al-Mufahras*, pp. 182 f; Reuven Firestone, "Jihad", in Gabriel Palmer-Fernandez, ed., *Encyclopedia of Religion and War* (New York: Routledge, 2004), p. 367.

4. Muḥammad Kheir Haykal, *Al-Jihād wa al-Qitāl fī al-Siyāsah al-Sharʿiyyah* (Beirut: Dār al-Bayāriq, third edn., 1417/1996), vol. 1, pp. 38 f.

5. Haykal, *Al-Jihād*, vol. 1, p. 38; Muḥammad ibn ʿAlī ibn Muḥammad al-Shawkānī, *Nayl al-Awṭār: Sharḥ Muntaqā al-Akhbār min Aḥādīth Sayyid al-Akhyār* (Cairo: Sharikat Maktabat wa Maṭbaʿat Muṣṭafā al-Bābī al-Ḥalābī wa Awlāduh, n.d.), vol. 7, p. 236.

6. Yūsuf ʿAbdullāh al-Qaraḍāwī, "Mafhūm al-Jihād: Ta'ṣīl wa Tarshīd", [article online]; available from http://www.islamonline.net/servlet/

Satellite?pagename=IslamOnline-Arabic-Ask_Scholar/FatwaA/FatwaA&cid=1122528621352; accessed 6 April 2009.

7. Gary R. Bunt, *Islam in the Digital Age: E-jihad, Online Fatwas and Cyber Islamic Environments* (London: Pluto Press, 2003), pp. 26 f; idem, *iMuslims: Rewiring the House of Islam* (Chapel Hill: University of North Carolina Press, 2009), p. 183.

8. ʿAlī As-Sayyid Ḥasan al-Ḥalawānī, "Some Aspects of Semantic Change and Religious Terminology" (MA diss., Department of English, Faculty of Languages, Minya University, Egypt, 2003), pp. 64–68, 85, 161.

9. Muḥammad Amīn ibn ʿUmar ibn ʿĀbidīn, *Ḥāshiyat Radd al-Muḥtār ʿalā al-Durr al-Mukhtār: Sharḥ Tanwīr al-Abṣār* (Beirut: Dār al-Fikr, 1421/2000), vol. 4, p. 121. For a comprehensive citation of and commentary on the four major Sunni juristic definitions of jihad see Abdulrahman Muhammad Alsumaih, "The Sunni Concept of Jihad in Classical Fiqh and Modern Islamic Thought" (PhD thesis, Department of Politics, University of Newcastle Upon Tyne, 1998), p. 14.

10. Haykal, *Al-Jihād*, vol. 1, p. 40; Rudolph Peters, *Jihad in Classical and Modern Islam: A Reader* (Princeton: Markus Wiener Publishers, second edn., 2005), p. 1.

11. Albert B. Randall, *Holy Scriptures as Justifications for War: Fundamentalist Interpretations of the Torah, the New Testament, and the Qur'an* (Lewiston, NY: Edwin Mellen Press, 2007), p. 2.

12. Carol Elzain, "Modern Islamic Terrorism, Jihad and the Perceptions of Melbourne's Muslim Leaders" (MA diss., School of Global Studies, Social Science and Planning, RMIT University, 2008), pp. 52–63.

13. Ṣubḥī ʿAbd al-Ra'ūf ʿAṣar, *Al-Muʿjam al-Mawḍūʿī li Āyāt al-Qur'ān al-Karīm* (Cairo: Dār al-Faḍīlah li al-Nashr wa al-Tawzīʿ wa al-Taṣdīr, 1990), pp. 217–230; Muḥammad, *Al-Fihris al-Mawḍūʿī*, pp. 223–340.

14. Brig. S.K. Malik, *The Quranic Concept of War* (Lahore: Wajidalis, 1979), pp. 22, 142.

15. Al-Alūsī, *Rūḥ al-Maʿānī*, vol. 20, p. 138; vol. 21, p. 14.

16. ʿAlī ibn al-Sayyid ʿAbd al-Raḥmān al-Hāshimī, "Al-Jihād: Maqāṣiduh wa Ḍawābiṭuh", in *The Truth about Islam in a Changing World*, Researches and Proceedings. The Fourteenth General Conference of the Supreme Council for Islamic Affairs (Cairo: Maṭābiʿ al-Ahrām al-Tujāriyyah, 1424/2003), p. 741.

17. Robert D. Crane, "Hirabah versus Jihad", [article online]; available from http://www.theamericanmuslim.org/tam.php/features/articles/terrorism_hirabah_versus_jihad/; accessed 11 July 2013.

18. Khaled Abou El Fadl, "Islam and Violence: Our Forgotten Legacy", in John J. Donohue and John L. Esposito, eds., *Islam in Transition: Muslim Perspectives* (Oxford: Oxford University Press, second edn., 2007), p. 463.

19. David Cook, *Understanding Jihad* (Berkeley: University of California Press, 2005), pp. 43, 218.

20. Riḍā, *Tafsīr al-Qur'ān al-Ḥakīm*, vol. 2, p. 254; al-Daqs, *Āyāt al-Jihād fī al-Qur'ān al-Karīm*, p. 13; Reuven Firestone, *Jihād: The Origin of Holy War in Islam* (Oxford: Oxford University Press, 1999), p. 74.

21. Mustansir Mir, "Jihād in Islam", in Hadia Dajani-Shakeel and Ronald A. Messier, eds., *The Jihād and Its Times* (Ann Arbor: Centre for Near Eastern and North African Studies, The University of Michigan, 1991), p. 114.

22. Muhammad Abdel Haleem, *Understanding the Qur'an: Themes and Style* (London: I.B. Tauris, 1999), p. 62.

23. 'Abd al-Ṣabūr Marzūq, *Mu'jam al-A'lām wa al-Mawḍū'āt fī al-Qur'ān al-Karīm* (Cairo: Dār al-Shurūq, 1415/1995), pp. 485–498.

24. For these few examples and others, see 'Abd al-Bāqī, *Al-Mu'jam al-Mufahras*, pp. 341–343.

25. Badawi and Abdel Haleem, *Arabic-English Dictionary of Qur'anic Usage*, pp. 736 f.

26. Alsumaih, "The Sunni Concept of Jihad", p. 15.

27. 'Abd al-'Aẓīm Badawī al-Khalafī, "Al-Ḥarb wa al-Salām fī al-Islām fī Ḍaw' Sūrat Muḥammad 'Alayhi al-Salām" (MA diss., Department of Da'wah and Islamic Culture, Faculty of Uṣūl al-Dīn, al-Azhar University, Cairo, 1415/1994), p. 7.

28. Muḥammad 'Azzah Darwazah, *Al-Jihād fī Sabīl Allāh fī al-Qur'ān wa al-Ḥadīth* (Beirut: Dār al-Nāshir li al-Ṭibā'ah wa al-Nashr wa al-Tawzī' wa al-I'lān, second edn., 1410/1990), pp. 5–7; L. Ali Khan, *A Theory of International Terrorism: Understanding Islamic Militancy*, Developments in International Law (Leiden: Martinus Nijhoff Publishers and VSP, 2006), vol. 56, pp. 186 f.

29. Firestone, "Jihad", *Encyclopedia of Religion*, p. 367; Ibn Manẓūr, *Lisān*, vol. 1, pp. 302 f.

30. Reuven Firestone, "Jihād", in Rippin, ed., *Blackwell Companion to the Qur'ān*, p. 312.

31. For a confirmation of this view, see the term *ḥarb* successively interpreted as "fighting" in al-Qurṭubī, *Al-Jāmi'*, vol. 6, p. 240; al-Rāzī, *Al-Tafsīr al-Kabīr*, vol. 15, p. 146; and al-Alūsī, *Rūḥ al-Ma'ānī*, vol. 26,

p. 41. On the Qur'anic usage of *ḥarb*, see 'Abd al-Bāqī, *Al-Mu'jam al-Mufahras*, p. 196; and Aḥmad Maḥmūd Karīmah, *Al-Jihād fī al-Islām: Dirāsah Fiqhiyyah Muqāranah* (Cairo: Maṭābi' al-Dār al-Handasiyyah, 1424/2003), p. 115.

32. Muḥammad al-Ḥabīb ibn al-Khūjah, *Al-Jihād fī al-Islām* (Tunis: Al-Dār al-Tūnisiyyah li al-Nashr, 1386/1968), p. 30.

33. Riḍā, *Tafsīr al-Qur'ān al-Ḥakīm*, vol. 10, p. 56; al-Sha'rāwī, *Tafsīr*, vol. 8, pp. 4,768 f.

34. Reuven Firestone, "Holy War Idea in the Biblical Tradition," in Palmer-Fernandez, ed., *Encyclopedia of Religion and War* (New York: Routledge, 2004), p. 282; Jamal Badawi, "Muslim/Non-Muslim Relations: Reflections on Some Qur'anic Texts", *Scientific Review of the European Council for Fatwa and Research*, no. 6, January 2005, p. 271.

35. James Turner Johnson, *The Holy War Idea in Western and Islamic Traditions* (University Park, Pa.: Pennsylvania State University Press, 1997), p. 25.

36. Abou El Fadl, *The Great Theft*, p. 226; A. Rashied Omar, "Conflict and Violence", in Richard C. Martin, ed., *Encyclopedia of Islam and the Muslim World* (New York: Macmillan Preference USA, 2004), vol. 1, p. 158.

37. The term rather has a Christian origin, beginning in Europe in the eleventh century during the Crusades. John L. Esposito and Dalia Mogahed, *Who Speaks for Islam?: What a Billion Muslims Really Think* (New York: Gallup Press, 2007), p. 75.

38. See for example Hector Avalos, *Fighting Words: The Origins of Religious Violence* (Amherst, N.Y.: Prometheus Books, 2005), pp. 283–299; D.R. Goyal, "International Terrorism: Challenge and Response", in Mahavir Singh, ed., *International Terrorism and Religious Extremism: Challenges to Central and South Asia* (New Delhi: Published for Maulana Abul Kalam Azad Institute of Asian Studies, Kolkata [by] Anamika Publishers & Distributors, 2004), p. 4.; Jerald F. Dirks, *Understanding Islam: A Guide for the Judaeo-Christian Reader* (Beltsville, Maryland: Amana Publications, 1424/2003), p. 321; Hassan Hathout, *Reading the Muslim Mind* (Plainfield, Ind.: American Trust Publications, 2005), pp. 107 f.; Noor Mohammad, "The Doctrine of Jihad: An Introduction", *Journal of Law and Religion*, vol. 3, no. 2, 1985, pp. 381–397, citation at p. 381.

39. Bernard Lewis, *The Political Language of Islam* (Chicago: The University of Chicago Press, 1988), pp. 71–72; see also Talal Asad, *On Suicide Bombing* (New York: Columbia University Press, 2007), p. 11.

40. Asma Barlas, "Jihad, Holy War, and Terrorism", pp. 46 f.

41. Rudolph Peters, *Islam and Colonialism: The Doctrine of Jihad in Modern History* (The Hague: Mouton, 1979), p. 4.

42. For a special reference as to why the term "Islamist" should be used and how it differs from other terms, especially the term "Islamic", see Jeremy D. Kowalski, "The Geographical and Spatial Imaginings of Islamist Extremism/Terrorism" (MA diss., University of Waterloo, Ontario, Canada, 2005), pp. 4 f. See also Mehdi Mozaffari, "What is Islamism? History and Definition of a Concept", *Totalitarian Movements and Political Religions*, vol. 8, no. 1, March 2007, pp. 17–33.

43. Bonney, *Jihād*, p. 28.

44. Firestone is a clear example of one of these scholars; see his *Jihād*, pp. 47 f.

45. Al-Qurṭubī, *Al-Jāmi'*, vol. 2, p. 247. See also Khan, *A Theory of International Terrorism*, pp. 172–177; Eric Bordenkircher, "An Analysis of Jihād in the Context of the Islamic Resistance Movement of Palestine" (MA diss., Faculty of Graduate Studies and Research, Institute of Islamic Studies, McGill University, Montreal, 2001), pp. 11 f.

46. The order of verses here follows al-Qurṭubī, see his *Al-Jāmi'*, vol. 2, p. 247.

47. Mohammad Hashim Kamali, "Issues in the Understanding of *Jihād* and *Ijtihād*", *Islamic Studies*, vol. 41, no. 4, Winter 1423/2002, pp. 617–634, citation at pp. 619 f.

48. Al-Daqs presents a distinguished survey of the most authentic classical narrations to reach this important conclusion, see his *Āyāt al-Jihād fī al-Qur'ān*, pp. 185–208. In peaceful jihad, a Muslim strives in the cause of Allah without resorting to violence, see Khan, *A Theory of International Terrorism*, p. 178.

49. Darwazah, *Al-Jihād fī Sabīl Allāh*, pp. 55 f.

50. Ibid., p. 56.

51. Quṭb, *Ẓilāl*, vol. 5, pp. 3,166 f.

52. Al-Ṭabarī, *Jāmi' al-Bayān*, vol. 25, p. 38.

53. For a modern study that takes much interest in explaining different stages of jihad with reference to the Qur'an, see Firestone, *Jihād*, pp. 51–65.

54. Abdullahi Ahmed An-Na'im, "Why Should Muslims Abandon Jihad? Human Rights and the Future of International Law", *Third World Quarterly*, vol. 27, no. 5, 2006, pp. 785–797, citation at p. 792.

55. Ibn al-'Arabī, *Aḥkām al-Qur'ān*, vol. 1, p. 456.

56. David Cook, *Martyrdom in Islam*, p. 14.

57. Abū al-Ḥasan ʿAlī ibn Aḥmad al-Nīsābūrī, *Asbāb al-Nuzūl*, ed. Sharīf Muḥammad ʿAbd al-Raḥmān (N.p.: Dār al-Taqwā, 2005), p. 195; ʿAbd al-Raḥmān ibn Abī Bakr al-Suyūṭī, *Lubāb al-Nuqūl fi Asbāb al-Nuzūl*, ed. Muḥammad Tāmir (N.p.: Dār al-Taqwā, 2004), p. 154.

58. Al-Ṭabarī, *Jāmiʿ al-Bayān*, vol. 17, p. 172; al-Alūsī, *Rūḥ al-Maʿānī*, vol. 17, p. 162; al-Daqs, *Āyāt al-Jihād fi al-Qur'ān*, p. 73; Silverman, "Just War, Jihad, and Terrorism", p. 78. This last article has been republished in David Cook, ed., *Jihad and Martyrdom: Critical Concepts in Islamic Studies* (London: Routledge, 2010), vol. 4, p. 7.

59. Al-Shaʿrāwī, *Tafsīr*, vol. 16, p. 9,836.

60. Al-Ṭabarī, *Jāmiʿ al-Bayān*, vol. 17, 172; al-Qurṭubī, *Al-Jāmiʿ*, vol. 12, p. 68.

61. Firestone, *Jihād*, pp. 51–56; idem, "Disparity and Resolution in the Quranic Teachings on War: A Reevaluation of a Traditional Problem", *Journal of Near Eastern Studies*, vol. 56, no. 1, January 1997, pp. 4–17.

62. Discussion of all the numerous verses that speak about each stage of fighting in the Qur'an is extremely difficult in a limited study such as this. The verses considered are therefore fairly representative of each stage. For a similar discussion of this point, see Silverman, "Just War, Jihad, and Terrorism", p. 81.

63. Al-Ṭabarī, *Jāmiʿ al-Bayān*, vol. 2, p. 189; Ibn Kathīr, *Tafsīr al-Qur'ān*, vol. 1, p. 227; David Dakake, "The Myth of a Militant Islam", in Aftab Ahmad Malik, ed., *The State We Are in: Identity, Terror and the Law of Jihad* (Bristol: Amal Press, 2006), p. 73; al-Nīsābūrī, *Asbāb al-Nuzūl*, p. 31; al-Suyūṭī, *Lubāb al-Nuqūl*, pp. 33 f.

64. See for example al-Ṭabarī, *Jāmiʿ al-Bayān*, vol. 2, p. 190; al-Rāzī, *Al-Tafsīr al-Kabīr*, vol. 5; p. 110; al-Alūsī, *Rūḥ al-Maʿānī*, vol. 2, p. 74; Quṭb, *Ẓilāl*, vol. 1, p. 188; idem, *In the Shade*, vol. 1, p. 210.

65. Ibn Kathīr, *Tafsīr al-Qur'ān*, vol. 1, p. 227.

66. Riḍā, *Tafsīr al-Qur'ān al-Ḥakīm*, vol. 2, pp. 208 f.

67. Firestone, *Jihād*, p. 77.

68. Wahbah al-Zuḥaylī, *Āthār al-Ḥarb fi al-Fiqh al-Islāmī: Dirāsah Muqāranah* (Damascus: Dār al-Fikr, third edn., 1419/1998), p. 91.

69. Haykal, *Al-Jihād*, vol. 1, pp. 611–613.

70. Aḥmad Ghunaym, *Al-Jihād al-Islāmī: Dirāsah ʿIlmiyyah fi Nuṣūṣ al-Qur'ān wa Ṣiḥāḥ al-Ḥadīth wa Wathā'iq al-Tārīkh* (Cairo: Dār al-Ḥamāmī li al-Ṭibāʿah, 1394/1975), p. 20.

71. According to Adams, *kufr* destabilizes the whole society because it entails the denial of the existence of God. This, in turn, leads to disorder and corruption in society. Charles J. Adams, "Kufr" in Esposito, ed., *Oxford Encyclopedia of the Modern Islamic World*, vol. 2, pp. 439 f.

72. Abdel Haleem, *Qur'an*, pp. 21 f.

73. Al-Ṭabarī, *Jāmiʿ al-Bayān*, vol. 2, pp. 194 f; al-Qurṭubī, *Al-Jāmiʿ*, vol. 2, p. 353; Ibn al-ʿArabī, *Aḥkām al-Qur'ān*, vol. 1, p. 155; al-Suyūṭī, *Al-Durr al-Manthūr*, vol. 1, p. 495; al-Jaṣṣāṣ, *Aḥkām al-Qur'ān*, vol. 1, pp. 324 f; al-Rāzī, *Al-Tafsīr al-Kabīr*, vol. 5, p. 113; al-Alūsī, *Rūḥ al-Maʿānī*, vol. 2, p. 76.

74. Ibn Kathīr, *Tafsīr al-Qur'ān*, vol. 1, p. 288.

75. S. Abdullah Schleifer, "Jihad: Modernist Apologists, Modern Apologetics", *The Islamic Quarterly*, vol. 28, no. 1, First Quarter 1984, pp. 25–46, citations at pp. 32, 45, n. 45.

76. Al-Ṭabarī, *Jāmiʿ al-Bayān*, vol. 2, p. 194.

77. Al-Qurṭubī, *Al-Jāmiʿ*, vol. 2, p. 353.

78. For an elaboration on the meanings of *naskh*, its types and various polemical issues related to it, see Ibn Manẓūr, *Lisān*, vol. 2, p 615; Abī Manṣūr ʿAbd al-Qāhir ibn Ṭāhir ibn Muḥammad al-Baghdādī, *Al-Nāsikh wa al-Mansūkh*, ed. Ḥilmī Kāmil Asʿad ʿAbd al-Hādī (Amman: Dār al-ʿAdawī, n.d.), pp. 39–267; Saeed, *Interpreting the Qur'ān*, pp. 77–89, 168–170; Abou El Fadl, *The Great Theft*, pp. 240 f.; Muṣṭafā Zayd, *Al-Naskh fī al-Qur'ān al-Karīm: Dirāsah Tashriʿiyyah Tārīkhiyyah Naqdiyyah* (Cairo: Dār al-Fikr al-ʿArabī, 1383/1963), vol. 2, pp. 503–547; John Burton, *The Collection of the Qur'ān* (Cambridge: Cambridge University Press, 1977), pp. 46–104.

79. McAuliffe, "The Tasks and Traditions of Interpretation", p. 187.

80. Bin Jani, "Sayyid Qutb's View of Jihād", p. 120. Al-Qaraḍāwī mentions several narratives stating that, according to some scholars, 9: 5 has abrogated 140 verses, see his *Fiqh al-Jihād*, vol. 1, p. 310.

81. Al-Qaraḍāwī, *Fiqh al-Jihād*, vol. 1, pp. 284–305.

82. Bin Jani, "Sayyid Qutb's View of Jihād", pp. 120 f.

83. International Union for Muslim Scholars, *Al-Mīthāq al-Islāmī* (N.p.: International Union for Muslim Scholars, n.d.), p. 55.

84. Riḍā, *Tafsīr al-Qur'ān al-Ḥakīm*, vol. 2, p. 209.

85. For a well-structured presentation of ʿAbduh's modernist views with special reference to this particular point, see Bordenkircher, "An Analysis of Jihād", pp. 34–40.

86. Ibid., p. 210. 87. Ibid., p. 199. 88. Ibid., p. 200.

89. Al-Alūsī, *Rūḥ al-Ma'ānī*, vol. 10, pp. 49–51.

90. Al-Sha'rāwī, *Tafsīr*, vol. 2, pp. 824–828.

91. Ibid., vol. 2, pp. 825 f.; also see his, *Al-Jihād fī al-Islām*, rev. and ed. Markaz al-Turāth li Khidmat al-Kitāb wa al-Sunnah (Cairo: Maktabat al-Turāth al-Islāmī, 1419/1998), pp. 157 f., 180–198.

92. Al-Sha'rāwī, *Tafsīr*, vol. 8, pp. 4,874–4,885, 5,092 f.

93. Darwazah, *Al-Tafsīr al-Ḥadīth*, vol. 9, p. 352. idem, *Al-Jihād fī Sabīl Allāh*, pp. 67–77; 'Abd al-'Azīz Zahrān, *Al-Silm wa al-Ḥarb fī al-Islām*, Kutub Islāmiyyah, no. 164 (Cairo: Supreme Council for Islamic Affairs, 1394/1974), p. 29.

94. Bin Jani, "Sayyid Qutb's View of Jihād", p. 269; see also Keith M. Trivasse, "Modern Perspectives on Jihad: Authoritative or Authoritarian?" (MA diss., University of Lancaster, 2004), pp. 7–10.

95. Mawdūdī, *Towards Understanding*, vol. 1, p. 152; idem, *Sharī'at al-Islām fī al-Jihād wa al-'Alāqāt al-Dawliyyah*, trans. Samīr 'Abd al-Ḥamīd Ibrāhīm, rev. 'Abd al-Ḥalīm 'Uways and Ibrāhīm Yūnus (Cairo: Dār al-Ṣaḥwah li al-Nashr, 1406/1985), p. 77

96. Mawdūdī, *Sharī'at al-Islām*, p. 85.

97. Abul A'lā Mawdūdī, *Al-Jihād fī Sabīl Allāh* (Beirut: Dār al-Fikr, n.d.), pp. 38 f.

98. Mawdūdī, *Al-Jihād*, pp. 38 f. See also Abul A'lā Mawdūdī, Ḥasan al-Bannā, and Sayyid Quṭb, *Thalāth Rasā'il fī al-Jihād* (Amman: Dār 'Ammār li al-Nashr, 1992), pp. 52–54.

99. According to al-Zuḥaylī, this dichotomous classification is postulated by the majority of classical Muslim jurists. Only the Shāfi'īs introduce a third classification: *dār al-ṣulḥ* or *dār al-'ahd* (territory of treaty), where non-Muslims offer to sign a peaceful agreement with Muslims in return for paying land tax. See al-Zuḥaylī, *Āthār al-Ḥarb*, pp. 168, 175. For al-Shāfi'ī's definition of *dār al-ṣulḥ*, see Muḥammad ibn Idrīs al-Shāfi'ī, *Al-Umm*, ed. Maḥmūd Maṭrajī (Beirut: Dār al-Kutub al-'Ilmiyyah, 1413/1993), vol. 4, p. 258.

100. According to Abou El Fadl, the only *dār* (territory, abode) the Qur'an speaks of is "the abode of the Hereafter and the abode of the earthly life, with the former described as clearly superior to the latter", Abou El Fadl, *The Great Theft*, p. 227. See also 29: 64.

101. According to Haykal, this hadith is: "The house of Islam constitutes the source of inviolability for its residents, and the house of polytheism constitutes the source of violability for its residents." He

states this "hadith" is only cited by al-Māwardī, and is not found in the authentic collections of Hadith, see Haykal, *Al-Jihād*, vol. 1, p. 660.

102. I.e. the Qur'an and the Sunnah. Al-Zuḥaylī stresses this view, arguing that there is no trace of this classical division in either the Qur'an or the Sunnah. See al-Zuḥaylī, *Āthār al-Ḥarb*, p. 193.

103. Majid Khadduri, trans., *The Islamic Law of Nations: Shaybānī's Siyar* (Baltimore, MD.: Johns Hopkins Press, 1966), p. 194.

104. Mawdūdī, *Sharī'at al-Islām*, p. 189. According to Mawdūdī, these people are known as *al-mu'āhadūn*. They are the ones who accepted the conditions set by Muslims, and submit themselves to obey them before or during fighting. See ibid., p. 213.

105. Bin Jani, "Sayyid Qutb's View of Jihād", p. 268. 106. Ibid., 294.

107. To limit the discussion, a special focus will be given to highlighting Quṭb's views concerning Muslim–non-Muslim relations, because his other jihad-related views go beyond the scope of this study, in which he is treated as one among a number of other exegetes.

108. It seems that Quṭb is not the only one who is influenced by the views of these two scholars. 'Umar 'Abd al-Raḥmān, an Azhar graduate whose views on jihad are very controversial and who is serving a life sentence in a US prison for his role in the first attack on the World Trade Center in New York in 1993, has also been inspired by both Ibn al-Qayyim and Mawdūdī. 'Abd al-Raḥmān's bulky PhD thesis (of 1,099 pages), with which he graduated in 1972, contains lengthy quotations from both Ibn al-Qayyim's *Zād al-Ma'ād* and the works of Mawdūdī. See 'Umar 'Abd al-Raḥmān, "Mawqif al-Qur'ān min Khuṣūmih Kamā Tuṣawwiruhu Sūrat al-Tawbah" (PhD thesis, Department of Qur'ān Interpretation, Faculty of Uṣūl al-Dīn, al-Azhar University, Cairo, 1972), pp. 838–840, 854–869. See also Gilles Kepel, *The Roots of Radical Islam*, trans. Jon Rothschild (London: Saqi, 2005), p. 11; Fawaz A. Gerges, *The Far Enemy: Why Jihad Went Global* (Cambridge: Cambridge University Press, 2005), p. 4.

109. Bin Jani, "Sayyid Qutb's View of Jihād", pp. 261 f.; Bonney, *Jihād*, p. 218.

110. S. Abdullah Schleifer, "Jihad: Sacred Struggle in Islam (V)", *Islamic Quarterly*, vol. 27, no. 3, Third Quarter 1984, pp. 135–149, citation at p. 143; Amritha Venkatraman, "Religious Basis for Islamic Terrorism: the Quran and Its Interpretation", *Studies in Conflict and Terrorism*, vol. 30, 2007, pp. 229–248, citation at p. 241.

111. Adnan A. Musallam, *From Secularism to Jihad: Sayyid Qutb and the Foundations of Radical Islamism* (Westport, Conn.: Praeger, 2005), pp. 151 f.

112. Muḥammad ibn Abī Bakr Ibn Qayyim al-Jawziyyah, *Zād al-Maʿād fī Hady Khayr al-ʿIbād*, rev. & eds. Shuʿayb al-Arnaʾūṭ and ʿAbd al-Qādir al-Arnaʾūṭ (Beirut: Muʾassasat al-Risālah, fifteen edn., 1407/1987), vol. 3, pp. 158–161.

113. For a detailed description of these stages and methods as outlined by Ibn al-Qayyim, see Ibid. See also Musallam, *From Secularism to Jihad*, pp. 181 f.

114. Quṭb, *Ẓilāl*, vol. 3, pp. 1,578–1,583; idem, *In the Shade*, vol. 8, pp. 20–25; idem, *Maʿālim fī al-Ṭarīq* (Beirut: The Holy Koran Publishing House, n.d.), p. 55–57; idem, *Milestones* (New Delhi: Islamic Book Service, n.d.), pp. 53–57.

115. Quṭb, *Ẓilāl*, vol. 3, p. 1,580; idem, *In the Shade*, vol. 8, pp. 24 f.

116. Ibn al-Qayyim, *Zād al-Maʿād*, vol. 3, pp. 159 f.; idem, *Kitāb al-Jihād fī Sabīlillāh* (Cairo: Markaz al-Kitāb li al-Nashr, 1991), pp. 56–58. See also Quṭb, *Fī Ẓilāl*, vol. 3, pp. 1,582 f.; idem, *In the Shade*, vol. 8, pp. 21 f.; Bin Jani, "Sayyid Qutb's View of Jihād", p. 264.

117. Bin Jani, "Sayyid Qutb's View of Jihād", p. 261.

118. According to Perry and Negrin, "Contemporary jihadist ideologues refer to Ibn Taymiyyah to legitimate their goals of overthrowing political leaders who do not govern in accordance with Islamic law; of waging war against foreign unbelievers who threaten the Muslim community." See Marvin Perry and Howard E. Negrin, "A Medieval Theorist of Jihad", in idem, eds., *The Theory and Practice of Islamic Terrorism: An Anthology* (New York: Palgrave Macmillan, 2008), p. 22.

119. Aḥmad ibn ʿAbd al-Ḥalīm ibn Taymiyyah, *Fiqh al-Jihād li Shaykh al-Islām al-Imām Ibn Taymiyyah*, ed. Zuhayr Shafīq al-Kabbī (Beirut: Dār al-Fikr al-ʿArabī li al-Ṭibāʿah wa al-Nashr, 1412/1992), p. 71.

120. Ibn Taymiyyah, *Fiqh al-Jihād*, p. 74.

121. Schleifer supports the view that Mawdūdī was influenced by Ibn Taymiyyah. See S. Abdullah Schleifer, "Jihad: Sacred Struggle in Islam (IV)", *The Islamic Quarterly*, vol. 28, no. 2, Second Quarter, 1983, pp. 87–102, citation at p. 93. Graham E. Fuller is one of the few Western authors who also refers to this fact, see his *The Future of Political Islam* (New York: Palgrave Macmillan, 2003), p. 52.

122. Quṭb, *Ẓilāl*, vol. 3, pp. 1,580–1,582; idem, *In the Shade*, vol. 8, pp. 24 f.

123. Quṭb, *Milestones*, p. 76.

124. Quṭb, *Ẓilāl*, vol. 3, pp. 1,580 f.; idem, *In the Shade*, vol. 8, p. 25.

125. Bin Jani, "Sayyid Qutb's View of Jihād", p. 305.

126. Quṭb, *Ẓilāl*, vol. 3, pp. 1,546 f.; idem, *In the Shade*, vol. 7, pp. 190 f.

127. Bin Jani, "Sayyid Qutb's View of Jihād", p. 305. Non-aggressive verses in Bin Jani's terminology refer to the verses pertaining to patience, co-existence and tolerance earlier discussed in this chapter.

128. Quṭb, *Milestones*, pp. 61 f.

129. Quṭb, *Ẓilāl*, vol. 3 p. 1,544; idem, *In the Shade*, vol. 7, p. 186.

130. Quṭb, *Ẓilāl*, vol. 3, pp. 1,588 f.; idem, *In the Shade*, vol. 8, p. 41. See also Bin Jani, "Sayyid Qutb's View of Jihād", p. 300.

131. Quṭb, *Ẓilāl*, vol. 3, pp. 1,589–1592; idem, *In the Shade*, vol. 8, pp. 41–46.

132. Bin Jani, "Sayyid Qutb's View of Jihād", p. 303.

133. Ibid., p. 301.

134. That is, "Sheikh" for Riḍā and "Mr" for Darwazah.

135. Quṭb, *Ẓilāl*, vol. 3, pp. 1,589–1,592; idem, *In the Shade*, vol. 8, pp. 41–46.

136. François Burgat, *Islamism in the Shadow of al-Qaeda,* trans. Patrick Hutchinson (Austin: University of Texas Press, 2008), p. 104; Bonney, *Jihād*, p. 219; Jalil Roshandel and Sharon Chadha, *Jihad and International Security* (New York: Palgrave Macmillan, 2006), p. 63; Nettler, "Guidelines for the Islamic Community", p. 189.

137. Bin Jani, "Sayyid Qutb's View of Jihād", p. 346.

138. Gilles Kepel, *Beyond Terror and Martyrdom: The Future of the Middle East*, trans. Pascale Ghazaleh (Cambridge, Mass: The Belknap Press of Harvard University Press, 2008), p. 161.

139. Yūsuf al-Qaraḍāwī, "Muzakkirāt al-Qaraḍāwī: Waqfah maʿa Sayyid Quṭb", [article online]; available from http://www.almotamar.net/news/10244.htm; accessed 5 July 2013. See also Musallam, *From Secularism to Jihad*, pp. 178 f., 230, nn. 33–34.

140. Yūsuf al-Qaraḍāwī, "Al-Qaraḍāwī: Kalimah Akhīrah ḥawla Sayyid Quṭb", [article online]; available from http://www.islamonline.net/servlet/Satellite?c=ArticleA_C&pagename=Zone-Arabic-Shariah%2FSRALayout&cid=1173694966860; accessed 3 June 2009. See also Ana Belén Soage, "Ḥasan al-Bannā and Sayyid Quṭb: Continuity or Rupture?", *The Muslim World*, vol. 99, no. 2, April 2009, pp. 294-311, citation at p. 295.

141. For details of the dramatic historical events Egypt witnessed at that time, see for example Jeffrey T. Kenney, *Muslim Rebels: Kharijites and the Politics of Extremism in Egypt* (Oxford: Oxford University Press, 2006), pp. 117–145; Omar Ashour, *The De-Radicalization of Jihadists: Transforming Armed Islamist Movements* (London; New York: Routledge, 2009), pp. 40–44.

4: The Modern Debate on Offensive Jihad

1. According to Abou El Fadl, "No aspect of Islamic religion is in the public eye and all over the media on a daily basis as much as the issue of jihad and terrorism." See his *The Great Theft*, p. 220.

2. According to one expert, "It is significant that terrorism has come to acquire extraordinary prominence in global discourse only after September 11, 2001," see D.R. Goyal, "International Terrorism", p. 4.

3. Bernard Lewis, *The Crisis of Islam: Holy War and Unholy Terror* (New York: The Modern Library, 2003), p. 137; John L. Esposito, *What Everyone Needs to Know about Islam* (Oxford: Oxford University Press, 2002), p. 120.

4. According to Soage, "Western scholarship has accepted this [i.e. the difference of views between al-Bannā and Quṭb on jihad] interpretation of events, neglecting al-Bannā, and concentrating on Quṭb when analysing Islamic radicalism." See Soage's "Ḥasan al-Bannā and Sayyid Quṭb", p. 295.

5. Ḥasan al-Bannā, *Majmū'at Rasā'il al-Imām al-Shahīd Ḥasan al-Bannā* (Cairo: Dār al-Tawzī' wa al-Nashr al-Islāmiyyah, 1412/1992), p. 433; idem, *Six Tracts of Ḥasan al-Bannā: A Selection from the Majmū'at Rasā'il al-Imam al-Shahīd Ḥasan al-Bannā* (Kuwait: International Islamic Federation of Student Organizations, n.d.), pp. 251 f.

6. Mawdūdī, al-Bannā, Quṭb, *Thalāth Rasā'il*, pp. 69–105; El-Awaisi, "The Conceptual Approach of the Egyptian Muslim Brothers", pp. 236 f.; Bordenkircher, "An Analysis of Jihād", pp. 42–50.

7. Muḥammad Abū Zahrah, *Al-'Alāqāt al-Dawliyyah fī al-Islām* (Cairo: Dār al-Fikr al-'Arabī, 1415/1995), pp. 50–55; 89–94; idem, *Al-Mujtama' al-Insānī fī Ẓill al-Islām* (Jeddah: Al-Dār al-Su'ūdiyyah li al-Nashr wa al-Tawzī', second edn., 1401/1981), pp. 152, 155; idem, *Concept of War in Islam*, trans. Muhammad al-Hady and Taha Omar, rev. & ed. Shawki Sukkary (Cairo: Ministry of Waqfs, Supreme Council for Islamic Affairs, 1987), p. 31; idem, "Al-Jihād", in *Kitāb al-Mu'tamar al-Rābi' li-Majma' al-Buḥūth al-Islāmiyyah* (Cairo: Majma' al-Buḥūth al-Islāmiyyah, 1388/1968), pp. 79–91.

8. Muḥammad Sa'īd Ramaḍān al-Būṭī, *Al-Jihād fī al-Islām: Kayf Nafhamuh? Wa Kayf Numārisuh?* (Damascus: Dār al-Fikr, second abridged edn., 1424/2003), pp. 227–231.

9. The first edition of al-Būṭī's book was published in 1997.

10. Ibid., p. 231.

11. Wahbah al-Zuḥaylī, *Al-'Alāqāt al-Dawliyyah fī al-Islām: Muqāranah bi al-*

Qānūn al-Dawlī al-Ḥadīth (Beirut: Mu'assasat al-Risālah, 1401/1981), pp. 94 f.

12. Al-Zuḥaylī, *Āthār al-Ḥarb*, p. 131.
13. Ibid., p. 131, n. 3.
14. Al-Zuḥaylī, *Al-'Alāqāt al-Dawliyyah fī al-Islām*, p. 95, n. 4.
15. Al-Ḥifnī, *Mawsū'at al-Qur'ān*, vol. 2, p. 1,878.
16. For the views of other scholars who maintain the same view, see for example 'Abd al-Wahhāb Khallāf, *Al-Siyāsah al-Shar'iyyah aw Niẓām al-Dawlah al-Islāmiyyah fī al-Shu'ūn al-Dustūriyyah wa al-Khārijiyyah wa al-Māliyyah* (Beirut: Mu'assasat al-Risālah, n.d.), pp. 76–80; 'Abd al-Ḥalīm Maḥmūd, *Al-Jihād fī al-Islām* (Cairo: Dār al-Ma'ārif, second edn., 1988), p. 21; Maher Hathout, *Jihad vs. Terrorism,* ed. Samer Hathout (Los Angeles: Multimedia Vera International, 2002), p. 67; Esposito, *What Everyone*, p. 120; Abou El Fadl, *The Great Theft*, p. 223; Bernard K. Freamon, "Martyrdom, Suicide, and the Islamic Law of War: A Short Legal History", *Fordham International Law Journal*, vol. 27, no. 1, December 2003, pp. 315 f.; Sherman A. Jackson, "Jihad and the Modern World", *Journal of Islamic Law and Culture*, vol. 7, no. 1, 2002, p. 25; Sayyid Sābiq, *Fiqh al-Sunnah* (Cairo: Al-Fatḥ li al-I'lām al-'Arabī, n.d.), vol. 3, p. 16; Shaheen Sardar Ali and Javaid Rehman, "The Concept of Jihad in Islamic International Law", *Journal of Conflict and Security Law*, vol. 10, no. 3, Winter 2005, pp. 321–343, citation at p. 335.
17. Samuel P. Huntington, *The Clash of Civilizations and the Remaking of World Order* (New York, NY: Simon & Schuster, 1996).
18. Maḥmūd Ḥamdī Zaqzūq, "Muqaddimah", in *Islam and the Future Dialogue between Civilizations*, Researches and Facts. The Eighth General Conference of the Supreme Council for Islamic Affairs (Cairo, n.p., 1418/1998), p. 5.
19. Mufīd Shihāb, "Al-Qānūn al-Dawlī wa al-Sharī'ah al-Islāmiyyah", in *Islam and the Future Dialogue between Civilizations*, Researches and Facts. The Eighth General Conference of the Supreme Council for Islamic Affairs (Cairo, n.p., 1418/1998), pp. 337 f.
20. Maḥmūd Ḥamdī Zaqzūq, "Taqdīm", in *The Truth about Islam in a Changing World*, Researches and Proceedings. The Fourteenth General Conference of the Supreme Council for Islamic Affairs (Cairo: Maṭābi' al-Ahrām al-Tujāriyyah, 1424/2003), p. 3.
21. See for example Ṣūfī Ḥasan Abū Ṭālib, "Al-Kifāḥ al-Mashrū' li al-Shu'ūb", in *The Truth about Islam in a Changing World*, Researches and Proceedings. The Fourteenth General Conference of the Supreme Council for Islamic Affairs (Cairo: Maṭābi' al-Ahrām al-Tujāriyyah,

1424/2003), pp. 679 f.; al-Najjār, "Taḥdīd al-Mafāhīm fi Majāl al-Ṣirā' al-Basharī", p. 795.

22. Abū Salīm Muḥammad 'Abd al-Raḥīm, "Al-Jihād", in *The Truth about Islam in a Changing World*, Researches and Proceedings. The Fourteenth General Conference of the Supreme Council for Islamic Affairs (Cairo: Maṭābi' al-Ahrām al-Tujāriyyah, 1424/2003), p. 752.

23. See for example 'Abbās al-Jarārī, "Mu'ādalat al-Silm wa al-Ḥarb fī Manẓūr al-Islām", in *Tolerance in the Islamic Civilization*, Researches and Facts. The Sixteenth General Conference of the Supreme Council for Islamic Affairs (Cairo: Maṭābi' al-Ahrām al-Tujāriyyah, 1425/2004), pp. 1,192 f; Jamāl al-Dīn Maḥmūd, "Al-Jihād wa Akhlāqiyyāt al-Ḥarb fī al-Islām", in *Tolerance in the Islamic Civilization*, Researches and Facts. The Sixteenth General Conference of the Supreme Council for Islamic Affairs (Cairo: Maṭābi' al-Ahrām al-Tujāriyyah, 1425/2004), p. 847.

24. Maḥmūd, "Al-Jihād wa Akhlāqiyyāt al-Ḥarb", p. 848.

25. See for example, Karen Armstrong, *The Battle for God* (New York: Alfred A. Knopf, 2000), p. 262; Gilles Kepel, *Jihad: The Trial of Political Islam*, trans. Anthony F. Roberts (Cambridge, Mass: Belknap Press of Harvard University Press, 2002), p. 86; idem, *Beyond Terror and Martyrdom*, p. 161; Musallam, *From Secularism to Jihad*, pp. 182–198; John L. Esposito, *Unholy War: Terror in the Name of Islam* (New York: Oxford University Press, 2002), p. 56; John C. Zimmerman, "Sayyid Qutb's Influence", p. 222; al-'Awwā, *Al-Jamā'ah al-Islāmiyyah*, p. 24; Assaf Moghadam, *The Globalization of Martyrdom: Al Qaeda, Salafi Jihad, and the Diffusion of Suicide Attacks* (Baltimore, MD: Johns Hopkins University Press, 2008), p. 109.

26. Ashour, *The De-Radicalization of Jihadists*, p. 8; See also idem, "A World Without Jihad?: The Causes of De-Radicalization of Armed Islamist Movements" (PhD Thesis, Department of Political Science, McGill University, Montreal, Canada, May 2008), p. 162.

27. One reason for specifically referring to the Group in Egypt is because it is probably one of the few groups that depends mainly on dogmatic religious understanding in formulating their view. See Abdelwahab El-Affendi, "The Terror of Belief and the Belief in Terror: On Violently Serving God and Nation", in Madawi Al-Rasheed and Marat Shterin, eds., *Dying for Faith: Religiously Motivated Violence in the Contemporary World* (London: I.B. Tauris, 2009), p. 74.

28. See for example Rif'at Sayyid Aḥmad, *Al-Nabī al-Musallaḥ (1): Al-Rāfiḍūn* (London: Riad El-Rayyes Books, 1991), vol. 1, pp. 57, 117, 123, 129, 132, 141, 169; idem, *Al-Nabī al-Musallaḥ (2): Al-Thā'rūn* (London:

Riad El-Rayyes Books, 1991), vol. 2., pp. 66, 162, 167, 173, 248, 259, 280, 297; Rachel Scott, "An 'Official' Islamic Response to the Egyptian al-Jihād Movement", *Journal of Political Ideologies*, vol. 8, no. 1, February 2003, p. 48.

29. Indeed, the views of Quṭb have had their influence not only on Egypt but also on other countries such as Lebanon and Palestine. See Esposito, *Unholy War*, p. 62.

30. For the purposes of limitation, the literature of the Islamic Group in Egypt with reference to the *Neglected Duty* will be highlighted here. It is also worth mentioning that various other extremist groups have adopted violence in the name of Islam to achieve political objectives inside and outside Egypt. See al-ʿAwwā, *Al-Jamāʿah al-Islāmiyyah*, pp. 24–27; and also Jeffrey B. Cozzens, "Al-Takfir wa'l Hijra: Unpacking an Enigma", *Studies in Conflict and Terrorism*, vol. 32, no. 6, June 2009, pp. 489–510.

31. Jansen, *The Neglected Duty*, pp. 1 f., 159–230; idem, "The Creed of Sadat's Assassins: The Contents of 'The Forgotten Duty' Analysed", *Die Welt des Islams*, New Series, vol. 25, no. 1, 1985, pp. 1–30, citation at p. 1. According to Kelsay, the translated title, which suggests the omission or absence of jihad, is a reference to the fact that such negligence is itself a sinful act. See John Kelsay, *Arguing the Just War in Islam* (Cambridge, Mass.: Harvard University Press, 2007), p. 133. In the remainder of this chapter, the *Neglected Duty* or *al-Farīḍah al-Ghā'ibah* will be referred to as the *Farīḍah*.

32. Jansen, *The Neglected Duty*, p. 167.

33. Ibid., p. 169.

34. Jansen, "The Creed of Sadat's Assassins", p. 30.

35. Muḥammad ʿImārah, *Al-Farīḍah al-Ghā'ibah: ʿArḍ wa Ḥiwār wa Taqyīm* (Cairo: Dār Thābit, 1402/1982), p. 9; Jansen, *The Neglected Duty*, p. 166.

36. Yasa is a mixture of the beliefs adopted by Genghis Khan, Judaism, Christianity and Islam. See ʿImārah, *Al-Farīḍah al-Ghā'ibah*, pp. 9, 33. According to Kepel, only very limited information is available about the Yasa, apart from some "fragments reported by rather unreliable Muslim authors", see Kepel, *Roots of Radical Islam*, p. 203, n. 1.

37. ʿImārah, *Al-Farīḍah al-Ghā'ibah*, pp. 9 f.

38. The Mardin Conference, "The New Mardin Declaration", [article online]; available from http://www.mardin-fatwa.com/about.php?id=4, accessed 27 July 2014.

39. Ibid.; importantly, the recommendations of this timely peace summit were reflected in major Western media outlets. See for example Tom Heneghan, "Muslim Scholars Recast Jihadists' Favourite Fatwa",

[article online]; available from http://www.reuters.com/article/idUSLDE62T2AC; accessed 16 July 2013; BBC Arabic Website, "Fuqahā' Muslimūn: Qirā'āt Fatwā Ibn Taymiyyah li al-Jihād 'Khāṭi'ah'", [article online]; available from http://www.bbc.co.uk/arabic/worldnews/2010/03/100331_mardin_fatwa_jihad_tc2.shtml; accessed 16 July 2013.

40. 'Imārah, *Al-Farīḍah al-Ghā'ibah*, pp. 33 f., 47.

41. See for example Jansen, *The Neglected Duty*, pp. 168, 170, 172, 174–177, 179–181, 192, 207, 215–216.

42. 'Imārah, *Al-Farīḍah al-Ghā'ibah*, p. 9.

43. For one of the very few references to Quṭb in the *Farīḍah*, see Jansen, *The Neglected Duty*, p. 226.

44. Al-'Awwā, *Al-Jamā'ah al-Islāmiyyah*, p. 24.

45. Jansen, *The Neglected Duty*, pp. 193, 195.

46. Ibid., pp. 195, 197, 199 f.

47. Al-Ḥifnī, *Mawsū'at al-Qur'ān*, p. 1,876.

48. 'Imārah, *Al-Farīḍah al-Ghā'ibah*, pp. 23 f.

49. Faraj was an electrician with only shallow theological knowledge, see Kepel, *Roots of Radical Islam*, p. 12.

50. Jansen, *The Neglected Duty*, pp. 144 f.

51. Al-'Awwā, *Al-Jamā'ah al-Islāmiyyah*, pp. 108 f.; Lisa Blaydes and Lawrence Rubin, "Ideological Reorientation and Counterterrorism: Confronting Militant Islam in Egypt", *Terrorism and Political Violence*, vol. 20, no. 4, October 2008, pp. 461–479, citation at p. 469.

52. Jād al-Ḥaqq 'Alī Jād al-Ḥaqq and 'Atiyyah Saqr, "*Naqd al-Farīḍah al-Ghā'ibah: Fatwā wa Munāqashah*", supplementary book to *Majallat al-Azhar*, vol. 66, Muharram 1414/July 1993, p. 7.

53. Kelsay, *Arguing the Just War*, p. 133.

54. This process is also referred to in Arabic as an "initiative to halt violence" (*mubādarat waqf al-'unf*), or in modern Western literature as "ideological reorientation". It is considered by Blaydes and Rubin to be "a counterterrorism approach that seeks to change core ideological or religious beliefs of the terrorist group, thus bringing the beliefs of group members in line with societal norms". Blaydes and Rubin, "Ideological Reorientation and Counterterrorism", p. 462. See also al-'Awwā, *Al-Jamā'ah al-Islāmiyyah*, p. 46; Stéphane Lacroix, "Ayman Al-Zawahiri, Veteran of Jihad", in Gilles Kepel and Jean-Pierre Milelli, eds., *Al-Qaeda in Its Own Words*, trans. Pascale Ghazaleh (Cambridge, Mass.: Belknap Press of Harvard University Press, 2008), p. 159.

55. It is not only the refutation literature that is hard to find, but also the historical background of the Group itself, see Ashour, *The De-Radicalization of Jihadists*, p. 45.

56. See for example ʿAlī Muḥammad ʿAlī al-Sharīf and Usāmah Ibrāhīm Ḥāfiẓ, *Al-Nuṣḥ wa al-Tabyīn fī Taṣḥīḥ Mafāhīm al-Muḥtasibīn*, ed. Karam Muḥammad Zuhdī et al. (Cairo: Maktabat al-Turāth al-Islāmī, 1422/2002); Karam Muḥammad Zuhdı, *Tafjırat al-Riyāḍ: Al-Aḥkām wa al-Āthār* (Cairo: Maktabat al-Turāth al-Islāmī, 1424/2003); Usāmah Ibrāhīm Ḥāfiẓ and ʿĀṣim ʿAbd al-Mājid Muḥammad, *Ḥurmat al-Ghuluww fī al-Dīn wa Takfīr al-Muslimīn*, ed. Karam Muḥammad Zuhdī et al. (Cairo: Maktabat al-ʿUbaykān, 1425/2004); Nājiḥ Muḥammad Ibrāhīm, *Al-Ḥākimiyyah: Naẓrah Sharʿiyyah wa Ru'yah Wāqiʿiyyah*, ed. Karam Muḥammad Zuhdī et al. (Cairo: Maktabat al-ʿUbaykān, 1425/2004).

57. The web address of the bilingual website of the Egyptian Islamic Group is: http://www.egyig.com; accessed 13 July 2013.

58. Ṣafwat ʿAbd al-Ghanī, "*Liqā'āt*", [article online]; available from http://www.egyig.com/Public/articles/interview/7/26176518.shtml; accessed 13 July 2013; Muṣṭafā Shaʿbān, "*Abnā' al-Jamāʿah al-Islāmiyyah Al-Amn Qabila Tawbatahum wa al-Mujtamaʿ Rafaḍahum*", [article online]; available from http://www.islamonline.net/servlet/Satellite?c=ArticleA_C&cid=1235402630534&pagename=Zone-Arabic-Daawa%2FDWALayout; accessed 29 June 2009.

59. In Zidane's published study, he refers to the fact that the Group members have distanced themselves from terrorist organizations such as al-Qaeda and have adopted a moderate approach. His deduction, however, does not depend on academic sources but on a cursory reading of an article by Derbala, one of the leaders of the Group, in a local Arab newspaper of *Al-Sharq al-Awsat*; an indication that *al-murājaʿāt* literature has not yet been given the attention it deserves, especially from an ideological perspective. See Zidane Mériboute, *Islam's Fateful Path: The Critical Choices Facing Modern Muslims*, trans. John King (London: I.B. Tauris, 2009), pp. 108, 230, n. 23, quoting Muhammed Essam Derbala, writing in *Al-Sharq al-Awsat*, 16 January 2004. Bar refers to *al-murājaʿāt* very briefly. See Shmuel Bar, *Warrant for Terror: Fatwās of Radical Islam and the Duty of Jihad* (Lanham, Md: Rowman & Littlefield, 2006), p. 84, n. 9. In addition to Zidane and Bar, Chertoff and Post refer to the initiative of Sayyid Imām al-Sharīf (better known as Dr Faḍl), in which the latter declared his rejection of al-Qaeda's violence. Michael Chertoff, "The Ideology of Terrorism: Radicalism Revisited", *Brown Journal of World Affairs*, vol. 15, no. 1, Fall/Winter 2008, pp. 11–20, citation at p. 14; Jerrold M. Post, "Reframing

of Martyrdom and Jihad and the Socialization of Suicide Terrorists", *Political Psychology*, vol. 30, no. 3, 2009, pp. 381–385, citation at p. 384. Apart from the above authors, it is hard to find any other reference to *al-murājaʿāt* by Western scholars.

60. Ibrāhīm, *Al-Ḥākimiyyah*, pp. 103, 189–211; Zuhdī, *Tafjīrāt al-Riyāḍ*, pp. 40–42.

61. Nājiḥ Muḥammad Ibrāhīm, *Taṭbīq al-Aḥkām min Ikhtiṣāṣ al-Ḥukkām: Al-Ḥudūd, Iʿlān al-Ḥarb, al-Jizyah – Naẓarāt fī Fiqh al-Taṭbīq*, eds. Karam Muḥammad Zuhdī and ʿAlī Muḥammad ʿAlī al-Sharīf et al. (Cairo: Maktabat al-ʿUbaykān, 1425/2004), p. 73; al-Sharīf and Ḥāfiẓ, *Al-Nuṣḥ wa al-Tabyīn*, p. 85; Muḥammad, *Ḥurmat al-Ghuluww fī al-Dīn*, pp. 100–114; al-Qaraḍāwī, *Fiqh al-Jihād*, vol. 1, pp. 16 f., vol. 2, p. 1,169.

62. Al-Qaraḍāwī, *Fiqh al-Jihād*, vol. 2, pp. 1,168 f; idem, *Al-Islām wa al-ʿUnf*, pp. 40–58.

63. Steven Brooke, "Jihadist Strategic Debates before 9/11", *Studies in Conflict and Terrorism*, vol. 31, no. 3, March 2008, pp. 201–226, citation at pp. 207 f.; al-Qaraḍāwī, *Al-Islām wa al-ʿUnf*, p. 54.

64. ʿAbd al-Raḥmān, "Mawqif al-Qur'ān min Khuṣūmih", pp. 1,016–1,029.

65. Ashour, *The De-Radicalization of Jihadists*, pp. 2, 56.

66. Kepel, *Roots of Radical Islam*, p. 12. See also idem, *The War for Muslim Minds: Islam and the West*, trans. Pascale Ghazaleh (Cambridge, Mass: The Belknap Press of Harvard University Press, 2004), p. 1; Madawi Al-Rasheed, "The Quest to Understand Global Jihad: The Terrorism Industry and Its Discontents", *Middle Eastern Studies*, vol. 45, no. 2, March 2009, pp. 329–338, citation at p. 330.

67. Chertoff, "The Ideology of Terrorism", p. 14.

68. Mark Sedgwick, "Al-Qaeda and the Nature of Religious Terrorism", *Terrorism and Political Violence*, vol. 16, no. 4, Winter 2004, pp. 795–814, citation at p. 795; Esposito, *Unholy War*, pp. 5–18; Robert A. Pape, *Dying to Win: The Strategic Logic of Suicide Terrorism* (New York: Random House Trade Paperbacks, 2006), p. 107; Osama Bin Laden, "Declaration of War against the Americans Occupying the Land of the Two Holy Places", in David C. Rapoport, ed., *Terrorism: Critical Concepts in Political Science* (London: Routledge, 2006), vol. 4, pp. 271–294; Kingshott, "Terrorism: The 'New' Religious War", p. 18. Bernard Lewis argues that al-Qaeda seek authority and legitimacy to "represent a truer, purer, and more authentic Islam than that currently practiced by the vast majority of Muslims", see his *Crisis of Islam*, p. 138.

69. Shah, *Self-defence in Islamic and International Law*, p. 48; Rosalind W. Gwynne, "Usama bin Ladin, the Qur'an and Jihad", *Religion*, vol. 36, 2006, pp. 60–91, citation at p. 61; Osama Bin Laden, *Messages to the World: The Statements of Osama Bin Laden*, ed. and intro. Bruce Lawrence, trans. James Howarth (London: Verso, 2005), pp. 19, 29, 30, 41, 61, 62, 92, 118, 122, 150, 161, 171, 180, 181, 185, 217, 267, 268, 272. See also Kenneth Payne, "Winning the Battle of Ideas: Propaganda, Ideology, and Terror", *Studies in Conflict and Terrorism*, vol. 32, no. 2, February 2009, pp. 109–128, citation at p. 113.

70. Bin Laden, *Messages to the World*, pp. 60, 118 for al-Qurṭubī; pp. 60 f., 80, 118, 249 f. for Ibn Taymiyyah; pp. 26, 32, 77 for ʿAbdullāh ʿAzzām; and on Quṭb's indirect influence see Zimmerman, "Sayyid Qutb's Influence", p. 237; Burgat, *Islamism*, pp. 103 f.; Sedgwick, "Al-Qaeda and the Nature of Religious Terrorism", p. 805. Authors such as Pape argue that Bin Laden and al-Ẓawāhirī fully embrace the extremist views of Quṭb as well, see his *Dying to Win*, p. 107. At other times, it is said that it is al-Ẓawāhirī who is much more influenced by Quṭb's ideology than Bin Laden was, see Lacroix, "Ayman Al-Zawahiri", p. 150.

71. Christina Hellmich, "Al-Qaeda – Terrorists, Hypocrites, Fundamentalists? The View from Within", *Third World Quarterly*, vol. 26, no. 1, 2005, pp. 39–54, citation at p. 47.

72. Bin Laden, *Messages to the World*, pp. 14, 140; Maria T. Miliora, "The Psychology and Ideology of an Islamic Terrorist Leader: Usama bin Laden", *International Journal of Applied Psychoanalytic Studies*, vol. 1, no. 2, 2004, pp. 121–139, citation at p. 126.

73. Osama Bin Laden, et al., "World Islamic Front Statement Urging Jihad against Jews and Crusaders", in Kepel and Milelli, eds., *Al-Qaeda*, p. 55. See also Said Mahmoudi, "The Islamic Perception of the Use of Force in the Contemporary World", in Mashood A. Baderin, ed., *International Law and Islamic Law* (Aldershot: Ashgate, 2008), p. 110; Shah, *Self-defence in Islamic and International Law*, pp. 57 f.

74. Shah, *Self-defense in Islamic and International Law*, p. 23; Katerina Dalacoura, "Violence, September 11 and the Interpretations of Islam", in Mashood A. Baderin, ed., *International Law and Islamic Law* (Aldershot: Ashgate, 2008), p. 236; Rehman, *Islamic State Practices*, p. 27.

75. Abdal Hakim Murad, "Bombing without Moonlight: The Origins of Suicidal Terrorism", *Encounters*, vol. 10, nos. 1–2, 2004, pp. 93–126, citation at p. 93.

76. Bin Laden, *Messages to the World*, pp. 41, 118; Gwynne, "Usama bin Ladin", pp. 64 f.

77. Bin Laden, *Messages to the World*, p. 61; Abdel Haleem, *Qur'an*, p. 22.
78. Bin Laden, *Messages to the World*, p. 61. 79. Ibid., p. 118.
80. Such as the attacks on the USS Cole in Yemen and the 1998 attacks on the US embassies in Kenya and Tanzania, and the London bombings of 2005, see Gerges, *The Far Enemy*, pp. 31, 59; Aaron David, *In Their Own Words: Voices of Jihad: Compilation and Commentary* (Santa Monica, Ca: RAND Corporation, 2008), pp. 225, 297, n. 17.
81. Abdel Haleem, *Qur'an*, p. 71.
82. Shah, *Self-defense in Islamic and International Law*, p. 53; John L. Esposito and Dalia Mogahed, "Who Will Speak for Islam?", *World Policy Journal*, vol. 25, no. 3, Fall 2008, pp. 47–57, citation at p. 49. According to Barlas, it is strange to consider Bin Laden, the hijackers and their followers and supporters as "exemplifying real Islam" with a total disregard to the world's one billion Muslims. See Barlas, "Jihad, Holy War, and Terrorism", p. 57.
83. Johnson, *The Holy War Idea*, p. 37; Abdulaziz Sachedina, *The Islamic Roots of Democratic Pluralism* (New York: Oxford University Press, 2001), p. 120.
84. Joseph M. Schwartz, "Misreading Islamist Terrorism: The 'War Against Terrorism' and Just-War Theory", *Metaphilosophy*, vol. 35, no. 3, April 2004, pp. 273–302, citation at p. 273.
85. Al-Qaraḍāwī, *Fiqh al-Jihād*, vol. 2, pp. 900–910, although he excludes Israel from this.
86. Shah, *Self-defense in Islamic and International Law*, p. 78, under 22: 39–40 referred to earlier in this chapter.
87. Bin Laden, *Messages to the World*, pp. 60, 93, 118 f., 122; Gwynne, "Usama bin Ladin", p. 65.
88. Lewis, *Crisis of Islam*, p. 138; Schwartz-Barcott, *War, Terror and Peace in the Qur'an and in Islam*, pp. 2 f.; Marvin Perry and Howard E. Negrin, "Introduction", in idem, eds., *The Theory and Practice of Islamic Terrorism: An Anthology* (New York: Palgrave Macmillan, 2008), p. 9.
89. Lewis, *Crisis of Islam*, p. 153.
90. Faysal Mawlawī, "Al-Tafjīrāt fī Amrīkā lā Tablugh Darajat al-Shahādah", [article online]; available from http://www.islamonline.net/servlet/Satellite?pagename=IslamOnline-Arabic-Ask_Scholar/FatwaA/FatwaA&cid=1122528615454; accessed 13 July 2009.
91. Farhana Ali and Jerrold Post, "The History and Evolution of Martyrdom in the Service of Defensive Jihad: An Analysis of Suicide Bombers in Current Conflicts", *Social Research*, vol. 75, no. 2, Summer

2008, pp. 615–654, citation at p. 645; Esposito and Mogahed, "Who Will Speak", p. 49.

92. Group of Muftis, "Sept 11 Attacks: Islamic Views", [article online]; available from http://www.islamonline.net/servlet/Satellite?pagename=IslamOnline-English Ask_Scholar/FatwaE/FatwaE&cid=1119503544428; accessed 15 July 2009; Muzammil Siddiqi, "Two Years after Sept 11: What Does Islam Have to Say?", [article online]; available from http://www.islamonline.net/servlet/Satellite?pagename=IslamOnline-English-Ask_Scholar/FatwaE/FatwaE&cid=1119503545852; accessed 15 July 2009.

93. Muḥammad Sayyid Ṭanṭāwī, "Bayān Majmaʿ al-Buḥūth al-Islāmiyyah bi al-Azhar bi Shaʿn Ẓāhirat al-Irhāb", [article online]; available from http://www.islamonline.net/Arabic/doc/2001/11/article3.shtml; accessed 15 July 2009; Ali and Post, "The History and Evolution of Martyrdom", p. 645.

94. Mbaye Lo, "Seeking the Roots of Terrorism: An Islamic Traditional Perspective", *Journal of Religion and Popular Culture*, vol. 10, Summer 2005, pp. 1–13 [article online]; available from http://www.usask.ca/relst/jrpc/art10-rootsofterrorism-print.html; accessed 26 January 2010.

95. Muhammad Abdel Haleem, *The "Sword Verse" Myth* (London: Centre of Islamic Studies, SOAS, 2007), p.33; idem, *Understanding the Qur'an*, p. 65.

96. Abou El Fadl, *The Great Theft*, p. 231.

97. Andrew F. March, "Sources of Moral Obligation to non-Muslims in the 'Jurisprudence of Muslim Minorities' (*Fiqh al-Aqalliyyāt*) Discourse", *Islamic Law and Society*, vol. 16, no. 1, 2009, pp. 34–94, citation at p. 72.

98. Khurshid Ahmad, "The World Situation after September 11, 2001", in Ibrahim M. Abu-Rabi' ed., *The Blackwell Companion to Contemporary Islamic Thought* (Malden, MA: Blackwell, 2006), pp. 408 f.

5: Terrorism and Its Qur'anic Punishment

1. Badawi and Abdel Haleem, *Arabic-English Dictionary of Qur'anic Usage*, p. 160; al-Aṣfahānī, *Mufradāt Alfāẓ*, p. 193.

2. Al-Shaʿrāwī, *Tafsīr*, vol. 15, p. 9,331; ʿAbd al-Bāqī, *Al-Muʿjam al-Mufahras*, p. 166.

3. Al-Alūsī, *Rūḥ al-Ma'ānī*, vol. 29, p. 60; 'Abd al-Bāqī, *Al-Mu'jam al-Mufahras*, p. 166.
4. Badawi and Abdel Haleem, *Arabic-English Dictionary of Qur'anic Usage*, p. 160. For a full citation of those fifty occurrences, see 'Abd al-Bāqī, *Al-Mu'jam al-Mufahras*, pp. 166 f.
5. Badawi and Abdel Haleem, *Arabic-English Dictionary of Qur'anic Usage*, p. 160.
6. Al-Aṣfahānī, *Mufradāt Alfāẓ*, p. 192; see also Yahaya Yunusa Bambale, *Crimes and Punishments under Islamic Law* (Lagos: Malthouse Press Limited, second edn., 2003), p. 1.
7. 'Abd al-Bāqī, *Al-Mu'jam al-Mufahras*, p. 167.
8. Majma' al-Lughah al-'Arabiyyah, *Al-Mu'jam al-Wajīz*, p. 101.
9. *Jarīmah* (crime), according to al-Māwardī, is a prohibited act for which Allah sets a deterring punishment either through *ḥadd* or through *ta'zīr* (discretionary punishment). 'Alī ibn Muḥammad Ḥabīb al-Baṣrī al-Māwardī, *Al-Aḥkām al-Sulṭāniyyah wa al-Wilāyāt al-Dīniyyah* (Cairo: Dār al-Fikr li al-Ṭibā'ah wa al-Nashr wa al-Tawzī', 1983), p. 189; idem, *Al-Ahkam As-Sultaniyyah: The Laws of Islamic Governance*, trans. Asadullah Yate (London: Ta-Ha Publishers, 1416/1966, repr. 2005), p. 309. Crimes in Islamic law can be divided into three main categories: *ḥudūd* crimes (whose punishments are set out by the scriptures), retaliatory crimes, and *ta'zīr* (crimes whose punishment is discretionary), see Frank E. Vogel, "The Trial of Terrorists under Classical Islamic Law", *Harvard International Law Journal*, vol. 43, no. 1, Winter 2002, pp. 53–64, citation at p. 58.
10. Al-Tartūrī and Guwayḥān, *'Ilm al-Irhāb*, pp. 64–65.
11. 'Abd al-Qādir 'Udah, *Al-Tashrī' al-Jinā'ī fi al-Islām: Muqāranan bi al-Qānūn al-Waḍ'ī* (Beirut: Mu'assasat al-Risālah li al-Tibā'h wa al-Nashr wa al-Tawzī', thirteen edn., 1994), vol. 1, pp. 110 f.; idem, *Criminal Law of Islam*, trans. S. Zakir Aijaz (New Delhi: Kitab Bhavan, 1999, repr. 2005), vol. 1, pp. 90 f.
12. Nājih Ibrāhīm 'Abdullāh, *Taṭbīq al-Aḥkām min Ikhtiṣāṣ al-Ḥukkām: Al-Ḥudūd, I'lān al-Ḥarb, al-Jizyah – Naẓarāt fi Fiqh al-Taṭbīq*, rev. and eds. Karam Muḥammad Zuhdī and 'Alī Muḥammad 'Alī al-Sharīf et al., (Cairo: Maktabat al-'Ubaykān, 1425/2004), p. 38; A.A.K. Sherwani, *Impact of Islamic Penal Laws on the Traditional Arab Society* (New Delhi: M D Publications Pvt, 1993), pp. 31–32.
13. According to 'Udah, an examination of the Qur'anic verses about juristic rulings (including 5: 33) shows that they refer to two punishments; one in this world and another in the Hereafter. 'Udah,

Al-Tashrī' al-Jinā'ī, vol. 1, p. 167; idem, *Criminal Law*, vol. 1, p. 196.

14. Nik Rahim Nik Wajis, "The Crime of *Ḥirāba* in Islamic Law" (PhD thesis, Glasgow Caledonian University, United Kingdom, 1996), p. 165; Abou El Fadl, *The Great Theft*, p. 243; Aḥmad ibn Sulaymān Ṣāliḥ al-Rubaysh, *Jarā'im al-Irhāb wa Taṭbīqātuhā al-Fiqhiyyah al-Mu'āṣirah* (Riyadh: Maṭābi' Akādimiyyat Nāyif al-'Arabiyyah li al-'Ulūm al-Amniyyah, 2003), p. 132.

15. Haytham, *Mafhūm al-Irhāb,* pp. 173–174; Sa'īd 'Abdullāh Ḥārib, *Al-Ta'aṣṣub wa al-'Unf: Fikran wa Sulūkan* (Kuwait: Wazārat al-Awqāf wa al-Shu'ūn al-Islāmiyyah, Al-Markaz al-'Ālamī li al-Wasaṭiyyah, 1427/2006), pp. 11–15.

16. Abdel Haleem, *Qur'an*, p. 71.

17. 'Abd al-Raḥīm Ṣidqī, *Al-Jarīmah wa al-'Uqūbah fī al-Sharī'ah al-Islāmiyyah: Dirāsah Taḥlīliyyah li Aḥkām al-Qiṣāṣ wa al-Ḥudūd wa al-Ta'zīr* (Cairo: Maktabat al-Nahḍah al-Miṣriyyah, 1408/1987), p. 249.

18. Al-Ṭabarī, *Jāmi' al-Bayān*, vol. 1, pp. 182 f.

19. Muḥammad Sa'īd al-'Ashmāwī, *Uṣūl al-Sharī'ah* (Cairo: Madbūlī al-Ṣaghīr, fourth edn., 1416/1996), pp. 128–130.

20. Ibn al-'Arabī, *Aḥkām al-Qur'ān*, vol. 2, pp. 91–94; al-Qurṭubī, *Al-Jāmi'*, vol. 6, pp. 148–150; al-Ṭabarī, *Jāmi' al-Bayān*, vol. 6, pp. 205–208; al-Ḥifnī, *Mawsū'at al-Qur'ān*, vol. 2, p. 1,306; al-Jaṣṣāṣ, *Aḥkām al-Qur'ān,* vol. 4, p. 53.

21. Al-Qurṭubī, *Al-Jāmi'*, vol. 6, p. 149.

22. Al-Jaṣṣāṣ, *Aḥkām al-Qur'ān*, vol. 4, p. 53.

23. Ibn al-'Arabī, *Aḥkām al-Qur'ān*, vol. 2, p. 92; al-Suyūṭī, *Al-Durr al-Manthūr*, vol. 3, p. 69.

24. Ibn al-'Arabī, *Aḥkām al-Qur'ān*, vol. 2, p. 92.

25. Khaled Abou El Fadl, *Rebellion and Violence in Islamic Law* (Cambridge: Cambridge University Press, 2001), p. 49.

26. Al-Bukhārī, *Ṣaḥīḥ al-Bukhārī*, no. 4,192, in *Mawsū'at al-Ḥadīth*, p. 344. There are other narrations of the hadith stating that the men were from 'Ukl; Ibid., no. 6,802, p. 567. One narration states that the men were from 'Uraynah, see al-Bukhārī, *Ṣaḥīḥ*, no. 1,501, p. 119; other narrations do not mention where the men were from, see al-Bukhārī, *Ṣaḥīḥ*, no. 4,610, p. 380; nos. 5,685–5,686, p. 487.

27. Abou El Fadl, *Rebellion*, p. 50.

28. Al-Ḥifnī, *Mawsū'at al-Qur'ān*, p. 2,463.

29. Al-Ṭabarī, *Jāmi' al-Bayān*, vol. 6, p. 208; Riḍā, *Tafsīr al-Qur'ān al-Ḥakīm*,

vol. 6, p. 354.

30. Muḥammad ʿAbdullāh al-Sammān, *Al-Islām wa al-Dimā'* (Cairo: Al-Maktab al-Fannī li al-Nashr, n.d.), p. 45.

31. Ibn Manẓūr, *Lisān*, vol. 1, pp. 302 f.

32. Al-Alūsī, *Rūḥ al-Maʿānī*, vol. 3, p. 53.

33. Muḥammad Ibn ʿAbdullāh al-ʿUmayrī, *Musqiṭāt Ḥadd al-Ḥirābah wa Taṭbīqātihā fī al-Mamlakah al-ʿArabiyyah al-Suʿūdiyyah* (Riyadh: Akādimiyyat Nāyif al-ʿArabiyyah li al-ʿUlūm al-Amniyyah, 1999), p. 16.

34. Muḥammad ʿAtrīs, *Al-Muʿjam al-Wāfī li-Kalimāt al-Qur'ān al-Karīm* (Cairo: Maktabat al-Ādāb, 2006), p. 950.

35. Shawqī Ḍayf, et al., *Al-Muʿjam al-Wasīṭ*, p. 163; Majmaʿ al-Lughah al-ʿArabiyyah, *Al-Muʿjam al-Wajīz*, p. 142.

36. Badawi and Abdel Haleem, *Arabic-English Dictionary of Qur'anic Usage*, p. 196; Riḍā, *Tafsīr al-Qur'ān al-Ḥakīm*, vol. 6, p. 356.

37. Riḍā, *Tafsīr al-Qur'ān al-Ḥakīm*, vol. 6, p. 356.

38. ʿUdah, *Al-Tashrīʿ al-Jinā'ī*, vol. 1, pp. 78 f.; idem, *Criminal Law*, vol. 1, pp. 85 f; Rudolph Peters, "The Islamization of Criminal Law: A Comparative Analysis", *Die Welt des Islams*, vol. 34, no. 2, Nov., 1994, pp. 246–274, citation at pp. 247 f.

39. Wajis, "The Crime of *Ḥirāba*", p. 63; Sobhi Mahmassani, "The Principles of International Law in the Light of Islamic Doctrine", *Recueil des Cours*, vol. 117, 1966, pp. 201–328, citation at p. 287.

40. Alā' al-Dīn al-Kāsānī, *Badā'iʿ al-Sanā'iʿ fī Tartīb al-Sharā'iʿ* (Beirut: Dār al-Kitāb al-ʿArabī, 1982), vol. 7, pp. 90 f.

41. Muḥammad ibn Aḥmad ibn Abī Sahl al-Sarakhsī, *Kitāb al-Mabsūṭ* (Beirut: Dār al-Maʿrifah, n.d.), vol. 9, p. 195.

42. Ibn ʿĀbidīn, *Ḥāshiyat Radd al-Muḥtār*, vol. 4, p. 113.

43. Al-Shāfiʿī, *Al-Umm*, vol. 6, p. 152.

44. Al-Māwardī, *Al-Aḥkām al-Sulṭāniyyah*, p. 56; idem, *Islamic Governance*, p. 93.

45. Mawil Izzi Dien, "Hiraba (Highway Robbery)", in Ian Richard Netton, ed., *Encyclopedia of Islamic Civilisation and Religion* (Abingdon, Oxon: Routledge, 2008), p. 239.

46. Wajis, "The Crime of *Ḥirāba*", p. 64.

47. Al-ʿUmayrī, *Ḥadd al-Ḥirābah*, p.20; ʿAbd al-Ḥamīd Ibrāhim al-Majālī, *Al-Taṭbīqāt al-Muʿāṣirah li Jarīmat al-Ḥirābah* (Amman: Dār Jarīr, 2005),

p. 21.

48. Muwaffaq al-Dīn ʿAbdallāh ibn Aḥmad ibn Qudāmah, *Al-Mughnī: fī Fiqh al-Imām Aḥmad Ibn Ḥanbal al-Shaybānī* (Beirut: Dār al-Fikr, 1405/1984–5), vol. 9, p. 124.

49. Mansūr ibn Yūnus ibn Idrīs al-Buhūtī, *Kashshāf al-Qināʿ ʿan Matn al-Iqnāʿ*, ed. Hilāl Muṣilhī Muṣṭafā Hilāl (Beirut: Dār al-Fikr, 1402/1981–2), vol. 6, p. 150.

50. Mālik ibn Anas, *Al-Mudawwanah al-Kubrā*, ed. Aḥmad ʿAbd al-Salām (Beirut: Dār al-Kutub al-ʿIlmiyyah, 1415/1994), vol. 4, p. 552.

51. Abū ʿUmar Yūsuf ibn ʿAbdullāh ibn Muḥammad al-Namirī ibn ʿAbd al-Barr, *Al-Kāfī fī Fiqh Ahl al-Madīnah* (Beirut: Dār al-Kutub al-ʿIlmiyyah, second edn., 1413/1992), p. 582. According to Abou El Fadl, the *muḥārib* is one who attacks defenceless victims by stealth, and spreads terror in society, see his "Islam and the Theology of Power", in Malik, ed., *With God on Our Side*, p. 303.

52. ʿAbd al-Barr, *Al-Kāfī fī Fiqh Ahl al-Madīnah*, p. 583.

53. Wajis, "The Crime of *Ḥirāba*", p. 63.

54. Al-Majālī, *Al-Taṭbīqāt al-Muʿāṣirah*, pp. 21 f.; al-ʿUmayrī, *Ḥadd al-Ḥirābah*, pp. 19–37.

55. Muḥammad Ṭalʿaṭ al-Ghunaymī, *Qānūn al-Salām fī al-Islām* (Alexandria, Egypt: Munsha'at al-Maʿārif, 2007), p. 815.

56. Wajis, "The Crime of *Ḥirāba*", p. 66.

57. ʿAbd al-Fattāḥ Muḥammad Qā'id, *Al-Ḥirābah fī al-Fiqh al-Islāmī: Dirāsah Muqāranah* (Cairo: Dār al-Ṭibāʿah al-Muḥammadiyyah, 1407/1987), p. 12.

58. Al-Majālī, *Al-Taṭbīqāt al-Muʿāṣirah*, p. 21 f.

59. Al-ʿUmayrī, *Ḥadd al-Ḥirābah,* p. 22.

60. Wajis, "The Crime of *Ḥirāba*", p. 66; al-Rubaysh, *Jarā'im al-Irhāb*, pp. 40–41; al-ʿUmayrī, *Ḥadd al-Ḥirābah,* p. 22; ʿAlī ʿAbd al-Qādir al-Qarālah, *Al-Muqāwamah wa al-Irhāb min Manẓūr Islāmī* (Amman: Dār ʿĀlam al-Thaqāfah li al-Nashr wa al-Tawzīʿ, 2005), p. 132.

61. I owe this term to Khaled Abou El Fadl, see his *Rebellion*, p. 49.

62. Jackson, "Domestic Terrorism", pp. 303 f.

63. Mālik, *Al-Mudawwanah*, vol. 4, p. 556.

64. According to Mohamed S. El-Awa, Aḥmad ibn Ḥanbal gave no answer concerning this point, and because of this the Ḥanbalī jurists have different views concerning this element, see Mohamed S. El-

Awa, *Punishment in Islamic Law: A Comparative Study* (Plainfield, IN: American Trust Publications, 1993), p. 9.

65. Al-Sarakhsī, *Al-Mabsūṭ*, vol. 9, p. 201; Ibn Qudāmah, *Al-Mughnī*, vol. 9, p. 124.
66. El-Awa, *Punishment*, p. 9.
67. Ibid., pp. 9 f.
68. Wajis, "The Crime of *Ḥirāba*", pp. 68 f.
69. Ibid., p. 70.
70. Chapter 1 dealt with the occurrences of the word *fasād* and the general Qur'anic attitude towards it. According to Wajis, the closest equivalent to the English word "corruption" is the Arabic word *fasād*, See his "The Crime of *Ḥirāba*", p. 71.
71. Abou El Fadl, *The Great Theft*, p. 242.
72. Frederick Mathewson Denny, "Corruption", in McAuliffe, ed., *Encyclopaedia of the Qur'ān*, vol. 1, p. 439.
73. Al-Sha'rāwī, *Tafsīr*, vol. 15, pp. 3,090 f.
74. Ibid., vol. 15, p. 3,090.
75. Mawdūdī, *Towards Understanding*, vol. 2, p. 156.
76. Al-Ṭabarī, *Jāmi' al-Bayān*, vol. 6, p. 211. Whether the targeted personnel in *ḥirābah* are Muslims or non-Muslims is a point to be discussed later in this chapter.
77. For the textual punishments for killing, adultery, and theft, see 2: 178; 24: 2; and 5: 38.
78. Riḍā, *Tafsīr al-Qur'ān al-Ḥakīm*, vol. 6, pp. 357 f.
79. Vogel's view here is apparently similar to al-Ṭabarī's by virtue of the fact that both speak of the verse as referring to more than one crime. Other than this limited aspect of similarity, there is no apparent commonality between al-Ṭabarī's view and Vogel's.
80. Vogel, "The Trial of Terrorists", p. 58.
81. E.g. al-Suyūṭī, *Al-Durr al-Manthūr*, vol. 3, p. 68; al-Alūsī, *Rūḥ al-Ma'ānī*, vol. 6, p. 120.
82. Al-Sha'rāwī, *Tafsīr*, vol. 15, pp. 3,090 f.
83. Ibid., vol. 15, p. 3,091.
84. Al-Qarālah, *Al-Muqāwamah*, p. 148.
85. Jackson, "Domestic Terrorism", p. 295.
86. Iqbāl Aḥmad Khān, "Mawqif al-Adyān Tijāh al-Irhāb wa al-Taṭarruf",

in *Islam and the Future Dialogue between Civilizations*, Researches and Facts. The Eighth General Conference of the Supreme Council for Islamic Affairs (Cairo: Supreme Council of the Islamic Affairs, 1418/1998), p. 326.

87. Abou El Fadl, *Rebellion*, p. 6; idem, *The Great Theft*, p. 243.

88. Personal correspondence with Professor Khaled Abou El Fadl, 25 March 2008.

89. Al-ʿAwwā, *Al-Jamāʿah al-Islāmiyyah*, p. 33.

90. E.g. see Muḥammad Fatḥī ʿĪd, *Wāqiʿ al-Irhāb fī al-Waṭan al-ʿArabī* (Riyadh: Akādimiyyat Nāyif al-ʿArabiyyah li al-ʿUlūm al-Amniyyah, 1420/1999), pp. 94 f.

91. Ḥārib, *Al-Taʿaṣṣub*, p. 13; Haytham, *Mafhūm al-Irhāb*, pp. 173–174; Salah as-Sawi, "Refutation of a Fatwa Issued Concerning the Permissibility of Muslims Participating in Military Operations against the Muslims in Afghanistan", [article online]; available from http://www.islamicawakening.com/viewarticle.php?articleID=864, accessed 28 July 2014.

92. Ḥārib, *Al-Taʿaṣṣub*, p. 13.

93. Al-ʿUmayrī, *Ḥadd al-Ḥirābah,* pp. 36 f.

94. Jackson, "Domestic Terrorism", p. 299.

95. Al-Rubaysh, *Jarāʾim al-Irhāb*, p. 30.

96. Ḥārib, *Al-Taʿaṣṣub*, pp. 13 f.

97. Basheer M. Nafi, "Al-Judhūr al-Fikriyyah li al-Tayyār al-Salafī wa Taʿbīrātuhū al-Mukhtalifah", in Mādī, et al., *Al-Irhāb*, p. 66.

98. This is in reference to the context of the American-led war against Afghanistan after 11 September 2001.

99. For a detailed discussion of the question submitted to al-Qaraḍāwī, as well as the various responses, see Basheer M. Nafi, "Fatwā and War: On the Allegiance of the American Muslim Soldiers in the Aftermath of September 11", *Islamic Law and Society*, vol. 11, no. 1, 2004, pp. 78–116; reprinted in David Cook, ed. *Jihad and Martyrdom*, vol. 4, pp. 204–235.

100. There is another opposing fatwa, written by the late Saudi scholar Ḥammūd ibn ʿUqalāʾ al-Shuʿaybī (d. 2002), which responds to "al-Qaraḍāwī's fatwa". However, al-Ṣāwī's refutation is highlighted here for two reasons: firstly, its treatment of *ḥirābah* and terrorism and secondly, its wide availability and accessibility compared with al-Shuʿaybī's. For a brief reference to the two opposing voices to "al-Qaraḍāwī's fatwa", see Nafi, "Al-Judhūr al-Fikriyyah", p. 50.

101. Ibid. 102. Ibid.

103. Ṣalāḥ al-Ṣāwī, "Al-Ishtirāk fī Qitāl al-Muslimīn taḥta Rāyat al-Amrīkān: Ijtihād Ākhar", [article online]; available from http://www.islamonline.net/servlet/Satellite?pagename=IslamOnline-Arabic-Ask_Scholar/FatwaA/FatwaA&cid=1122528600884; accessed 27 August 2008; As-Sawi, "Refutation of a Fatwa".

104. Nafi, "Al-Judhūr al-Fikriyyah", p. 68.

105. As-Sawi, "Refutation of a Fatwa".

106. The Arabic word *baghy* literally refers to injustice or transgression. The *bughāh* (sing. *bāghī*) are those who attempt the violent overthrow of a legitimate ruler, see al-Nawawī, *Al-Majmū'*, vol. 20, p. 337; Nafi, "Al-Judhūr al-Fikriyyah", pp. 50 f. According to al-Jazzār, "*Baghy* is a purely political crime that has nothing to do with the crime of terrorism," see Muḥammad Bahjat Muṣṭafā al-Jazzār, "Al-Jarā'im al-Irhābiyyah: Bayna al-Qānūn al-Waḍ'ī wa al-Sharī'ah al-Islāmiyyah fī Ḍaw' Aḥkām al-Qaḍā'" (PhD thesis, Faculty of Law, Zagazig University, Egypt, 2002), pp. 284, 586.

107. For the Arabic version, see al-Ṣāwī, "Al-Ishtirāk fī Qitāl al-Muslimīn"; for the English version, see As-Sawi, "Refutation of a Fatwa".

108. Haytham, *Mafhūm al-Irhāb*, pp. 173–174.

109. Chapter 1 of this book deals with some institutional definitions of terrorism and their evaluations.

110. The terrorism meant here is the comprehensive concept that transcends politically-motivated terrorism to focus on terrorism where the souls of innocents, their properties and their interests are threatened. For a detailed handling of this concept of terrorism, see al-Rubaysh, *Jarā'im al-Irhāb*, pp. 30 f.

111. This view is further established by al-Azhar scholar 'Abdul-Majeed Hamid Subh. See 'Abdul-Majeed Hamid Subh, "General Fatwa Session", [article online]; available from http://www.islamonline.net/livefatwa/english/Browse.asp?hGuestID=4F3k3y; accessed 3 February 2010.

112. Wajis, "The Crime of *Ḥirāba*", p. 164.

113. Ibid., p. 164. 114. Ibid., pp. 164 f.

115. Vogel, "The Trial of Terrorists", p. 59.

116. From this point onwards in the discussion, *ḥirābah* and terrorism will be used interchangeably, as will *muḥāribūn* and terrorists.

117. Darwazah, *Al-Tafsīr al-Ḥadīth*, vol. 9, p. 105.

118. Al-Maṭrūdī, "Al-Irhāb", pp. 167 f.; idem, *Naẓrah fī Mafhūm al-Irhāb wa*

al-Mawqif minhu fi al-Islām, Dirāsāt Mu'āṣirah 17 (Riyadh: King Faisal Center for Research and Islamic Studies, 1425/2004), p. 48.

119. Sherwani, *Impact of Islamic Penal Laws*, p. 33.

120. Mohammad Hashim Kamali, *Punishment in Islamic Law: An Enquiry into the Hudud Bill of Kelantan* (Kuala Lumpur: Institute Kajan Dasar, 1995, repr. Ilmiah Publishers, 2000), p. 77.

121. Sherwani, *Impact of Islamic Penal Laws*, p. 33.

122. Punishment here refers to the two forms of worldly punishment to be discussed in the remaining part of this chapter.

123. Al-Ṭabarī, *Jāmi' al-Bayān*, vol. 6, p. 219; Ibn Kathīr, *Tafsīr al-Qur'ān*, vol. 2, p. 52.

124. Quṭb, *Ẓilāl*, vol. 2, p. 880; idem, *In the Shade*, vol. 4, p. 92; al-Sha'rāwī, *Tafsīr*, vol. 5, p. 3,103.

125. Al-Sha'rāwī, *Tafsīr*, vol. 5, p. 3,103.

126. These are given as two different linguistic meanings for the word *khizy* by Ibn Manẓūr, al-Aṣfahānī, Badawi and Abdel Haleem. See Ibn Manẓūr, *Lisān*, vol. 14, pp. 226 f.; al-Aṣfahānī, *Mufradāt Alfāẓ*, p. 281; Badawi and Abdel Haleem, *Arabic-English Dictionary of Qur'anic Usage*, p. 261.

127. Al-Sha'rāwī, *Tafsīr*, vol. 5, p. 3,103.

128. Quṭb, *Ẓilāl*, vol. 2, p. 880; idem, *In the Shade*, vol. 4, p. 92; Darwazah, *Al-Tafsīr al-Ḥadīth*, vol. 9, p. 109.

129. Quṭb, *Ẓilāl*, vol. 2, pp. 880 f.; idem, *In the Shade*, vol. 4, p. 89.

130. Quṭb, *Ẓilāl*, vol. 6, pp. 3,544 f.

131. Al-Qurṭubī, *Al-Jāmi'*, vol. 6, p. 157; Bambale, *Crimes*, p. 70.

132. Sābiq, *Fiqh*, vol. 2, p. 296; Jackson, "Domestic Terrorism", p. 295.

133. Vogel, "The Trial of Terrorists", p. 59; Muḥammad 'Ārif Muṣṭafā Fahmī, *Al-Ḥudūd wa al-Qiṣāṣ bayna al-Sharī'ah wa al-Qānūn: Dirāsah Muqāranah* (Cairo: Maktabat al-Anglū al-Miṣriyyah, second edn., 1399/1979), p. 169.

134. Abou El Fadl, *Rebellion*, p. 57.

135. Badawi and Abdel Haleem, *Arabic-English Dictionary of Qur'anic Usage*, pp. 61 f. For the detailed linguistic meanings of the conjunction *aw* with reference to the Qur'an, see Ibn Manẓūr, *Lisān*, vol. 14, pp. 54 f., e.g. on 2: 135 for the use of *aw* to connote division, and on 34: 24 for the use of *aw* to connote vagueness.

136. Al-Ṭabarī, *Jāmi' al-Bayān*, vol. 6, pp. 215 f. The absence of this narration in the authentic collections of Hadith is based here on

the exhaustive research of the researcher in *Mawsū'at al-Ḥadīth al-Sharīf al-Kutub al-Sittah* quoted earlier in this chapter. Online search ascribes this narration to al-Ṭabarī stating that its authenticity is questionable, see 'Alī ibn 'Abd al-Qādir al-Saqāf, "Al-Ḍurar al-Saniyyah", [article online]; available from http://www.dorar.net/enc/hadith/وأصابوا+الفرج+/+yj&page=1; accessed 23 July 2013.

137. Al-Alūsī, *Rūḥ al-Ma'ānī*, vol. 6, pp. 119 f.

138. Al-Bukhārī, *Ṣaḥīḥ al-Bukhārī*, no. 6,878, in *Mawsū'at al-Ḥadīth*, p. 573; Qā'id, *Al-Ḥirābah*, pp. 97 f.

139. Muḥammad Abū Zahrah, *Al-Jarīmah wa al-'Uqūbah fī al-Fiqh al-Islāmī: Al-'Uqūbah* (Cairo: Dār al-Fikr al-'Arabī, n.d.), p. 155; 'Abd al-Ḥamīd 'Alī al-Maghrabī, *Al-Mushārakah fī al-Ḥirābah wa 'Uqūbatuhā fī al-Sharī'ah al-Islāmiyyah* (Cairo: Dār al-Ṭibā'ah al-Muḥammadiyyah, 1404/1983), p. 30.

140. Al-Ṭabarī, *Jāmi' al-Bayān*, vol. 6, p. 214; al-Alūsī, *Rūḥ al-Ma'ānī*, vol. 6, p. 119; Qā'id, *Al-Ḥirābah*, pp. 93–95.

141. Al-Qurṭubī, *Al-Jāmi'*, vol. 6, p. 152.

142. Sābiq, *Fiqh*, vol. 2, p. 300.

143. 'Abd al-Karīm Zidān, *Al-Wajīz fī Uṣūl al-Fiqh* (Beirut: Mu'assasat al-Risālah li al-Ṭibā'ah wa al-Nashr wa al-Tawzī', 1987), p. 240; al-Maghrabī, *Al-Mushārakah fī al-Ḥirābah*, p. 35.

144. For a comprehensive discussion of *istiḥsān* and *maṣlaḥah* as two examples of the science of the principles of Islamic jurisprudence and the difference between them, see Zidān, *Al-Wajīz*, pp. 230–244; Wahbah al-Zuḥaylī, *Al-Wajīz fī 'Ilm Uṣūl al-Fiqh* (Damascus: Dār al-Fikr, second edn., 1419/1999), pp. 86–96; Mohammad Hashim Kamali, *Principles of Islamic Jurisprudence* (Cambridge: Islamic Texts Society, third edn., 2006), pp. 323–368.

145. Ibn al-'Arabī, *Aḥkām al-Qur'ān*, vol. 2, pp. 98 f.

146. Quṭb, *Ẓilāl*, vol. 2, p. 880; idem, *In the Shade*, vol. 4, p. 91.

147. Al-Sha'rāwī, *Tafsīr*, vol. 5, p. 3,095; Riḍā, *Tafsīr al-Qur'ān al-Ḥakīm*, vol. 6, p. 363.

148. Al-Suyūṭī, *Al-Durr al-Manthūr*, vol. 3, p. 68; Ibn Kathīr, *Tafsīr al-Qur'ān*, vol. 2, pp. 51 f.; al-Jaṣṣāṣ, *Aḥkām al-Qur'ān*, vol. 4, p. 54.

149. E.g. see Sidqī, *Al-Jarīmah wa al-'Uqūbah*, p. 171; Muḥammad ibn 'Abdullāh al-'Umayrī, *Mawqif al-Islām min al-Irhāb* (Riyadh: Jāmi'at Nāyif al-'Arabiyyah li al-'Ulūm al-Amniyyah, 1425/2004), p. 377; Haytham, *Mafhūm al-Irhāb*, p. 188; al-Maghrabī, *Al-Mushārakah fī al-Ḥirābah*, p. 35.

150. Haytham, *Mafhūm al-Irhāb*, p. 188
151. Muḥammad Abū Zahrah, *Al-Jarīmah wa al-ʿUqūbah fī al-Fiqh al-Islāmī: Al-Jarīmah* (Cairo: Dār al-Fikr al-ʿArabī, 1998), p. 51.
152. Nevertheless, this should not necessarily lead to the dismissal of the *tartīb* approach as a workable system of punishment supported by the majority of scholars, see Abū Zahrah, *Al-Jarīmah*, p. 151.
153. It is worth noting that the Indonesian authorities have applied execution as a punishment for the perpetrators of the 2002 Bali bombings. See BBC News, "Indonesia executes Bali bombers", [article online]; available from http://news.bbc.co.uk/2/hi/south_asia/7718053.stm, accessed 28 July 2014.
154. Al-Alūsī, *Rūḥ al-Maʿānī*, vol. 6, p. 119.
155. Qā'id, *Al-Ḥirābah*, pp. 100–111.
156. Wajis, "The Crime of *Ḥirāba*", p. 85.
157. For the Qur'an, see 21: 107, and for the Sunnah, see Abū Dāwūd, *Sunan Abū Dāwūd*, no. 2,814, in *Mawsūʿat al-Ḥadīth*, p. 1,433. For an excellent treatment of execution as a punishment, see Kulliyyat al-Sharīʿah wa al-Qanūn bi Jāmiʿat al-Imārāt al-ʿArabiyyah al-Muttāḥidah, *Waqāʾiʿ Nadwat al-Bayān al-Urubbī wa Ḥadd al-Ḥirābah fī al-Fiqh al-Islāmī* (UAE, Ein: Kulliyyat al-Sharīʿah wa al-Qānūn, 1418/1997), p. 57.
158. Abou El Fadl, *Rebellion*, p. 47; Arne A. Ambros, *A Concise Dictionary of Koranic Arabic* (Wiesbaden: Reichert, 2004), p. 162.
159. Badawi and Abdel Haleem, *Arabic-English Dictionary of Qur'anic Usage*, p. 530.
160. Al-Aṣfahānī, *Mufradāt Alfāẓ*, p. 489.
161. Riḍā, *Tafsīr al-Qur'ān al-Ḥakīm*, vol. 6, p. 356. Thus, *ṣalb* in Islam has nothing to do with nailing someone to a cross, as can be easily inferred from the word crucifixion itself in Roman practice, see Abou El Fadl, *Rebellion*, p. 47.
162. Darwazah, *Al-Tafsīr al-Ḥadīth*, vol. 9, p. 108.
163. Al-Jaṣṣāṣ, *Aḥkām al-Qur'ān*, vol. 4, p. 58.
164. Al-Bukhārī, *Ṣaḥīḥ al-Bukhārī*, no. 1,315, in *Mawsūʿat al-Ḥadīth*, p. 102.
165. Mālik, *Al-Mudawwanah*, vol. 4, p. 553.
166. Al-Alūsī, *Rūḥ al-Maʿānī*, vol. 6, p. 119.
167. Riḍā, *Tafsīr al-Qur'ān al-Ḥakīm*, vol. 6, p. 360.
168. Majmaʿ al-Lughah al-ʿArabiyyah, *Al-Muʿjam al-Wajīz*, p. 629.
169. Al-Shaʿrāwī, *Tafsīr*, vol. 15, p. 3,096.

170. Ibn al-ʿArabī, *Aḥkām al-Qur'ān*, vol. 2, p. 99.

171. Al-Shaʿrāwī, *Tafsīr*, vol. 15, p. 3,102.

172. Al-Ṭabarī, *Jāmiʿ al-Bayān*, vol. 6, p. 218.

173. Badawi and Abdel Haleem, *Arabic-English Dictionary of Qur'anic Usage*, p. 137.

174. Qā'id, *Al-Ḥirābah*, p. 155.

175. Muḥyī al-Dīn ibn Sharaf al-Nawawī, *Riyāḍ al-Ṣāliḥīn* (Cairo: Dār al-Rayyān, n.d.), p. 9.

176. Riḍā, *Tafsīr al-Qur'ān al-Ḥakīm*, vol. 6, p. 364. See also Quṭb, *Ẓilāl*, vol. 2, pp. 880 f.; idem, *In the Shade*, vol. 4, p. 92.

177. Riḍā, *Tafsīr al-Qur'ān al-Ḥakīm*, vol. 6, p. 365.

178. Muhammad Abdel Haleem, "Compensation for Homicide in Islamic Sharīʿa", in Muhammad Abdel Haleem, Adel Omar Sharef and Kate Daniels, eds., *Criminal Justice in Islam: Judicial Procedure in the Sharīʿa* (London: I.B. Tauris, 2003), pp. 97 f.

179. For a study on how the application of legal punishments can bring about positive change in society, see Muḥammad Ḥusayn al-Dhahabī, *Athar Iqāmat al-Ḥudūd fī Istiqrār al-Mujtamaʿ* (Cairo: Maktabat Wahbah, 1407/1986), pp. 19–65.

180. Jack Nelson-Pallmeyer, *Is Religion Killing Us? Violence in the Bible and the Quran* (London: Continuum, 2005), pp. 84–88.

INDEX

(NOTE: THE FIRST FULL REFERENCE TO BIBLIOGRAPHICAL SOURCES IN THE ENDNOTES IS INDEXED BY AUTHOR.)